ALL THEY
DID WAS
WIN

Also by Van Allen Plexico and John Ringer:

First Time Ever: The Untold Story of How Auburn First Brought Undefeated Alabama to Jordan-Hare Stadium—and Beat Them

Auburn Basketball: From Barkley to Bruce

We Believed: A Lifetime of Auburn Football, Vol. 1: 1975-1998

Decades of Dominance: Auburn Football in the Modern Era

Season of Our Dreams: The 2010 Auburn Tigers

More Auburn Football, from White Rocket Books:

Lorendo, by Ken Ringer

ALL THEY DID WAS WIN

SHOOTOUTS, SHOCKERS AND CAMBACKS ON THE ROAD TO AUBURN'S IMPROBABLE 2010 NATIONAL CHAMPIONSHIP

VAN ALLEN PLEXICO & JOHN RINGER

HOSTS OF THE AU WISHBONE AUBURN PODCAST

WHITE ROCKET BOOKS

ALL THEY DID WAS WIN:
SHOOTOUTS, SHOCKERS AND CAMBACKS ON THE ROAD TO
AUBURN'S IMPROBABLE 2010 NATIONAL CHAMPIONSHIP

Copyright 2025 by Van Allen Plexico and John Ringer

Cover design by Van Allen Plexico for White Rocket Books

Interior illustrations by Jarrod Alberich.

All rights reserved, including the right to reproduce this book, or portions thereof, in any form, save for brief passages to be quoted in reviews.

A White Rocket Book
www.whiterocketbooks.com

ISBN-13: 978-1-962993-14-2

This book is set in Times and Calibri.

First printing: July 2025

0 9 8 7 6 5 4 3 2 1

Camzilla; the Blessed Individual; Cameron Newton.
Artwork Copyright 2025 by Jarrod Alberich.

For Rod Bramblett, Chette Williams and John Feinstein.
—Van & John

All I do is win, win, win
No matter what

—DJ Khaled

I've got a feeling
That tonight's gonna be a good night
That tonight's gonna be a good good night

—The Black-Eyed Peas

Two songs closely associated with Auburn's 2010 season.

The DJ Khaled song was featured on the stadium "hype video" all year long, while the Black-Eyed Peas song was the backing track for the popular "AU HD" celebratory highlight video after the national championship game.

– THE AU WISHBONE FAMILY –

Van and John extend their eternal thanks and appreciation to these fine members of the Auburn Family and the AU Wishbone Family (as of May 2025) whose support helps to make our podcasts and other projects (such as this book) a reality. *War Eagle!*

Samuel Salvatore
Ben Spooner
Carl Von Drunker
Chris and Clinton Stewart
Logan Chilton
Mark Brown
Wilson Beard
Anne Pridgen
Bradley Blackmon
David WDE Sammons, Esq
Earl Ricks
Eric Morgan
Gary Grant aka AU_Fan@KSC
Harry Zagger
Matte Flowers
Michael Kirshner
Phil Amthor
Richard Stephens
Shane Bailey
Steve Trawick
Susan Trawick
Trombone Tiger
Mark Sandy
William Cardin
William Morgan
Winn from Norman, OK
Robbie Pressley
Ben Bloodworth
Brandon Smith
Chad McDowell
Chris Hilton
Chris Thrash
Dan Thompson
Daniel Odom
Lane Middleton

Josh Corbett
HTown Danny
In-Home Hugh
Jacob and Robyn Fleming
Jeff Hunter
Kathryn England
Luther and Kelly Ottaway
Mike Bradley
George Gaston c/o 2001
OwlGoRhythm and Blues
Reynolds Wolf
Rhodesian Mudflap
Rich Reimer
Rusty Owens
Steve Harlan
Theodore Gary
Bob Sammons, official sleazy shyster for the AU Wishbone
Wade Ward
War Eagle Always
WDErichie Butler
Wes Atkinson
Jason Valentine, Class of '97
Winston Boddie
Woody the Jag
ABB
Antionne Morris
AuburnBlue
Blake Herrin
Boris the Tiger
Charles Mauney
Constructiontiger
David D.
David Simpson
Parker Neill

VAN ALLEN PLEXICO & JOHN RINGER

Josh Teal
Kevin Mahan
Melissa Blackstone
Papa Todd
Patrick Williams
Phillip Martin
Randall Walker
Rob Morgan
Russell Milling
Sarah Hines
Todd Gray '88
Shannon Butson
Steven Huston
Tim Pittman
Timothy
Tony Perry
Tyler Ward
Walt Austin
Mandy Thompson
Bill Minor
Brett Wiggins & Randy Wiggins
Alex Brouns
Alex Nguyen
AU falling up
Ben Amos
Ben Rigas
Bobby Politte
Chris Comeaux
chris_brAUn
Clay Henson
Auburn Elvis
CT Tiger
Daniel Barnett
Daniel Whitten

Darren Pyle
David Garner
David Smilie
Elizabeth Donald
Michael Nobles
I'll buy this for a dollar!!!
James Taylor
Jim McCrory
Jim Myers
John Otsuki
John Stubbs
Joey Miller
Justin Bean
Kenneth Brent Raines
Mark Squire
Kathy Bright MVP
Jeanne Davis Swart, who believes in Auburn & loves it
Paul Bankson
Rich Hammett
Royce Alvarez
Russell Suther
Ruth and Darrin Sutherland
Spanky
Stephen Thompson
Steve Bailey
The Slinko Family
Tiger (who is sometimes a bad kitty)
Tim Sauls
Trevor Johnson
Trey Jackson
Plus 1-time & anonymous!

To join their illustrious ranks, go to **www.auwishbone.com** and click on the big orange button that says "Become a Patron!"
Thank you—and *War Patron Eagle!*

– CONTENTS –

PREFACE	13
PROLOGUE	15
1: WE WANT A WINNER	19
2: A DREAM JOB	35
3: ANGLES AND GEOMETRY	45
4: AN ENVIRONMENT OF CONFIDENCE	57
5: GOOD THINGS HAPPEN	63
6: WE HAD TO WIN THE GAME FOUR TIMES	77
7: AN ATHLETIC FREAK OF NATURE	91
8: DEFINITELY DIFFERENT	103
9: SUPERMAN	121
10: BREAKING THE HEX	133

11: THAT HEISMAN MOMENT	143
12: NUMBER ONE	153
13: COMING SO CLOSE	159
14: BOMBSHELL	169
15: A BLESSED INDIVIDUAL	179
16: BAD DIRT	189
17: THE FIRST QUARTER: GETTING WHIPPED	195
18: THE SECOND QUARTER: AN AWFUL BEAUTIFUL THING	209
19: HALFTIME: LET'S GO, LET'S GO, LET'S GO	227
20: THIRD QUARTER: RIGHT WHERE THEY WANT TO BE	231
21: THE FOURTH QUARTER: FIVE DELAY	245
22: THE FOURTH QUARTER: KEEP THE PRESSURE ON	253
23: THE FOURTH QUARTER: NEWTON'S LAW	259

24: POST-GAME: WE HUNG OUR HATS ON THAT	271
25: FREAKISH AS USUAL	279
26: TWO LETTERS	295
27: UNPRECEDENTED	301
28: ANYBODY'S BALLGAME	311
29: HERE IN THE DESERT	319
30: CELEBRATION DAY	331
31: ONE MORE BRICK	339
EPILOGUE	345
A NOTE ON SOURCES	351
APPENDIX 1: 2009 TEAM ROSTER	363
APPENDIX 2: 2010 TEAM ROSTER	366
APPENDIX 3: THE 1,000-YARD RUSHING STREAK	369
APPENDIX 4: MEMORIES	370

PREFACE

In the aftermath of the 2010 season, and before their audio podcast existed, Van Allen Plexico and John Ringer assembled a collection of their weekly *War Eagle Reader* columns from the Tigers' national championship year into a book. *Season of Our Dreams* tracked the thoughts and reactions of the AU Wishbone duo week-to-week in real time as they experienced that incredible 14-0 season and shared the joy with the rest of the Auburn Family.

But that book was a series of snapshots taken in the moment, not a comprehensive history of the season. Nor was it meant to be the story of the coaches and players and fans who made that year so unforgettable.

Now, fifteen years later, Van and John have taken up the challenge of revisiting that season and telling the story from start to finish.

This is the *complete* story of the 2010 Auburn Tigers. And, as the song the team and fans embraced as their theme all year long stated so clearly:

All they did was win.

– PROLOGUE –

"The most important thing in coaching is the will *to win. If you have that, you're going to figure out* how *to win."*
—Bob Knight

It was all falling apart.

After a season of last-second escapes, miracle plays and mind-bending super-heroics, it looked as if Auburn's chances—dare we say Auburn's *luck?*—had run out. The Tigers were on their way to losing to Alabama in the final regular-season game of the 2010 season.

Auburn would still win the SEC West and go to Atlanta with a shot at a conference title, even with a loss to the Crimson Tide. In that scenario, the Tigers would finish at 7-1, a game ahead of Alabama, Arkansas and LSU, who would all be tied at 6-2.

But if Auburn were to lose to Alabama on that cold, damp, miserable Friday in Tuscaloosa, their chances to play for a national title would dwindle away, probably to nothing. After all, both Oregon and TCU would end the season undefeated, and Auburn would become just another of several one-loss teams with good arguments for why they should have a spot in the BCS Championship Game. Only by finishing 12-0, and then winning the SEC Championship Game in Atlanta, could the Tigers all but guarantee themselves a shot at the title—the title that had eluded them on so many frustrating occasions over the past fifty-three years.

And it definitely looked as if the Tigers were going to lose. In fact, as halftime approached, it looked increasingly like they were going to get *blown out*.

Nothing was working. The run game was being stuffed. The passing game was nonexistent. The defense was giving up vast chunks of yardage to Alabama, not to mention touchdowns. The team's miracle-worker on offense, Cam Newton, had been harassed and stymied from the get-go. His counterpart on defense, Nick Fairley, had managed one monstrous sack of the Alabama quarterback—only to have the referees instantly flag him for a highly questionable, 15-yard personal foul penalty for alleged "excessive celebration."

As horrifying as the spectacle in Bryant-Denny looked, midway through the second quarter, it was not completely unprecedented. We'd seen this very movie before, only six years earlier. Tommy Tuberville had brought an undefeated 2004 Auburn squad to Tuscaloosa with visions of conference and national titles floating in their heads. Two quarters later, Mike Shula's Tide had stifled them at every turn and led at the half, 6-0.

Tuberville's team had rallied for the win. But then, a deficit of six points is much easier to overcome than one of 21 points—and the Tide was driving for more. After just over a quarter of football, Alabama was averaging 9.0 yards per play. For Auburn's average yardage, one needed only move the decimal place one spot to the left: a shocking 0.9 yards per play.

And it appeared for all the world like things were about to get even worse.

With 12:42 to go before halftime, Alabama had a first-and-10 on their own 40-yard line. Tide quarterback Greg McElroy took the snap and completed a short pass to Mark Ingram just past the line of scrimmage. Ingram, the previous season's Heisman Trophy winner, caught the ball and immediately slipped the attempted tackle of linebacker Eltoro Freeman. He then proceeded to weave his way down the field, almost untouched. Strong safety Zac Etheridge dove at him and didn't make the tackle, but did knock him slightly off his stride. Ingram's path ahead, however, remained clear.

If he continued on and took the ball into the end zone for a demoralizing fourth touchdown for the Tide, Auburn would find themselves down 28-0. That was likely a hole too deep for any team to climb out of—even one with magicians like Newton and Fairley on the roster. After all, why would anyone believe the remaining three quarters would unfold any differently than the first one had? The Tigers had fought back from behind in multiple games that season, and had prevailed in all of them. But they'd never faced a situation like this. The 2010 Iron Bowl held the potential to get seriously out of hand, and to bring Auburn's season of infinite promise crashing down to earth in the most humiliating fashion imaginable.

But then something truly remarkable happened, there at the end of a truly remarkable regular season.

As Ingram, still stumbling from his brush with Etheridge, crossed Auburn's 20-yard line, on his way to what everyone watching in Bryant-Denny and at home on television must surely have believed was an inevitable touchdown, defensive end Antoine Carter caught up to him from behind. Carter had been in hot pursuit from the start of the play, but never could have caught up with the Alabama running back if not for Ethridge's disruptive efforts. Carter reached out, jabbing at Ingram with one big mitt. He reached out, out, and…

…And what happened next was impossible. It was unthinkable. It was the stuff of legends.

A football, as we all know, has a funny shape. Because of that, it almost always bounces in funny ways.

In this instance, the ball chose to bounce in the funniest way possible: not at all.

Instead it rolled. And rolled. And rolled. In a straight line. Right down the sideline, like a bowling ball headed for a strike. Like it was being steered by the hand of God Almighty. Somehow, improbably, it remained in bounds the entire way, right into the end zone.

In doing so, it turned around a play, a game, and a season. It changed the trajectory of the 2010 national championship and put the Tigers back on track to end a 53-year wait.

Before we finish that story, however—and in order to fully appreciate all that came just before, and just after—we must go back. Back two years, to the end of the 2008 season, when Auburn suddenly separated itself from a head coach that had only recently won six Iron Bowls in a row, only to hire as his replacement a coach who'd managed five wins in his past 24 games.

The road to that epic, unthinkable, unimaginable victory in the 2010 Iron Bowl—plus the eleven games before it and the two huge games that followed it—began with the hiring of Gene Chizik as the Tigers' 25th head coach, and his hiring in turn of Gus Malzahn as offensive coordinator. And then, of course, his (and assistant coach Curtis Luper's) recruitment of a junior college transfer quarterback from College Park, Georgia, by the name of Cameron Newton.

The road to Tuscaloosa, and to Atlanta, and to Glendale, Arizona began in that same Bryant-Denny Stadium, two years earlier, as the Tigers endured a 36-0 shellacking at the hands of the Crimson Tide.

After that game, Tommy Tuberville and his staff departed. And then Athletic Director Jay Jacobs set out to find a new head coach.

No one on earth could have predicted what would happen next.

- 1 -

WE WANT A WINNER

At long last, the Auburn Tigers had done it.

Behind the passing of Jason Campbell, the rushing attack of Carnell "Cadillac" Williams and Ronnie Brown, and the powerful defense constructed by defensive coordinator Gene Chizik, they had won the SEC. More than that, they were undefeated: the undefeated champions of the toughest conference in college football.

Surely *this* was the year.

As bowl season rolled around, one would surely think they were on their way to play the winner of some other major conference in the BCS title game, for the undisputed national championship.

Well, not quite.

They had begun the season too far down in the rankings, and had never risen higher than number 3.

At that time, only the top two teams in the BCS rankings got to play for the national championship.

Number 1 USC and number 2 Oklahoma were also undefeated, and they had remained ahead of Auburn the entire season in the polls. There would be no chance for this undefeated SEC champion to even compete for the big trophy. In terms of trying to win the national championship, going undefeated in the SEC meant absolutely nothing that year. It was almost unthinkable, and yet it was reality.

Instead of playing one of the other undefeated contenders for the biggest prize in the sport, they were relegated to the Sugar Bowl, where they would meet 10-2 Virginia Tech in a meaningless contest.

It marked quite a comedown for the once-prestigious Sugar Bowl, as well. There were years, not long before, when the winner of the Sugar Bowl won the national championship. In 2004, however, the Sugar Bowl was as relevant to the title chase as the Weedeater Independence Bowl.

As the Tigers finished off Virginia Tech, wrapping up their undefeated and now 13-0 season, all they could do was watch helplessly as two other teams played for the title they believed was rightfully theirs.

Auburn fans were despondent. After close calls and disappointments in 1983, 1988 and 1993, the 2004 squad had seemed like the team they'd been waiting decades for. It had seemed like the real deal. A team that could legitimately compete and win a long-elusive national championship.

But through no fault of their own, the 2004 Auburn team and its coaches and fans had to watch as they were cruelly deprived of any opportunity to win the title. They would never get the chance to show the country what they could do.

That 2004 team had been led by an impressive group of seniors, but now they were done. Cadillac, Jason and Ronnie graduated and moved on to the NFL. Two weeks after the bowl game, Gene Chizik packed up his belongings and moved out of the football complex in Auburn, headed for a new job in Austin, Texas. There he would spend the next two seasons as defensive coordinator for Mack Brown and the Longhorns.

Back in Auburn, the circumstances were changing. The next two Tigers teams were very good, but unexpected losses knocked them down in the polls both years. When Nick Saban arrived in Tuscaloosa at the end of 2006, the balance of power in the state began to slide back to the west. Some had questioned for years if Auburn could ever win a national championship. Now they openly speculated it would be impossible. Not with Saban gobbling up the state's best players and constructing such a powerhouse on their rival's campus.

ALL THEY DID WAS WIN

What Tommy Tuberville could accomplish at Auburn, in the face of such a challenge, remained to be seen.

For most of his decade-long tenure as head coach of Auburn University, Tommy Tuberville was a winner.

Hired away from Ole Miss, where he'd enjoyed a fair amount of success as the Rebels' head coach, Tuberville managed to win only five games in his first season on the Plains. In year two, however, he coached the Tigers back to respectability. Bringing in rugged junior college transfer running back Rudi Johnson, he was able to add a powerful rushing attack to the team's existing Ben Leard-to-Ronney Daniels passing game. That 2000 Auburn team won nine games and the SEC West title. A year after finishing 5-6, and only two years removed from 3-8, they made it to Atlanta for the SEC Championship Game, and battled Michigan in the Citrus Bowl.

Following a disappointing 2001 season, Tuberville fired both of his coordinators. He brought in Bobby Petrino from the NFL to freshen up the offense, and Gene Chizik from Central Florida to run the defense.

These new coordinators experienced immediate success on the Plains in 2002, coaching the Tigers to a 9-4 finish and tying for a share of the SEC West title. They did it despite star running back Cadillac Williams suffering a season-ending injury in game seven at Florida. Ronnie Brown, replacing Williams in the featured back role, emerged as a true star over the second half of the season and kept the offense moving.

Following the Tigers' Capital One Bowl win over Penn State, a now-in-demand Petrino—who had run that offense—departed to take the head coaching job at Louisville. Gene Chizik meanwhile opted to remain at Auburn. He would go on to coach the defense for the Tigers for two more seasons. During that time, he would have additional opportunities to make an impression on the powers-that-be at Auburn.

Chizik had begun coaching college defenses as a graduate assistant at Clemson under famed coordinator Bill "Brother" Oliver in 1988 and 1989. Oliver would later serve as Auburn's defensive coordinator from 1996-1998, including a brief stint as interim head coach.

About the time Oliver was finishing his Auburn tenure, Chizik was starting his new job as defensive coordinator at the University of Central Florida. It turned out he was in the right place at the right time. During his four years at UCF in Orlando, Chizik lived and worked in close proximity to the NFL's Tampa Bay Buccaneers. He was able to study their defensive scheme up close, learning the cutting-edge "Tampa 2" system being assembled there by the likes of Tony Dungy, Monte Kiffin and Lovie Smith. The system has been described as "simple" and relies on two main factors: fast players who will gang-tackle and swarm to the ball, and defensive backs in the secondary who can create turnovers through aggressive hitting.

Chizik bought into the concept and introduced it to his UCF players, who enjoyed much success in the system. Their relatively gaudy defensive numbers caught Tuberville's attention.

> *"We're looking forward to having Gene join our staff. He has been extremely successful as a defensive coordinator and a secondary coach. I think he will be a great fit for our staff and program."*
> —*Tommy Tuberville*

> *"Our goal will be to field an attacking, aggressive, physical defensive team that will help Auburn be successful each and every week."*
> —*Gene Chizik, upon accepting the Auburn DC job*

Chizik's first defensive squad at Auburn in 2002 was very good, but in 2003 and 2004, he produced exceptionally powerful units. The 2003 team finished fifth in the country in total defense, and in 2004 Auburn led the country in scoring defense, giving up just over 11 points per game. During those three seasons, the Tigers went 30-9, played in the Capital One Bowl, Music City Bowl and Sugar Bowl, and finished undefeated and ranked second in the country after 2004. Following that season, Chizik won the Frank Broyles Award for best assistant coach in the country.

And then Mack Brown came calling, and Chizik exited the Plains to become assistant head coach, co-defensive coordinator and linebackers coach at Texas. There he would remain for two years—

including a second straight undefeated season, in 2005, adding up to twenty-eight consecutive wins across both programs. Speaking to reporters prior to the national championship game that year, he was asked about that win streak, and replied: "I haven't thought much about it. It's been mentioned a couple of times, but when you are in the forest looking up you can't see much. Just trying to win another game. I remember the last game I lost, but I don't think about it much."

After two years at Texas, he had earned about as good a reputation for success as any assistant in the country. ESPN's Kirk Herbstreit had named him the "Top Future Coach" and "Best Defensive Mind" after 2006, and it wasn't long before schools in search of a new head coach came calling. He accepted the top job at Iowa State in 2007.

"Gene Chizik is about winning championships," said Iowa State Athletic Director Jamie Pollard at Chizik's welcoming press conference in Ames. "He has a thorough understanding of what's involved in building a championship program. He has had an integral role on teams that won national, conference and conference playoff titles. Gene is one of, if not the, top coaching prospects in the nation."

Meanwhile, back at Auburn, Tommy Tuberville would bring in three more defensive coordinators in the four seasons after Chizik departed for Texas. That side of the ball struggled a bit, but it never quite faltered the way the offense did during those seasons. As a result of that inconsistent play, the 2005 team—despite suffering only one conference loss—felt disappointing, as it won a share of the Western Division title but failed to make it back to the SEC Championship Game. The following year the Tigers only lost two games, but they again missed out on a trip to Atlanta due to a surprising home loss to Arkansas.

Van Allen Plexico

The Razorbacks had an innovative offensive coordinator on their staff that season by the name of Gus Malzahn, and he tied the Tigers in knots all game long. How interesting might things have been if Tuberville had hired Malzahn away from Arkansas after that season?

The 2007 Tigers failed to live up to expectations, suffering four regular-season losses and finishing second in the West again.

Even so, and at first glance, Auburn's situation appeared quite rosy as the 2007 season ended. By that point, the Tigers had won the Iron Bowl a shocking six years in a row. Their last really disappointing season had been in 2003; in the four years since, they had finished first in the Western Division twice and second twice.

For all of that, however, the fans were growing frustrated. Despite those good teams and successful seasons, the Tigers had made it to the SEC Championship Game only once in seven years. The offense had grown stagnant and the team was relying on grinding out unexciting, low-scoring, defensive victories. It felt to many as if things were headed in the wrong direction—a situation that became all too clear the following year, 2008, as the wheels finally started to fall off.

The first and most obvious problem was that Nick Saban had arrived at Alabama the previous season, changing the game and upending the rivalry. Some had accused the Tuberville staff of coasting—of settling into an easy routine, as they had faced the likes of Dennis Franchione and Mike Shula on the opposite side of the state. With Saban on board in Tuscaloosa, however, coasting along easily was no longer an option. He quickly grasped control of recruiting in the state and beyond, as he moved rapidly to turn Alabama into a football power of historical proportions. Even in the best of years, Auburn had never totally dominated recruiting in Alabama. Now the situation was about to get much, much worse for the Tigers and for Tuberville. He needed to shake things up, and do it quickly.

His solution was to make a radical change with the hiring of his new offensive coordinator: Tony Franklin, late of Troy University.

Franklin was a firm disciple of the hurry-up Spread offense. It was a radically different system from the one the previous OC, Al Borges, had been running on the Plains for the last four years. Borges, along with Tuberville, preferred to lean on the running game as the primary weapon. That's not to say the passing game was unimportant to them. They would mix in the occasional play-action pass, in which the quarterback fakes the hand off to the back, rolls out to one side, and then looks down field to a receiver or tied end. And quarterback Jason Campbell in 2004 had been particularly adept at throwing the deep ball. But the passing game was not designed to be the primary aspect of that offense.

Franklin's Spread offense, on the other hand, was absolutely built around the passing game.

The Spread passing attack gets its name from the way it attempts to spread the defense both horizontally and vertically on the field. As many as five wide receivers are arrayed from one sideline to the other, in an effort to open up spaces in the defense along that axis. Meanwhile, it employs deep passing routes to create vertical seams in the defense. When executed properly by a talented quarterback with several good receiving targets, it can literally spread the defensive players all over the field and leave plenty of space for the ball carrier to operate. In this way it has the potential to be devastating. When there is a problem either with personnel or execution, however, a team using the Spread can find itself in deep trouble. The quarterback ends up running for his life, receivers wander aimlessly downfield, and running backs are left with little blocking help at the line of scrimmage. It can be very much an all-or-nothing approach. And because the entire offense is based around that concept, if it's not working, there's nowhere else to turn.

Tuberville had flirted with moving to the Spread once before, in 2004, but said later that the candidates he interviewed that used it hadn't had good answers to the question, "What are your halftime adjustments if it's not working?" Ultimately, he'd decided to hire Borges and go with his more conventional approach.

Things had changed by the end of 2007. Saban was stealing most of the public's attention and pulling the best recruits in the state to Alabama. Tuberville, known during his Ole Miss days as "the Riverboat Gambler," needed to rock the boat and pump some excitement back into the Auburn program. This time, unlike after 2003, he was willing to gamble on the Spread. And Tony Franklin would be the guy to bring that offense to the Plains.

Franklin arrived just after the end of the regular season and got to work immediately. The talk after the Iron Bowl was that the Tigers would continue to use the Borges offense through the bowl game and then make the transition to the Spread the following spring. This turned out to be disinformation. As it played out, Franklin was able to install enough bits and pieces of his system in eight practices to score 23 points and beat Clemson, 23-20, in overtime in the Chick-Fil-A Bowl on December 31.

A promising start, yes—but one with a very big warning sign attached.

In game three, at Mississippi State, the still-strong Auburn defense shut the Bulldogs out. Franklin's offense, however, managed only 3 points the entire game. A holding penalty in Auburn's end zone, resulting in a safety for MSU, brought the final score to 3-2, the very epitome of an "ugly win."

After that, the situation deteriorated rapidly. Tuberville began insisting on changes to how the offense was run. Franklin resented any interference in his system.

The players were not making the transition to the Spread as quickly as Franklin wanted, and weren't moving the ball as successfully as Tuberville demanded. For Franklin, the perceived meddling by his head coach was only making matters worse. Add to that the lack of knowledge and experience with that particular offense by the coaching staff, and Franklin felt he faced an almost impossible task.

Franklin had wanted to bring some of his assistants with him from Troy, to work with the players and help them better understand their roles in the offense.

"I have always had a rule that to take another job I have to be able to bring at least two assistants with me. (Tuberville) said I couldn't do that. I asked if I could bring one. He said he'd think about it, and I never heard another word."
—Tony Franklin, 2008

That meant the players would be taught Franklin's Spread offense by assistant coaches he didn't know, who had never run that system before. Those coaches had been able to adapt very quickly and successfully to Al Borges' more run-heavy, play action-oriented West Coast Offense (or, as it was quickly renamed in Auburn, the "Gulf Coast Offense") in 2004. That offense had fit closely with what Tuberville and his staff had run for most of their careers. The Spread, however, was a very different animal.

It was an awkward fit from the beginning. And, very quickly, things started to fall apart.

ALL THEY DID WAS WIN

At the start of the season, Franklin wanted to go with quarterback Chris Todd, who had committed to him at Troy and then followed him over to Auburn. Tuberville preferred Kodi Burns, whom he had recruited, to start at QB. Franklin wanted to run the Spread his way. Tuberville wanted to be able to interject changes here and there, mainly consisting of more running the ball, continuing the approach his teams had relied upon for so many years. In short, Tuberville wanted to be able to say he'd embraced a radically new offense while actually sticking with much of what he'd always done. This, understandably, rankled Franklin.

> *"At the first sign of trouble on offense—and it came quickly—Tuberville pressed Franklin to run more I-formation plays. The I-formation was not part of Franklin's offense."*
> —*Philip Marshall, Auburn Undercover*

Perhaps it might have worked out if the team had won more games. Unfortunately for all concerned, after an early Top 10 ranking and a hot, 3-0 start against lesser competition, Auburn's fortunes soured.

The troubles began when they lost a last-second heartbreaker to defending national champions LSU at home. Losing such a game was disappointing, sure, but it seemed to be a promising sign that Auburn could compete so closely with the previous year's top team, and very nearly beat them. This, unfortunately, turned out to be a mirage. The Bayou Bengals stumbled to a losing record in the SEC, finishing only one game ahead of Auburn in the SEC West, and 8-5 overall.

A win over Tennessee in Knoxville lifted the Tigers to a respectable 4-1, but then they traveled to visit 19th ranked Vanderbilt and managed only 13 points in a 14-13 loss.

Some of the players were, understandably, upset—if not bewildered—by what had happened against the Commodores.

> *"This isn't the program I signed with."*
> —*Kodi Burns, Auburn quarterback, after the Vanderbilt game*

> "I'm pretty sure not many Auburn teams have ever lost to Vanderbilt."
> —Ryan Pugh, Auburn center, after the Vanderbilt game

By this point, Auburn was tied for last nationally with Washington State in plays resulting in negative yardage, having run 57 of them.

Already displeased about the state of the offense, Tuberville grew even more upset following the Vandy game. Back in Auburn, Franklin responded to the growing pressure by frantically attempting to coach many of the skill-position players at practice that week himself, making clear without saying so out loud that he didn't believe Tuberville's assistants were properly teaching the players how to function in the offense.

At that point, Tommy Tuberville had seen enough. He unceremoniously fired Franklin.

> "It hurts. It hurts bad (to fire Franklin). That's a difficult situation and a difficult thing to do in the middle of the season. My responsibility is this football team and it always will be. Tony is a good person, a good guy. He's got a great family, and he's a good family man. Basically when it all comes down to it, it's about production. I didn't think the last few weeks we were making any progress. I came to the decision this morning that we would make that change."
> —Tommy Tuberville, quoted by Chris Low of ESPN, October 8, 2008

> "I told (Tuberville) when he hired me, 'If you don't want to do what I do, don't hire me. I don't know how to do anything else.'"
> —Tony Franklin, to Philip Marshall, after the Vanderbilt game

Franklin vacated his office in the football complex quickly, even as Tuberville held a pre-practice meeting to inform the players.

> "Everyone was shocked. There were blank stares on everyone's faces."
> —anonymous individual at Auburn pre-practice meeting

Tuberville told reporters that his removal of Franklin as OC was "not going to change our philosophy. This is a good offense. Our guys like it. They understand it. They're getting better at it." But clearly that was not to be the case. Tuberville had big changes in mind.

The reins of the offense were abruptly handed over to tight ends coach Steve Ensminger, who was tasked with bringing back the old, smashmouth approach in mid-season. Ensminger had been made co-offensive coordinator (along with offensive line coach Hugh Nall) in 2003, after the departure of OC Bobby Petrino. That experiment had resulted in an offense with stellar players like Jason Campbell, Cadillac Williams and Ronnie Brown being unable to score a single touchdown until three games into the season. This time Ensminger had far less time to prepare, with players who weren't future NFL first-round draft picks. The results were about what one might expect.

"Steve Ensminger had the unenviable task of changing offenses at midseason. He was miserable. Players were miserable. Everyone connected with Auburn football was miserable."
—*Philip Marshall, Auburn Undercover*

Van Allen Plexico
I can testify that *I* was definitely miserable.

The Tigers would win only two more games the rest of the season, finishing a disappointing 5-7 and missing out on a bowl game for the first time since Tuberville's first year, 1999. Their fortunes didn't improve after the midseason switch back to the old style of play. They ended up 11th out of 12 teams in the SEC in scoring offense, and 110th of 119 teams nationally. After four years of finishing first or second in the SEC West, they concluded the 2008 season in a three-way tie for last place. Perhaps even worse, their winning streak in the Iron Bowl came to a crashing halt, losing 36-0 to Nick Saban's Alabama.

> "Because it was the last regular-season game, Auburn's players didn't have to return to the Loveliest Village on the Plains on the team buses (after the Iron Bowl) that day, and for that, (Auburn center Ryan) Pugh was thankful. Then a sophomore, the center knew what was coming next back in Auburn.
>
> "Pugh finally escaped the crush (of celebrating Alabama fans) by hopping a metal barricade. Once he got free of the mob, Pugh tucked his Auburn hat into his backpack and zipped his name tag inside. No need to invite any more attention. Pugh's season was over. His coach was about to get fired. He just wanted to find his family and get the hell out of Tuscaloosa."
> —Andy Staples, the New York Times, 2020

The slow downward trend that had begun three years earlier had become a precipitous decline. At that point, Tuberville had spent a decade as Auburn's head coach. He'd managed to reinvigorate the program after nearly being fired at the end of the 2003 season, and now it looked like he'd have to repeat that trick again, if he wanted to make it to year eleven. To make matters worse, he now faced a far more formidable coach at the arch-rival school on the other side of the state. Was he up for the challenge of taking on Saban while simultaneously trying to rebuild the Tigers program? Could he reinvent himself one more time at Auburn? Did he trust his superiors at the university enough, and did he feel he had their backing enough, to make it worth trying?

As one might expect, Tuberville was called in to visit with the university president, Jay Gogue, on Monday. He then spoke with Athletic Director Jay Jacobs on Tuesday and again on Wednesday. He was not, as they say, feeling the love, and he wasn't sure whom he could trust.

> "After almost losing his job at the end of the 2003 season, he had little trust in anybody. Four years removed from a perfect season and two years removed from an 11-win season, he thought Jacobs and Gogue should have, during the season, forcefully stopped speculation about his job security. They didn't.
>
> "Jacobs and Gogue told Tuberville they wanted him to stay and put it in writing. But he had decided he didn't want to stay.

He told Jacobs he wanted to leave but he couldn't because he would lose his buyout of some $5 million. Jacobs was left in a quandary. Should he keep a coach who had told him he didn't want to be there or should he give him his buyout and move on? He chose to do the latter, and Tuberville was gone."
—Philip Marshall, Auburn Undercover

Van Allen Plexico

There is a theory out there that a "Jetgate II" happened near the end of the 2008 season, and ultimately led to Tuberville's departure.

The original event known as "Jetgate" had occurred at the end of the 2003 season. Auburn officials, frustrated with the team's failure to live up to high expectations that year, quietly reached out to Bobby Petrino about his interest in returning to Auburn, this time as the head coach. Petrino was still the head man at Louisville after leaving Auburn for that job in 2002. When the Auburn jet was spotted on the runway in Louisville, the story blew wide open, leading to many fans vocally rallying behind Tuberville. Faced with a backlash from the alumni and fans, Auburn officials ultimately decided to stick with their existing coach.

After that incident, Tuberville's agent, Jimmy Sexton, had inserted a clause into the coach's contract stating that if another such "Jetgate" incident happened, Tuberville would be owed his full buyout and could walk away.

The "Jetgate II" story goes that Auburn officials quietly reached out to Houston Nutt at Ole Miss about taking over the Auburn job after 2008, just as they had to Petrino five years earlier. Nutt informed his agent, who also happened to be Sexton, about the Auburn query. Sexton in turn passed word of this on to his other client, Tommy Tuberville.

Some believe this version of events in part because it sheds more light on why Tuberville had become so distrustful of Jacobs and company by the end of the 2008 season that he preferred to walk away. It would also explain why Auburn paid Tuberville his buyout despite not firing him: because his renegotiated contract required that payment if another "Jetgate" incident had taken place.

Which version of events is true? We may never know.

"The last 10 years have been a great time in my life, both professionally and personally. It's been a great place to coach and live, and we've had a lot of success along the way. I'm going to remain in Auburn and help the Auburn family however I can. I'm very appreciative of the coaches, players, staff and Auburn fans over the last decade."
—*Tommy Tuberville, written statement after separating from Auburn*

"Tommy and I have had the opportunity to discuss the direction of the program. Through those discussions, Tommy felt it would be in his and the program's best interest to step aside as Auburn's head football coach."
—*Jay Jacobs, Auburn Athletic Director, written statement*

Five years earlier, and with the help of the fans, Tuberville had managed to save his job at Auburn, when the administration had made moves to replace him. This time, he didn't make the effort. This time, he simply walked away.

"None of this—not one word—comes from 'sources.' I was there, in and out of Tuberville's office and Jacobs' office as it all came down. Tuberville was not fired. He didn't trust Jacobs or (President) Gouge or the Board of Trustees. He felt unappreciated if not unwanted and left of his own accord."
—*Philip Marshall, Auburn Undercover*

Tuberville quit. He quit because he felt he couldn't trust the Board of Trustees or the Auburn administration. The issue was confused a bit in public perception because he was then paid his $5 million buyout, something that normally only happens when a coach is fired. Auburn may have paid him the buyout because they felt he'd remain in the job, but only half-heartedly, if they didn't. They may have paid him because they felt he had earned it over his full tenure at the school. Or perhaps they did it because they'd violated the terms of his contract and were required to do so.

ALL THEY DID WAS WIN

"We took it hard. There was a week or so there where we were on a roller coaster of emotion. There is that relationship you build with coaches. People who become mentors to young men. And when they lose that mentor, how people react, how people handle those things emotionally, I think, is the challenging part."
—Ryan Pugh, Auburn center

John Ringer
It seemed like there were people in the Auburn fan base that were more Tuberville people than Auburn people at one point. But with all coaches in all sports, there's a certain period of time when the coaches and the fans kind of grow tired of each other, unless you're winning the national title every year. Tuberville had had some great success. But I think the offensive coordinator thing was an issue, and people saw how things were improving in other parts of the SEC, and were concerned that he couldn't keep up with them.

Van Allen Plexico
Yeah, I agree.
When he was nearly fired after 2003, I was among the Auburn fans that were upset and wanted him to stay.
When I saw the story on television at the end of 2008 that he was leaving or had been fired (it was never clear), my reaction was, "Yeah, it's probably time."
I still appreciate all that his teams accomplished, but I was ready for something new in 2009.

Tuberville went 85-40 in his ten years at Auburn. In the four seasons prior to the disastrous 2008 campaign, he'd guided the Tigers to 42 victories and an 82.4 percent winning percentage. And now he was gone, and the job of head football coach at Auburn was open.
The Tigers needed a new coach. And the fans wanted a winner.
Re-enter: Gene Chizik.

- 2 -

A DREAM JOB

It wasn't just the Auburn Family that was interested in who Auburn would hire as its next head football coach. The national media jumped in with both feet—and Jay Jacobs felt they were often getting the story wrong from the start. Not only were reports surfacing that he'd fired Tuberville—something Jacobs strenuously denied—there were also suggestions the hiring process for the new coach was well underway.

> *"It (the end of the Tuberville regime) all went down on a Thursday, when Tommy and I went to the president and Tommy said, 'I'm done. I'm out.' We hadn't even thought to interview anybody yet. And on Saturday on ESPN... they're talking about who we've interviewed. And we hadn't even left campus yet."*
> —Jay Jacobs, interview on Auburn Undercover podcast, 2025

Jacobs went on to suggest that some coaches were telling their athletic directors that Auburn was talking to them, in the hopes of getting more money from their current schools. He had to call a couple of those ADs and reassure them that he hadn't actually spoken to anyone on their staff. "This is crazy stuff," he told one AD.

Soon enough, however, the search process for the new coach did begin.

Auburn fans wanted a winner. Despite a couple of mediocre seasons in Ames, Iowa, Gene Chizik had been just that his entire career: *A winner*. The problem was, not everybody remembered that fact.

But Jay Jacobs did.

When word began to spread among the Auburn Family that Jacobs had apparently narrowed his coaching search down to Chizik and perhaps one or two other finalists, reaction was mixed, to say the least.

Chizik himself found the idea far-fetched. He couldn't believe any school—even one as familiar with him and his qualities as Auburn—would pursue him after his Cyclones had won only five games over the previous two seasons. He firmly believed he had Iowa State on the right track, but he also felt that reviving the Cyclones' fortunes would be a long and sometimes painful process. That meant losing some games—maybe a lot of games—before they could start winning. And piling up that many losses likely meant he wouldn't appear on the radar of any other programs for some time to come.

Apparently, Jay Jacobs thought otherwise.

Jacobs could see past the 5-19 record to what Chizik had accomplished everywhere else he'd been before that. He believed Chizik was still a prize catch of a coach, and one with the added benefit of being intimately familiar with the Auburn program.

"We flew into Dallas and talked to Gene," Jacobs told the Auburn Undercover podcast in 2025, "and he put it all out there for us, on 'how are we going to do this.' And we just knew, having worked with him, and his values and how he fit Auburn. We just knew he was the right guy at the time, compared to the others."

Jacobs also tells the story of how, during the search, "One prominent alumnus called me and said, 'This (big time coach) will come to Auburn. So I called that coach—and he said, 'I'm not coming to Auburn!'

"So you try to manage that. It's a little bit challenging sometimes. But it's (also) wonderful, because people care."

John Ringer
These are the people that Auburn interviewed before they hired Gene Chizik: Ball State's Brady Hoke, who went on to be Michigan's coach; Louisiana Tech's Derek Dooley...

Van Allen Plexico
Derek Dooley? Oh, good lord! We dodged a bullet! We dodged a bullet, John!!

John Ringer
Buffalo's Turner Gill; TCU's Gary Patterson...

Van Allen Plexico
With every coaching opening back then, here comes Gary Patterson's name.

John Ringer
Wake Forest's Jim Grobe—out of this list, he's the second-best coach after Patterson. Tulsa's Todd Graham; Georgia assistant coach Rodney Garner, and Miami assistant Patrick Nix. Houston Nutt and Bobby Petrino were under discussion. Supposedly we reached out to Petrino, but he'd just gotten to Arkansas and wasn't interested in leaving.

Van Allen Plexico
You can vouch for me here: I was saying for a long time (on the AU Wishbone Podcast), "Why not just get Gene Chizik? He had an undefeated season as the defensive coordinator at Auburn, and then the next season was undefeated at Texas. He was a very good defensive coordinator for us. He knows Auburn."

John Ringer
Oh yes. You were carrying the flag for Chizik.

Van Allen Plexico
So, when we hired him, I was excited. It was like, "They're listening to me!"

Of course, whether that would turn out to be a good thing or not, we didn't know yet.

When Jacobs spoke with him on the phone, Chizik—still incredulous at being considered—wanted to be absolutely sure he was a serious candidate for Auburn. "Iowa State has been great to me," he told the Auburn AD, "and I'm extremely happy."

"If we weren't serious about this," Jacobs replied, "we wouldn't be having this conversation right now."

Even so, Chizik was reluctant to even sit down with Jacobs and Auburn.

> *"If any news leaked out about my showing interest in another job, that would cause nothing but problems back in Iowa. It just wasn't worth the risk to interview for a job that was a longshot at best."*
> —Gene Chizik, All In (2011)

The two men found a compromise. Chizik was planning to fly to Dallas for back surgery to repair a ruptured disc that had been causing him extreme pain. Jacobs agreed to meet him in Dallas and conduct the interview there. The operation made for a good cover story, since it gave him a legitimate reason to be there. Chizik was convinced everything would blow up if he flew directly to Auburn to interview. And he still felt there was little chance he'd get the job, so it was scarcely worth the risk.

Barely able to walk, pumped full of pain medications and described by his wife as looking "green," he hobbled into the interview with the Auburn search committee carrying no notes. He'd had little time to prepare any, and wasn't in the right state of mind to draw up anything very sophisticated. He instead spoke off the cuff, basing his presentation to them on his personal experiences as a head coach at Iowa State the past two years.

The question he'd been expecting all along was brought up by Tim Jackson, one of the associate athletic directors: If they hired him, how would they explain his 5-19 record at Iowa State to the public?

Chizik countered that he would be a much better head coach now than he would've been before taking the Iowa State job, because of everything he had learned while going 5-19. In his 2011 autobiographical book, *All In*, he notes that when he first arrived at Ames, Iowa, he wasn't even sure how to be a head coach. He had to figure out how to divide his time between the offense, defense, and special teams, and learn how to be an administrator over the entire program rather than just a coach of one specific area. It didn't come easily to him, and he figured it out as he went along. Now, two years later—two very trying years, but important ones—he believed he was ready.

The interview lasted only ninety minutes. The candidate just before him had been in with Jacobs and the others much longer. When it was over, he told his wife he was sure he hadn't swayed the decision-makers.

> *"We both felt deflated and filled with a certain measure of regret. Here we'd agreed to this interview for a position I didn't really think I had a shot at, aware that more harm than good could come of it if people back home (in Ames) found out. The fact that my interview had been much shorter than the previous interviewee's, not to mention Jay's reluctance to commit to a firm timetable on making a decision, made me sure this risk would be all for nothing."*
> —Gene Chizik, All In (2011)

Before leaving Dallas, Chizik decided to call Jacobs and withdraw his name from consideration for the job. His call was sent to voicemail, where he left Jacobs a message to that effect. Then he and his wife boarded the plane for Iowa.

Upon landing in Des Moines, he saw that Jacobs had attempted to call him multiple times. When they finally connected, he tried again to take his name out of consideration. Jacobs interrupted him. "Chiz. I want you to be the next head football coach at Auburn."

Chizik was shocked. He honestly had not believed he would get the offer. He'd felt that Auburn must be interviewing other names. Bigger names. Most of all, he had concluded his losing record at Iowa State would be a dealbreaker.

He had been wrong. A job he considered one of the best in the country was his for the taking.

He then shocked Jacobs in turn by saying he needed to talk to his wife about it, and would get back to him. He was still deeply conflicted. He knew it was his dream job, but he had poured his heart and soul into building up Iowa State the last two years, and believed he had them on the cusp of being truly competitive. He liked the people there, his kids were in school there, they'd all made friends and were settling into the community. The thought of suddenly just walking away made him sick.

But this was Auburn. The head coaching job at Auburn. The one place he and his wife had always said they dreamed of getting back to someday. It was just that someday had come a lot sooner than anyone expected.

Meanwhile, back in the state of Alabama, Jay Jacobs wasn't the only one surprised by how this search was playing out.

Somehow, inevitably, the news got out that the search committee had chosen Gene Chizik. Despite his impressive coaching credentials that stretched back well into the 1980s, including a 29-game winning streak as defensive coordinator at Auburn and Texas, quite a few Auburn fans were underwhelmed by the news. They felt Auburn required an established head coach with a winning record.

Some Auburn fans made their opinion of the potential hire very public. One fan greeted Jacobs at the airport on his return from negotiations with the infamous cry, "Boo! We want a winner, not a loser!" He continued to shout at Jacobs as the athletic director walked by, throwing out various names of coaches he considered better candidates, peppered with the occasional "Five and nineteen!"

John Ringer

One of the most iconic moments in Auburn history. Jay Jacobs lands at the airport in Opelika in the Auburn jet and gets off, and there's one guy at the fence, yelling, "We want a winner, not a loser."

Before leaving the airport, Jacobs was asked by a reporter, "Got your man?" Jacobs responded, "Nope, still in the process." Another reporter noted that multiple reports had come out saying Auburn was focused on hiring Chizik. Jacobs responded, "We're still processing right now. There's a lot of stuff going on."

Back in Iowa, Chizik made his decision. After weighing the pros and cons, discussing it with his wife and praying about it, he called Jacobs and accepted the job.

In the end, and to the chagrin of the airport heckler, the new head football coach of Auburn University was Gene Chizik. The hiring was announced on Saturday, December 13, 2008. He and his family flew down over the weekend and he was introduced to the public at a press conference the following Monday.

Van Allen Plexico
There had been a lot of talk that he was disorganized as a head coach at Iowa State. That they'd had a lot of sideline problems there. In other words, it wasn't just his win-loss record there. The talk was that he hadn't run the most buttoned-down, disciplined program—and, indeed, that would come back to haunt us later, though not really until midway through the 2011 season.

And so, even though the Chizik Era was only going to last four years, I'd argue we got our money's worth out of him.

John Ringer
Absolutely we did.

Van Allen Plexico
I wouldn't change a thing. There's an unwritten rule in football that you don't take points off the board. You don't take the field goal off the scoreboard, even if the other team gets called for a penalty. Well, even though it doesn't last very long or end very well, you don't take 2010 off the scoreboard and say, 'What if we could've gotten a better coach.' We might have gotten a better long-term coach—Pat Dye was a better long-term coach; Tommy Tuberville was a better long-term coach—but Gene Chizik coached us to a national championship in just two years.

I never understood the shortsightedness of people who would dwell on his record at Iowa State and couldn't see past that to how big of a winner he had been literally everywhere else before that. It's like if Alabama had refused to hire Nick Saban because he didn't do well with the Dolphins, or South Carolina rejected Steve

Spurrier because he didn't do great with the Redskins. The only difference is that Chizik hadn't been a head coach before, but that scarcely seemed like a dealbreaker to me. I felt like we were getting him at just the right time, maybe while we still could.

Many fans were happy with the hire. Some were not. And some folks back in Ames, Iowa, were also quite upset. And not just a little bit salty.

> *"Gene confirmed for me today that he is accepting the head coaching position at Auburn. I'm disappointed for our Iowa State fans and student-athletes that he has chosen to leave our program after only two seasons.*
>
> *"I understand that it is a dream job for him, but the timing and the way it played out has been hurtful and disappointing. Although this is a significant setback, we will get through the challenge because the Iowa State University athletics program is far greater than one person."*
> —Jamie Pollard, Iowa State Athletic Director

Chizik had earned $1.05 million in base salary and guaranteed pay from Iowa State the previous season, and owed Iowa State a $750,000 buyout.

> *"I'm extremely proud and excited to have Gene returning to Auburn to take over as head football coach of this program. I know that we have found the right fit for Auburn. Gene's body of work during his 23 years in this profession is remarkable. He has a strong knowledge of this athletics program, this university and the community, and he knows how to be successful in the Southeastern Conference. He is a high-energy coach that is an outstanding motivator and demands a tough, physical style of football.*
>
> *"I'm confident that Gene can build upon the foundation that has been established and make this a program that competes for championships on a consistent basis."*
> —Jay Jacobs, Auburn Athletic Director

Speaking about the Chizik hire on the Auburn Undercover podcast in 2025, Jay Jacobs returned to the concept of "fit" for a coach.

"Finding the right fit is so important," Jacobs said. "Gene Chizik—we worked with him (as defensive coordinator) and went undefeated at Auburn in 2004, and then he goes to Texas as defensive coordinator and goes undefeated there and wins the national championship. Man, if we'd hired him then, there probably wouldn't have been any controversy at all.

"It certainly didn't end the way we wanted it to, and there's a lot of factors there, but if he's not here, we don't win a national championship.

"And the fit for him was that he had been here before. He knew what Auburn is all about. He's a guy that is honest and has integrity. He just thinks about ball. He's a ball coach. And he cares about his players. That was a great fit for us, even though it was controversial. And the interesting thing about it is, the popular coaches that some people wanted, ended up only coaching a year or two at other places before getting fired.

"You have to have the tangible and the intangible. You have to be able to win games, but you also have to fit the program. The creed requires that."

> *"Through my travels in coaching over the last twenty-three years, there's one place that I've always wanted to return to and that is Auburn. The tradition of the Auburn football program combined with the passionate fans and their love for Auburn are second to none. My family and I are Auburn through and through, and look forward to being part of the Auburn family and community."*
>
> —Gene Chizik, December 15, 2008

> *"In two years he'll be gone. Book it."*
> —Clay Travis, Deadspin

- 3 -

ANGLES AND GEOMETRY

Once ensconced in the head coach's office, Gene Chizik began assembling his staff.

And it would be a *new* staff. In his book, *All In*, he states that his 5-19 record at Iowa State was the main reason he was reluctant to bring assistants from that staff with him to the new job:

> "With the perception battle I would be facing at Auburn, I knew I wouldn't be able to take most of (his Iowa State assistants) to Alabama with me. I would be a tough enough sell on my own; there was no way I could convince the folks at Auburn to take on an entire staff with a losing record.
>
> "I... informed the (Iowa State) coaches that I would meet with each one individually to give him an idea of whether I would be considering him for a position at Auburn. I knew that people would be hurt in this process, but I tried to convey that none of it was purposeful on my part.
>
> "Unfortunately, I did wind up damaging some friendships by the time I had filled my staff at Auburn."
>
> —Gene Chizik, All In

Ultimately, he brought only one assistant coach from Iowa State—Jay Boulware—for his Auburn staff.

Van Allen Plexico
Chizik doesn't come right out and say it in his book, but you have to wonder if he felt he could hire a higher caliber of assistant coaches for the Auburn staff then he was able to get to come to Ames, Iowa.

Things didn't go much better for Tuberville's old Auburn staff. Chizik told them, "There's a good chance that no one in here is going to be able to stay with me. So my advice to you is to go out and look for a job... Right now, you have to assume that you don't have a job."
Likewise, from that group of assistants, he immediately retained only one member. Kevin Yoxall, the Strength and Conditioning coach, had been at Auburn for a decade, and Chizik knew him from his previous stint there. Philip Lolley, who had been working in an administrative role under Tuberville, was kept around to maintain continuity in recruiting. Everyone else from the previous Auburn staff, barring the chaplain, Chette Williams, was dismissed. Chizik appreciated having a team chaplain and—controversially—had even pressed for one to be instituted at Iowa State when he first took that job.

Van Allen Plexico
He wasn't interested in keeping Tuberville's assistants, either. It seems as if he'd made up his mind that he wanted an entirely new staff of coaches that would operate at a higher level than either Iowa State or Auburn had had in 2008. I would say for the most part he succeeded.

On December 26, Chizik and Auburn decided to rehire linebackers coach James Willis, who'd been let go from the previous staff. A former star player for Auburn, Willis had served as a defensive graduate assistant under Chizik in 2003, so there was some familiarity.
Willis initially agreed to join the new staff, but his second tenure on the Plains didn't last a month. Nick Saban and Alabama swooped

in and hired him away on January 21. The job of coaching linebackers in 2009 would eventually be added to the defensive coordinator's plate.

Van Allen Plexico
It was cool to see Chizik try to rehire James Willis, who had played for the Tigers during Pat Dye's final years in charge and was always a favorite. Seeing Alabama lure him away was pretty depressing.

Interestingly enough, after just one season in Tuscaloosa, he followed Tommy Tuberville to his new job at Texas Tech, accepting the role of defensive coordinator for the Red Raiders.

Next came the hire that made possibly the biggest splash among assistant coaches: Gus Malzahn as offensive coordinator.

John Ringer
I think the big thing that sold Chizik to the Auburn folks as head coach early on—and people were skeptical, because of his record—was that he put a really good staff together.

Malzahn was the hot hire. Chizik getting him, with Chizik's defensive background, getting the up-and-coming offensive guy, that was really exciting.

Van Allen Plexico
I was so excited about Malzahn. I remembered what he'd done to us at Arkansas in 2006, and what he'd accomplished at Tulsa.

The offense had been the main problem the previous few seasons. It ultimately got Tony Franklin and then Tommy Tuberville run off. With Chizik being a defensive-minded coach, it was understood from the beginning that he was going to have to find a coordinator who could assemble and run a successful offense for him. Malzahn appeared to check every box.

Some concerned fans and commentators pointed out that the situation here seemed not that different from the one that had so recently brought Tommy Tuberville's tenure to a sudden conclusion. Once again you had a defensive-minded head coach who brought in an offensive coordinator with a somewhat radical system, based around spread concepts. How would this be any different? Could they work together? Would they clash?

Similarities existed, yes—but beyond the superficial, the comparisons ended.

Malzahn's system was much more run-oriented than Franklin's, so it fit with Auburn's traditional approach. It relied on extremely simple, easy-to-learn schemes. A young player only needed to absorb what he personally had to do, not how to read the defense. And it was predicated on tempo—going fast on offense. Everything else sprang from that simple concept.

Van Allen Plexico

Gus's philosophy always seemed to me as, "If my players are going fast enough from play to play, and I'm doing enough things to pull your players out of position and open up vulnerabilities in your defense, my guys don't have to be able to read your formations or whatever."

That's why the "hurry-up" as well as the fabled "eye-candy" pre-snap motion aspects of his offense are so important. The offense doesn't have to figure as much out, if the defense doesn't have time to figure anything out, either!

"If some no-huddle teams, like (Tony) Franklin's, are light-speed, then Malzahn's spends the entire game in something akin to 'ludicrous speed.'

"The key to his offense is to... have the ball snapped within four to five seconds of it being set... It requires endurance and discipline.

"The other side of Malzahn's attack, apart from the no-huddle aspect (I can't emphasize enough how unique it is to base your offensive philosophy around a tempo rather than simply schemes), is that Malzahn wants to formation you to death.

"But Malzahn is less spread and formation to run than he is infatuated with angles and geometry: he passes to set up the run, he uses a lot of shotgun, multiple receivers, and he does a lot of innovative things with wing-backs, tight-ends, fullbacks, and with guys in motion to get any advantage he can.

"In this way his offense has advantages over what Franklin was doing at Auburn. If done correctly, the tempo and formations really are what eats the defense up."
—Chris Brown, Smart Football website, December 29, 2008

Van Allen Plexico
I loved everything about Gus's offense from day one. Unfortunately, I think he rarely got to run it the way he wanted. Even when he later became coach, and Auburn was promoting "Auburn Fast" on the football schedules and posters and so forth, he slowed things way down.

What often happens is head coaches are attracted by the fireworks and high-scoring nature of a hurry-up, no-huddle offense. But once they install it, they realize it often results in their defense having to go back out on the field a lot, with very little time being taken off the game clock. That lengthens the game for the defense and wears them down. Consequently, head coaches often begin to interfere with the offensive coordinator—who, again, is mostly thinking in terms of what he wants the offense to be doing, and isn't really concerned with the defense. The head coach tells the OC to slow down, so the defense can get some rest and the game can be shortened. In Gus Malzahn's case, he didn't just like to go fast, he actually kept track of how many plays his offense was running in a game. He was convinced his teams wouldn't lose if they reached a certain number of offensive plays in a game. So he wanted to go fast and to squeeze in as many plays as possible. But if you're not making first downs, what that results in is punting the ball back to the other team with only a few seconds taken off the game clock.

That means you tend to have offensive coordinators saying "Go go go! Go faster! Run more plays!" while the head coach is saying "Slow down! Run fewer plays! Let the defense rest!" Inevitably you get clashes between the two coaches. And since the head coach usually wins those clashes, the offensive coordinator often becomes disgruntled and wants to leave.

Once those offensive coordinators become head coaches in their own rights, however, they then are responsible for the entire team—and suddenly they understand why it is important to let their defense rest. So *they* start slowing their offense down.

Gus was a perfect example of this. When he later became a head coach, he drastically slowed down his offense. Maybe those head coaches weren't so crazy after all!

Tony Franklin's offense, like that of Air Raid gurus like Mike Leach, called upon a quarterback to survey the field and make decisions. It therefore required a smart, seasoned QB to operate it. Malzahn's offense was able to cover up for deficiencies in personnel of that nature—young players; players new to the system—by drastically simplifying the process.

Malzahn had coached high school football in Springdale, Arkansas for five years, where he was able to employ his radical, tempo-based schemes to great success. His teams reached the state championship game twice in that time, winning in his final season of 2005 with a 14-0 record, while outscoring opponents 664-118. During that time, he turned down multiple offers to coach at the college level.

Then came 2006, and a call from Fayetteville, Arkansas.

Houston Nutt had been head coach for the Razorbacks for eight seasons at that point, and the offense he was running—while calling the plays himself—had grown stale, in the eyes of many. That included athletic director Frank Broyles. Broyles had become familiar with Malzahn's high school exploits in-state, and urged Nutt to consider him.

> *"He (Broyles) said the thing that would be really good for this state right now would be to hire Gus Malzahn. I visited with Gus. I was impressed with him. I was impressed with some of the things he did in high school. I said 'OK, that's probably going to work.'*
>
> *"He also had five good players (on his Springdale High team he could bring) with him."*
>
> —Houston Nutt, quoted by Greg Ostendorf, ESPN website

The "Springdale Five," as they came to be called, were seen as something of a package deal Arkansas would be receiving along with Malzahn's services as offensive coordinator. All five were committed to big-time, out-of-state schools like Notre Dame and Florida, but four of them flipped to Arkansas when Nutt made the hire. Those four included Mitch Mustain, the 2005 Gatorade

ALL THEY DID WAS WIN

National Player of the Year, who had flourished in Malzahn's system at Springdale High.

> *"The only reason we went to the University of Arkansas was because of Malzahn."*
> —Ben Cleveland, one of the Springdale Five

The Razorbacks enjoyed a successful season in 2006. After dropping their opener to USC, they reeled off ten straight wins, including one over Tommy Tuberville's 11-2 Auburn squad in Jordan-Hare. That game ultimately knocked Auburn out of the SEC Championship Game and put Arkansas in. It also gave Auburn fans and administrators a good look at what Malzahn's offense could do.

Behind the scenes, however, there were clashes of personality and philosophy between Nutt and Malzahn. The Arkansas head coach didn't like the "no-huddle" part of the offense, and wasn't that thrilled with the "hurry-up" part either. The locker room became divided between the Springdale crowd and the rest of the team. Players complained about playing time; parents complained about that and more. Chafing under Nutt's restrictions and limitations, not to mention the team dissension, Malzahn looked for an escape hatch. He found it in the form of the Golden Hurricanes of Tulsa.

At Tulsa the following season, Malzahn's offense flourished.

> *"I think it was a deal of having a common philosophy in our values and how we run a program and what we believed in, and it was a great combination."*
> —Todd Graham, Tulsa head coach during Malzahn's tenure as OC, 2007-2008

At Tulsa, Malzahn served as assistant head coach to Todd Graham while splitting the offensive coordinator duties with offensive line coach Herb Hand. The arrangement worked; their offense in 2007 and 2008 racked up gaudy numbers. They led the nation in total offense the first year and finished second in total offense and scoring offense the second year, averaging 565 yards and over 47 points per game. This attracted considerable national attention—including that of Gene Chizik, who was searching for a splashy hire as offensive coordinator.

Auburn officially hired Malzahn away from Tulsa on December 28. Chizik had the big-name, hot-commodity assistant coach he'd wanted.

"It's fair to say (Malzahn) is an attention-grabbing hire for new coach Gene Chizik."
—Deric Winslett, The Bleacher Report, December 28, 2008

Sources told ESPN reporters that Malzahn was "teary-eyed" when he broke the news to his colleagues and players at Tulsa that he was departing for Auburn. But he couldn't pass up the chance to return to the SEC at a big-time program.

"This is an exciting opportunity to coach at Auburn, get involved with the Auburn family and work for Coach Chizik. I can't wait to get to Auburn and get started."
—Gus Malzahn, Auburn offensive coordinator

"Gus is one of the great offensive minds in college football and we are very excited to have him join the Auburn staff. His track record at all levels of coaching is remarkable and his offenses have been extremely successful both running and passing the ball."
—Gene Chizik

But the task of hiring a staff wasn't over. The Tigers needed a coordinator for the other side of the ball, plus assistant coaches for the skill positions.

Ted Roof had spent five years as interim head coach and then head coach of the Duke Blue Devils, where he compiled a record of 6-45. His teams didn't win much, but the defenses showed marked improvement from the years before he arrived. After Duke let him go, he was hired as defensive coordinator by Minnesota. There he brought about improvements in defensive stats similar to those he'd accomplished at Duke, thereby catching the notice of Gene Chizik.

John Ringer
Ted Roof was fine as defensive coordinator. He was solid. Trooper Taylor and Curtis Luper were big-time recruiters at the time, and we *needed* coaches who were big-time recruiters, because we were going against Alabama and LSU and Georgia. They added energy. They brought a much-needed injection of energy to the staff.

Van Allen Plexico
For me, even this many years later, the jury is still out on Roof as a defensive coordinator. There's no question he was able to make some parts of the Auburn defense much better. But there always seemed to be a tradeoff, where other parts would become deficient. The run defense was usually terrific under Roof, but the pass defense struggled at times—especially early in games, meaning we'd start out in the hole. But then, late in games, the same defenses with the same players would be rock-solid.

It was bewildering.

On January 2, 2009, Chizik hired Curtis Luper away from Oklahoma State to coach the Tigers' running backs and serve as recruiting coordinator. Chizik and Luper had worked together from 1995-1997 when Luper was an assistant to defensive coordinator Chizik at Stephen F. Austin.

> *"The opportunity to reconnect with my mentor in Coach Chizik and have the chance to coach at a program known as Running Back U was something that I could not pass up."*
> *— Curtis Luper*

While in the neighborhood of Stillwater, and at the urging of Luper, Chizik also snatched up wide receivers coach Trooper Taylor. Chizik gave him the same responsibility on the Tigers staff along with the added title of assistant head coach. Taylor was at times a divisive figure but had been a successful recruiter as well as a coach, and was beloved by many. He was known for his infectious enthusiasm, often waving a towel on the sideline in an effort to fire up the crowd.

> *"Trooper Taylor is another solid hire for Gene Chizik, as the new Auburn head coach looks to continue the trend of bringing excellent coach and recruiter combinations to the plains. Those who doubted Chizik's leadership early on obviously underestimated the man.*
>
> *"Nationally known as a successful and relentless recruiter, Taylor was recognized by Rivals.com as a top-25 recruiter in 2005 and 2007."*
> —Deric Winslett, The Bleacher Report, January 5, 2009

Four days later, Chizik made the hire of Ted Roof official. In addition to assuming the defensive coordinator job—and due to the departure of James Willis—Roof would coach the linebackers. He received a $20,000 a year raise over the $350,000 salary he'd been earning at Minnesota—plus the opportunity to coach in the SEC.

> *"Ted has a wealth of experience and success as a defensive coach, and philosophically, we think alike. Ted took a Minnesota defense and made dramatic improvements in his one year as defensive coordinator. It was a defense that was very physical and aggressive, and created a lot of turnovers."*
> —Gene Chizik, 2009

Despite Willis's move to Alabama, the defensive staff would have a strong Auburn pedigree, thanks to the assistant coach Chizik hired just a few days later. Tracy Rocker, the All-American lineman who had anchored Auburn's great defensive units of 1985-1988, announced he would be leaving Ole Miss to come home to the Plains. Upon his arrival in Auburn, he was given responsibility over the entire defensive line for the Tigers.

"We have our work cut out," he told reporters. "The thing I'm looking forward to is hard work."

He expressed enthusiasm for new defensive coordinator Ted Roof, saying "I always heard he was a great guy to work for." He stated that returning to his alma mater was "a great honor," adding, "I always wanted to be known as a great coach. I'm not a player anymore. I'm a coach."

Van Allen Plexico

Having Tracy Rocker as defensive line coach really was a dream come true. We had loved those incredible Pat Dye defenses of the late Eighties. Despite those teams being loaded with talent, Rocker was always the star of those defenses. His NFL career had ended prematurely due to injury, but everyone expected he would be a great coach if he chose to pursue that line of work, and the previous decade had proven that.

The rest of the staff took well into February to assemble. Chizik hired Jeff Grimes away from Colorado to coach the offensive line. Jay Boulware followed Chizik from Iowa State to coach tight ends and special teams, though the hire wasn't finalized until later in January. Philip Lolley had served as a strength and conditioning coach for Tuberville earlier in his career, but was then moved to an administrative role for several years. Chizik, familiar with him from his previous stint at Auburn, pressed him into service to help with recruiting during the coaching transition. He then raised a few eyebrows when he decided to hire Lolley as an on-field coach, working with cornerbacks. Tommy Thigpen rounded out the staff by leaving North Carolina to take the job at Auburn coaching the safeties.

In a matter of weeks, Chizik had assembled a staff worthy of the Auburn name.

Van Allen Plexico

It wasn't necessarily the greatest coaching staff ever, but there was plenty to like about it. Probably the highlights were Malzahn running the offense and Tracy Rocker coaching the defensive front. Luper and Taylor brought in energy and excitement—and recruiting acumen, we hoped. I remember we weren't sure about Ted Roof, but we knew the head coach had been a great defensive coordinator for us and at other schools. So the general feeling was, "If Roof works out, great—and if not, Chizik can surely set it all straight."

I remember the main thing I was wondering about, as the team transitioned into preparing for their first season under Chizik, was, "Will he allow Gus to do all the unorthodox, super-fast things on offense that Gus is known for?" College and pro football are both littered with the remains of football teams where the offensive coordinator wanted to go fast and run lots of plays, and the defensive coordinator wanted just as badly to keep his unit off the field as much as possible, and the head coach got caught in the middle.

Houston DC Buddy Ryan infamously punching OC Kevin Gilbride on the Oilers sideline, for not running enough clock before sending the defense back out on the field, is just one vivid example.

Only time would tell if this staff could gel—if they could win over the players, bring in top new recruits and work together as a cohesive unit. And if Chizik and Roof would be comfortable with Gus Malzahn and his "ludicrous speed" hurry-up, no-huddle offense, and let him run it the way he wanted to.

But without a doubt the fans couldn't wait to see it in action.

- 4 -

AN ENVIRONMENT OF CONFIDENCE

Gene Chizik arrived in Auburn to discover a team divided.

Immediately after taking up his new post, the head coach began meeting with the returning players. He discovered the team was fragmented in more ways than one—not just racially, in some cases, but also between younger and older players, between the offense and the defense, and even among the various position groups. The players rarely spent any time together outside of the football building. Even there, they were usually divided into different personnel meeting rooms. They barely knew one another, the confidence of many was shot, and their overall morale was low.

The young men that would together make up the 2009 Auburn Tigers barely looked capable of beating a single opponent, much less returning to winning seasons and bowl games.

Chizik addressed this situation in a multitude of ways, from team-building exercises to visits to a local water park to fishing trips. He had players' locker assignments rearranged to mix players from different position groups together, created a lounge with games and pool tables in the football building so the players would mingle, changed up which units used which meeting rooms, and even had the walls repainted to provide a fresh start for everyone. "Little by little," he said later, "we were creating an environment of confidence in and reliance on one another," and, "the lines of separation...were being erased."

In addition to the "carrot" of new ways for the players to mix and get to know one another, however, he also wielded the metaphorical "stick" of not hesitating to boot out players that wouldn't get with the new program.

> *"Initially I wouldn't say (the transition to Chizik) was the smoothest. Chiz came in and just set the tone from the beginning. He's like, 'This is my way or the highway. We're gonna be a team, we're gonna have leaders.' Guys (were out) left and right. 'You're out. You're out.' He was getting rid of guys who weren't on the same page as us, and not trying to make this transition. Because he knew what kind of team we were capable of (becoming), and what he wanted."*
>
> —Josh Bynes, Auburn linebacker

When Tommy Tuberville had exited the Auburn job, he'd left behind quite a few very talented players. Players like offensive lineman Lee Ziemba, running backs Ben Tate and Mario Fannin, linebacker Josh Bynes and kicker Wes Byrum.

He also left behind a pair of quarterbacks whose roles on the team had never quite been settled. Chizik there inherited a dilemma of multiple dimensions.

The offensive coordinator in 2007, Al Borges, had recruited high school star Kodi Burns to be the next great Auburn quarterback. Burns was very good when running the ball, but his passing skills were rough and underdeveloped. When Tony Franklin replaced Borges as OC the following year, he brought in Chris Todd, more of a pocket passer, from junior college. Burns was the better athlete but Franklin wasn't convinced he could run the Spread properly, while Todd was more familiar with it. Tuberville had pushed for Burns to be the starter, while Franklin preferred Todd. Both had played a good bit for the Tigers in 2008, starting roughly half the games each. Neither had seized control of the job. In the bowl game at the end of 2007, Franklin had literally swapped them out every other play. To make matters more complicated, Burns was African American while Todd was white. As a result, the locker room was divided, with each quarterback having his supporters and detractors. The offensive players and defensive players were also divided, with the defense feeling the offense wasn't carrying its weight.

Chizik and his staff had to figure out quickly who would be the starter, and then get the team—the entire team—to accept that decision and move forward together.

> "We had to convince our players that this quarterback call wasn't about Kodi or Chris. This was about Auburn football. We wouldn't give an ounce of consideration to how the two had arrived at Auburn. It wouldn't matter who the players favored. Nothing outside of football would influence our choice. We would pick the quarterback who would win the most games for the Auburn Tigers. That was the only factor."
> —Gene Chizik, All In

Chizik and the offensive coaches huddled up. They watched game film. They debated. At last, the decision was made: The Tigers were going with Chris Todd as the starting quarterback.

Chizik and Malzahn met with both players individually to break the news. They told Burns they were sure he could start at quarterback for many other teams, and understood he might consider transferring, but they wanted him to stay with Auburn and play wide receiver.

"Kodi is a very talented young man and he's an Auburn man," Chizik said after the decision was announced. "He's very unselfish. We feel like Kodi can help our football team somewhere on this offense."

Burns was deeply disappointed, "but it's a good thing for the team, and I'm a hundred percent behind it. Chris is the guy and we're behind him." He said he looked forward to trying the receiver position so he could get some touches of the ball.

Meanwhile, Todd told reporters he was excited for the opportunity he'd earned. "I have the utmost respect for the other quarterbacks. They made me better every single day. I'm definitely excited."

He'd had very little time to make an impression on the coaches—"a really short window of opportunity," as he called it. He'd been injured back at Hutchinson Community College in Kansas, two years earlier, and his passing had suffered. Surgery had corrected the problem but the recovery period had caused him to miss actively participating in spring practice. Instead he took the time to soak up all he could of Malzahn's offense. When fall practice arrived, he had only nine days to impress the coaches. Somehow he managed it.

Auburn had its starting quarterback for 2009. Now all that remained was to inform the team. That presented another opportunity for a disaster, if handled poorly. Chizik and the staff needed to do as much as possible to unite the players behind Todd.

And there was one person who could do more than anybody else to help with that.

Kodi Burns knew he was that person. Toward that end, he stepped up and did all that was humanly possible to help. He asked permission to address the entire team, and Chizik agreed. The coach had no idea what the player intended to say, but he'd already begun to trust him.

Chizik gathered the entire team together. After informing the players that Todd would be the starter, Chizik nodded to Burns, who stood and faced his teammates.

What he said next began the healing process with the team. Beyond that, it might well have set the Tigers on their way to greater glory.

> *"This is really hard for me today. But you know what? I don't want this to split our team up. I don't want there to be any discussion. I trust the coaches. If this is what they want us to do, this is what we're gonna do. I'm here to help us win games, and that's what I want to do. I'm not gonna lie—this hurts me. But you know what? I'm gonna do what the coaches ask me to do."*
> —*Kodi Burns, quoted by Gene Chizik in* All In

John Ringer

Kodi Burns said he would move to another position and do whatever he could do to help the team in that way. That paved the way for Todd to be the starting quarterback, and Burns moved to receiver, and played as a slot receiver, made a lot of plays, was very selfless out there, gave himself up, blocking a lot. And that move kind of set the tone for the team to be an unselfish team, because if he could do that, nobody else could say, "I want my touches," or "I want my playing time at this position."

Van Allen Plexico
Video of Kodi's speech was shown on the news and on the Internet over and over for the next couple of days. It was amazing how the Auburn Family immediately embraced Burns in an almost universal outpouring of love and respect you rarely see. He might not have won the starting quarterback job, but he definitely won over the Auburn Family. I never heard a single bad thing about him the rest of the time he played at Auburn. He remains absolutely beloved.

It worked out for Chris Todd, too. He ended up setting some single-season passing records. He did pretty well.

As soon as Burns finished his statement, senior running back Ben Tate stood and echoed the former quarterback's words. "Nothing's gonna divide this team," he stated emphatically to the assembled players. "We're all moving forward now."

It was time to start learning the new systems—including Malzahn's hurry-up, no huddle attack—and find out just how dangerous this formerly divided team could truly be.

- 5 -

GOOD THINGS HAPPEN

With the internal team situation seemingly on the road to resolution, Coach Chizik and his staff went to work immediately, recruiting more players. They needed difference-makers. Players that could almost single-handedly turn the program around.

They would be more successful at that than anyone could have imagined.

Some high school players had committed to Auburn during the last year of the Tuberville regime, and had decided to stick with their pledges. Others were brought in by the new staff in 2009. On paper they didn't look like the greatest class ever. But there were some diamonds in the rough—diamonds that would go on to contribute massively in the days and years to come.

They found Onterrio McCalebb.

Thin as a rail but quick as lightning, the six-foot-tall, 175-pound McCalebb—known for his ability to catch squirrels bare-handed!—was not a prototypical SEC running back. But Luper and Malzahn would find ways to utilize his remarkable speed and skills without getting him killed by the defense.

They signed Emory Blake.

Son of NFL quarterback Jeff Blake, Emory would join a surprisingly good wide receiver corps starting in 2009, and become a major contributor the following year—including making a key play in the biggest regular-season game of the year.

They found Nosa Eguae, Dee Ford and Eltoro Freeman.

All three would make an impact on the defensive side of the ball, some sooner and some later.

They found Philip Lutzenkirchen.

The tight end from Marietta, Georgia would go on to set the Auburn record for most touchdown catches by a tight end, at fourteen. But his most memorable moment would come in the 2010 Iron Bowl, when he river-danced his way into everyone's hearts.

And they brought in a former three-star offensive guard commit— a young man who had failed to qualify for enrollment at Auburn out of high school in 2007, but had spent a couple of years at Copiah-Lincoln Community College, getting his grades in order and moving over to play on the defensive line.

His name was Nicholas Lachester Fairley.

Nick Fairley wouldn't accomplish a ton as a freshman in 2009. But the following year, under the continuing tutelage of Tracy Rocker, he would amaze the entire college football world.

Meanwhile, the Tigers had players already on the roster that were hungry for more. In particular, senior running back Ben Tate.

Tate had been a heralded recruit back in 2006, but he'd never managed to have a 1,000-yard rushing season. Now, in his senior year, he wanted that. Coach Curtis Luper promised him it would happen.

John Ringer

From 2009 to 2017, Auburn had at least one running back gain 1,000 yards every season. Nine straight years—an SEC record. Ben Tate was the first.

With the pieces now in place, the 2009 season began.

The Tigers came roaring out of the gate to start the season, winning their first five games. That included home wins over Louisiana Tech and Mississippi State in the first two contests, with the formerly pedestrian offense now rolling. The Tigers rang up a combined 86 points on those two opponents. Kodi Burns even scored the first touchdown of the season for the Tigers, playing as the Wildcat quarterback and running the ball in against Tech. In the same game, Chris Todd set a school record by throwing a 93-yard touchdown pass to Terrell Zachery. The following week, against the Bulldogs, Burns scored four more times, running it in himself three times and tossing the ball to new tight end Philip Lutzenkirchen for the fourth score. Todd failed to score, but passed for 186 yards to 6 different receivers, with no interceptions.

After the Louisiana Tech game, Gene Chizik was asked about the significance of Kodi Burns scoring the first touchdown of the season. His reply was succinct, but it spoke volumes: "Good things happen to good people."

Having scored the first touchdown in the first Auburn game of 2009, Burns would later score the first touchdown in the last game of 2010. Other players got more of the spotlight over those two seasons, but in many ways Kodi Burns bookends this entire story.

In week three, the Tigers played in one of the more memorable games in Jordan-Hare Stadium history. The start of the West Virginia "Rain Game" was delayed due to a massive downpour that looked just about capable of washing the entire stadium away.

> "Right now, it feels a little more like Woodstock than it does a football game. It is a torrential downpour, and we are officially in a weather delay, and it has been raining like crazy.
>
> "They have asked the fans to go underneath the seats, in the concourse area. Most of them have obliged. The student section, though, have come with their game faces on. They ain't budging one inch."
> —Rod Bramblett, Auburn Network broadcast

The Jordan-Hare draining system was put to the toughest test imaginable that night, but it came through with flying colors. Pipes beneath the field drained the water away rapidly.

Van Allen Plexico

A lot was made for the next couple of days after that game about how well the field drained all that water, and so quickly. The groundskeepers were interviewed by TV and print media, explaining how it all worked. They got their fifteen minutes of celebrity, and it was well-deserved.

Meanwhile, many fans and students remained in the stands despite the deluge. Their determination to stick with the team and be there when play resumed was a key emotional moment in the season, pulling everyone together even tighter. The Auburn Family had bought into this new coaching staff and the first team they had assembled, and they appeared determined to not let anything get in the way.

John Ringer
That was the game that was delayed because the rain and the storms were so bad, but a lot of the Auburn students and fans stayed in the stands and they sang in the rain and enjoyed it, and I think it was inspiring. They had a great time. I think, despite the weather, the stadium had a lot of life in it when the Auburn team came back out, and they fed on that.

When the rain at last died down enough for the game to be played, those who remained in the stands and who watched on TV were treated to a wild, back-and-forth affair. In a pattern that would become familiar over the remainder of this season and much of the next, Auburn's opponent scored big early in the game, as the Auburn defense was struggling. West Virginia rang up 14 points in the first five minutes of the game, on the strength of a long pass and a long run. They led 21-10 after the first quarter, and looked to be cruising toward an easy win. In another pattern that would become familiar, however, Auburn's defense finally woke up, playing much better late.

From the second quarter on, the Tigers held the Mountaineers to just 9 more points. This was no easy task. West Virginia featured Jarrett Brown, a massive, talented, dual-threat quarterback—something Auburn fans would get to experience themselves only a year later. Auburn's defense that night, however, gave Brown fits, sacking him and turning the ball over. The Tigers' offense meanwhile rang up four more touchdowns and a field goal. When the dust—or rather the rain—cleared, Auburn had won, 41-30. The Auburn game would be West Virginia's only loss in its first seven games.

ALL THEY DID WAS WIN

Van Allen Plexico

For me, at least, the West Virginia "Rain Game" was the true start of this new era. It was the first game where I honestly said to myself, "Maybe we're back." We'd gone out and beaten a good team with very good players—a team that had beaten us the year before. For our guys to sit through the rain delays and slog through that mess and somehow survive their big, talented quarterback and everything else they threw at us, and to win... It felt like Auburn Football had accomplished something really satisfying for the first time in a very long time. Maybe since the 2007 Iron Bowl.

After a 54-30 home win over Ball State, the Tigers left Jordan-Hare for their first away game of the season and visited Tennessee. Wes Byrum kicked four field goals and Ben Tate scored an early touchdown to put Auburn ahead. After trailing the entire game, the Vols tried a late comeback, scoring 16 points in the final frame. It wasn't enough. Auburn prevailed, 26-22. The Tigers were now 5-0. Gene Chizik had already matched the win total of his entire two-year tenure at Iowa State in just over a month.

The promising start to the season ran into a big dose of reality the following Saturday, as Auburn stalled out during a visit to Arkansas. Nothing seemed to go right for the Tigers at first, and they gave up four touchdowns before halftime. The Razorbacks added two more late, keeping them well ahead of Auburn, who managed a couple of Ben Tate touchdowns and another by Onterio McCalebb, to try to make it respectable. With a final score of 44-23, the Hogs reminded the Tigers of what some had come to call the "Hawg Hex"—that Arkansas had a remarkable knack for knocking off Auburn in unexpected moments.

Auburn lost its second game in a row the next week against Kentucky. The Tigers led at the half, 14-7, but the Wildcats blanked the Tigers in the second half to win, 21-14.

LSU added to the misery on October 24. They led 17-0 at halftime in Baton Rouge, scored again immediately to start the third quarter, and at one point were up by a score of 31-3. Philip Lutzenkirchen caught another touchdown with three seconds remaining in the game to make the final score a slightly more respectable 31-10. Tiger Stadium has always been a tough place to play, but this game showed the Tigers from Auburn they still had a way to go to be truly competitive in the SEC.

The Tigers had fought hard against LSU, but simply were not quite ready yet for the bruising style of football Les Miles's squad played. Some came out of this game worse off than others, including Kodi Burns:

> *"When the team met on Sunday after the loss, I talked about how there would be no whining. I gave Kodi Burns as an example of how I wanted our players to "man up." Kodi had gotten two teeth knocked out during the game—his teeth literally had to be picked up off the field. He'd also had his lip busted open to the point that he had to have it stitched up during play. But despite the pain and the stitches, Kodi had come back to finish the game. I wanted all of our players to have this mindset of not making any excuses or looking for an easy way out."*
> —Gene Chizik, All In

Auburn finally got back to winning ways on Halloween, against Ole Miss. Most of the action took place in the third quarter of this one, with the Tigers scoring on a Kodi Burns pass to tight end Tommy Trott and then capitalizing on a 29-yard interception return by Walter McFadden. Add in a 53-yard romp by Ben Tate and a 98-yard blocked extra point return by Demond Washington and Ole Miss found themselves in a hole too deep to dig out of. The final score was 33-20. Auburn was 6-3, back to winning again, and with a weak non-conference opponent next up. It felt like the Tigers had perhaps turned something of a corner, and could finish strong.

Van Allen Plexico

I always felt like the Ole Miss game was so important that year. It was pivotal for the season. If we'd lost to Ole Miss, we'd have been 5-4, on a 4-game losing streak, with Georgia and Alabama still to come. By winning this game, it meant we were 6-3 and probably going to a bowl game, and it was no longer imperative that we find a way to upset one of those big rivals at the end of the year.

ALL THEY DID WAS WIN

Something dramatic occurred during the Ole Miss game—something that stopped the game for half an hour and scared to death everyone who was watching in the stands, from the sidelines and on television. Safety Zac Etheridge collided with defensive end Antonio Coleman while attempting to tackle Rebels running back Rodney Scott. The impact resulted in torn neck ligaments and a fractured vertebra for Etheridge, who suffered temporary paralysis as he lay unmoving on the field. In most cases like this, the injured player inevitably gets jostled about as the players separate from one another and move back to their respective huddles or sidelines. As this particular scrum was pulling itself apart, however, the Ole Miss back trapped beneath Etheridge somehow realized something was amiss. Etheridge wasn't moving. Rather than impatiently pushing him off, Scott lay still and waited to see what might be wrong.

He lay there for twenty minutes, never moving.

At last, medical personnel were able to safely place Etheridge onto a backboard, allowing Scott to get up. His decision to remain still and not try to shove the Auburn safety off of him likely saved Etheridge from permanent paralysis, if not worse.

For his efforts, Scott was later awarded the SEC Sportsmanship Award.

"He was just amazing. He said it was a God thing. He just knew that something was different. It was almost like he couldn't explain it, but he just knew it was different and he just, he lay there. And it was pretty amazing."
—Gene Chizik, on Rodney Scott

Etheridge would fully recover and play safety for the Tigers the following season.

Now 6-3 overall, the Tigers welcomed Furman to Jordan-Hare on November 7, and heaped 63 points on them. Chris Todd completed 17 of 18 passes for 256 yards and 4 touchdowns. Darvin Adams caught 3 of those scores. Neil Caudle, playing in the second half in relief of Todd, threw for another 117 yards on 10 of 12 passing. Meanwhile, walk-on running back Anthony Gulley led all rushers with 77 yards on just 5 carries, scoring 2 touchdowns.

The following week, the 7-3 Tigers traveled to Athens to take on 6-4 Georgia. Just as they had the previous season, the Bulldogs managed a very tight, one-score win, despite trailing Auburn 14-0 in the first quarter. The two teams were tied at 17 at the half. Georgia pulled ahead by 7 in the final quarter on an 11-yard Caleb King run.

John Ringer

I remember the 2009 Alabama game, but I have no memories at all of the Georgia game that year. It turns out Auburn was actually higher-ranked, had a better record, and was favored to beat them in Athens.

After Georgia went up by 7 late, we had a 100-yard kickoff return with Demond Washington that tied the game. Then Georgia scored to go up 7 again. We were driving at the end, but they knocked down a sure touchdown pass before Mario Fannin could catch it. Georgia's safety, Bacari Rambo, knocked it away.

Georgia held Auburn in check at the end to win, 31-24. A scenario very much like this played out again in the next game, against Alabama.

And speaking of the Crimson Tide: they would close out the regular season with a visit to Jordan-Hare Stadium.

Nick Saban's second Alabama team had abused Auburn the previous year, shutting the Tigers out, 36-0, and ending their six-year winning streak in the Iron Bowl in emphatic fashion.

Auburn was a better team in 2009, and they had the Tide at home. But Alabama was better, too. They had the leading Heisman Trophy candidate in running back Mark Ingram. They were undefeated, on course for a conference title and cruising toward a date in the BCS national championship game. Against all of that, the Auburn coaches were looking for any edge they could find.

"(The Iron Bowl) needed to be personal. When you take something personally, you are more intent on doing what needs to be done. That's how humans are wired. I wanted our guys to know this game was for their pride. This game was for Zac (Etheridge). This game was for Auburn. Anything less than our absolute best would be unacceptable.

ALL THEY DID WAS WIN

> *"We didn't have a game the weekend after playing Georgia, so for the entire two weeks leading up to the Alabama game, we talked about making the game personal."*
> —Gene Chizik, All In

In the Iron Bowl, as they had done against Georgia, the Tigers scored twice early. They capitalized on a 67-yard Terrell Zachery reverse run to take the first lead of the game. Wes Byrum then executed a perfect onsides kick and the Tigers punched it in again. For a brief moment, the Tigers gave all their fans a bit of hope.

Unfortunately, Alabama came back to tie the game at the half, 14-14, with two scoring drives of their own. Auburn pulled ahead once more to start the third quarter, 21-14, this time on a 72-yard Darvin Adams pass from Chris Todd. From there, however, Alabama chipped away before delivering the knockout blow. They managed two short Leigh Tiffin field goals before the quarter ended, making it 21-20, Auburn. Then, with less than two minutes remaining in the game, they capped off a final drive with a short pass to fullback Roy Upchurch that gave the Tide the win, 26-21.

It marked the only time the entire game that Alabama had led.

The Tigers had come so close to knocking off both Georgia and Alabama. It was disappointing to have lost, but the Tigers' level of competitiveness in both games promised better times ahead.

After the game, Alabama's players realized what they'd just gone up against, how close they'd come to losing, and how prepared the Auburn team had been for them.

> *"Their game plan against us was so detailed. Everything they did against us defensively was incredibly well thought-out. I actually got a chance to interview (Auburn defensive coordinator) Ted Roof on the radio (years later) and I said to him, 'That's the best game plan I've ever seen.' And he said, 'We told our kids we weren't going to let Mark Ingram win the Heisman in Jordan-Hare Stadium.'"*
> —Mike Johnson, Alabama offensive lineman and senior on the 2009 team

Indeed, Ingram finished the game with 16 carries for only 30 yards, for an average of 1.9 yards per carry, and no touchdowns. He won the Heisman at the end of that season, but he did not win it against Auburn.

John Ringer
It was the closest game anybody played against Alabama that year, and it was a revelation in terms of, we talk about how, if the other team is better, you have to take chances to win. Chizik and his staff were prepared. They took chances from the opening kickoff.

We ran tricky plays on offense; we ran trick plays on special teams; our defense kept us in the game and didn't give up many big plays. It really was a masterful job by the entire coaching staff. And I felt like Malzahn did the thing he's done so many times over the years, where he pulled out a bunch of stuff that Alabama hadn't seen and wasn't prepared for, and we were able to get some big gains. It really was a valiant effort by the 2009 team. Did we want to win? Sure. But I don't think any Auburn fan could've walked out of that stadium and not said the team had given everything they had, and tried everything they could, to try to win.

The change in coaching regimes had definitely resulted in major turnarounds with regard to both the offense and the defense—for good and for ill.

The defense had been solid in Tuberville's final years, but by 2009 it was struggling. Help was needed, and quickly, on that side of the ball.

Meanwhile, the offense took a quantum leap forward, finishing the season second in the SEC and 16th in the nation in total yards. In 2008, they'd been shut out by Alabama, held to 3 points by Mississippi State, and managed only 7 points against Ole Miss. In four other games, the 2008 team had scored only in the teens. The 2009 team, on the other hand, scored in double figures in every single game, and in only two of them did Auburn score fewer than 21 points. They rang Mississippi State up for 49 points and hung 33 on Ole Miss. Their 21 points against soon-to-be national champions

Alabama was the second-most anyone scored against them that season, and the most of any SEC team.

Van Allen Plexico

Our defense gave up the following points to our twelve regular-season opponents in 2009:

13, 24, 30, 30, 22, 44, 21, 31, 20, 31, 31, 26.

That's 323 points, for an average of allowing 26.9 points per game.

And the amazing thing is, we actually *won* seven of those games!

Not exactly pitching a lot of shutouts on defense that season.

John Ringer

It was tough as a fan of defensive football to get through that season. But there was a big injection of life into the offense that had not been there. The offense had gotten very stale under Tuberville. They'd tried to go to the Spread but it didn't work. This was the Spread unleashed, and it was exciting and fun.

Van Allen Plexico

It was definitely fun. We lost five games, but the offense did look a lot better. They were doing the opposite of the old option-type, grind-it-out offenses. They did crazy things. Plus, they'd go for 2 randomly. They'd do onside kicks randomly. It was exciting football for a change.

In those same twelve regular-season games that year, our *offense* scored:

37, 49, 41, 54, 26, 23, 14, 10, 33, 63, 24, 21.

Not a lot of dreaded 3-2 games there.

That's 395 points, for an average of 32.9 points per game.

When you include the bowl game—which we'll get to shortly—that's 433 points, for an average of 33.3 points per game. That's a lot.

Now get this: The 2010 offense would score 577 points, for an average of 41.2 points per game. So it's only going to get better. Incredibly better.

John Ringer
Gus's offense in 2009 was an offense that was well-conceived. It was smart. It could keep the opponent's defense off balance, move guys around and take advantage of the defense. And even when it seemed like it was doing simple things, it could get big, exciting plays out of it. And the speed sweep, the running game that he put in, Todd passing the ball to those receivers—the offense just had a life and an explosion with Gus's offense that it hadn't had in a long time, and it was really fun.

With the conclusion of the regular season, Auburn's record stood at 7-5, a two-game improvement from the previous season. They'd also come much closer to beating Alabama and had avenged the previous season's loss to West Virginia. Their reward was an invitation to a New Year's Day bowl: the Outback Bowl in Tampa, Florida. They would play Northwestern in a game that would feature the wildest finish of the season.

> *"Our team was off-the-charts ecstatic to be invited to play on New Year's Day. This was a major improvement from the previous season, when they missed playing in a bowl and were home before Christmas."*
> *—Gene Chizik, All In*

As the Tigers were practicing in Tampa the day before the bowl game, they got word of a player commitment for the following season. A junior college quarterback by the name of Cameron Newton had decided to transfer to Auburn.

> *"Cameron Newton, the nation's top junior college recruit, on Thursday announced plans to sign with Auburn and enroll later (in January).*
> *"The 6-foot-6 quarterback, who spent his first two seasons at Florida, will have two seasons of eligibility on the Plains. he led Blinn (Texas) College to a junior college national title in 2009.*

ALL THEY DID WAS WIN

"At Blinn, Newton rushed for 655 yards and scored 16 touchdowns. He also completed 61 percent of his throws, including 21 touchdown passes."
—*Jay Tate, Montgomery Advertiser, January 1, 2010*

How Auburn came to recruit him, and how he came to choose Auburn, were only the opening movements in a drama of vast, Shakespearean proportions.

For Auburn, nothing would ever be the same again.

- 6 -

WE HAD TO WIN THE GAME FOUR TIMES

Before anyone could turn their attention to the 2010 season, however, the 2009 campaign had to be concluded. No one was complaining, though, because the final game was in the Sunshine State on New Year's Day. After a one-year absence, Auburn was going bowling again.

The Tigers would wrap up the 2009 season by playing Northwestern in the Outback Bowl. After all the disappointments of the previous season, and all the drama the program had dealt with over the past year, the players, coaches and fans alike were thrilled.

It wasn't just a vacation, though—despite the fact that they'd surely earned one. It was, as some like to say, a business trip.

> *"From the moment we received the invitation, we (coaches) communicated this unwavering message to our players: we were going to Tampa with the sole purpose of returning home with our eighth win. Our school deserved at least eight wins, and it was up to us to deliver."*
> —*Gene Chizik*, All In

The regular season had ended with the Tigers making history on both sides of the ball, for good and for bad. They ranked 13th among all FBS programs in rushing offense, averaging 5.0 yards rushing per carry. That was the team's highest average in fourteen years; higher than any of the Cadillac Williams-Ronnie Brown years under Tommy Tuberville; the best, in fact, since Patrick Nix was handing the ball to Stephen Davis. They outscored opponents in the first quarter by a combined 41 points, and scored 50 touchdowns, double what they'd scored in 2008.

Unfortunately, the defensive stats were as bad as the offensive numbers were good. They ranked 80th in rushing defense, and their fourth quarter scoring margin was -14. They had allowed 323 points to opponents, the most any Auburn team had ever given up.

After the loss to Arkansas, the coaches realized their depth on defense was becoming an issue for the team. Malzahn had to adjust his hyper-speed approach to the offense, in order to give the defenders a chance to breathe. He didn't like doing it, but realized it had become a necessity. As a result, Auburn's average number of offensive plays run per game dropped from 74 in the first half of the season to 66 in the second half.

Van Allen Plexico

This is what I'd been concerned about from the beginning, when we changed to the hurry-up, no-huddle offense: That kind of approach always seemed in the past to result in the defensive coordinator wanting to punch the offensive coordinator.

I was afraid the first time Gus heard the words "Slow Down" from Chizik, we'd lose him to some other team that promised, "No, really—we *actually will* let you go the speed you want to go!"

Of course, head coaches never liked running that super-high-speed offense, because, when it's not clicking and you're having to punt a lot, it wears your defense down. Sure enough—as soon as Gus became a head coach, what did he do? He slowed the offense way down!

Chizik must have told him to ease up on the gas pedal, later in the season. To Gus's credit, he did it.

But, since his entire offensive approach is built around fast tempo, I'm sure he wasn't happy about it.

Chizik stated publicly that throttling down Gus's schemes was not his preferred approach. Furthermore, he planned to kick the offense back into high gear as soon as it became more feasible to do so. "When you're not as deep and as experienced, you have to do whatever gives your team the best chance for winning," he explained. "At times, we had to (slow down). In the future, we will strive to have more plays and run at a faster pace."

The sense was that, between injuries and lack of depth, they simply hadn't had the horses on that side of the ball to be truly competitive at the highest levels that season. Getting the injured players back and bringing in some new ones might, it was believed, go a long way toward transforming the Tigers into a truly competitive squad the following year.

Despite the defensive struggles, the players came into the bowl game excited, energized and hungry for success.

Some of the players had a personal stake in performing well in Tampa.

Onterio McCalebb grew up in south Florida, near the site of the bowl game. He looked forward to making a strong impression on the folks back home.

> "It's awesome to show people. In high school, people thought I was going to drop out. I had a rough family life. I had to prove them wrong. I prayed every night. I ended up here doing good things."
> —Onterio McCalebb, Auburn running back, before the Outback Bowl

It would be the final football game of Chris Todd's college career. He looked back on all he'd gone through to get there—to be Auburn's starter in a New Year's Day bowl game.

> "Situations present themselves in a lot of different ways. I'm a strong believer in situations like that making you stronger and making you a better player and ultimately a better person. I think I grew a lot from my experience, and I think I gained from it."
> —Chris Todd, Auburn quarterback, prior to the Outback Bowl

Todd ended the season having set the Auburn single-season touchdown passes record, at 21. He would add one more in the bowl game, for a total of 22, surpassing Pat Sullivan and Jason Campbell by 2.

It was a record that would last all of one year, whereupon the books would be completely rewritten and the old records shattered by a certain transfer quarterback.

Van Allen Plexico

Looking at the Auburn all-time touchdown passes chart, it's a real testament to how much the game of football has changed in recent years. Five of the top six single-season passing touchdown records were set since 2000. And that also shows just how great Pat Sullivan was, because he still holds the 4-spot, and he did it way back in 1971.

It's also interesting to note that while Gus Malzahn is not known for having a sophisticated passing offense—he's generally much better regarded for his run schemes—his quarterbacks command the top two spots here, and five of the top ten overall.

Auburn Single-Season Touchdown Passing (through 2024)

	Player	TDs	Year
1	Cam Newton	30	2010
2	Chris Todd	22	2009
3	Payton Thorne	21	2024
4	Pat Sullivan	20	1971
	Jason Campbell	20	2004
	Nick Marshall	20	2014
7	Dameyune Craig	18	1997
	Jarrett Stidham	18	2017
	Jarrett Stidham	18	2018
10	Pat Sullivan	17	1970

It was safe to say the Auburn players had adjusted relatively quickly to their new and unorthodox offense.

ALL THEY DID WAS WIN

> *"All the experiences (our players have) had before, there was probably some hesitancy, but they bought in (to the hurry-up/no-huddle). We ask a lot of them and they've bought in completely offensively to what we've done."*
> —Gus Malzahn, Auburn offensive coordinator

They seemed to be more relaxed and at ease with the new regime in charge.

> *"It's more about the personalities. Last year, it was all about football. When we're out there now, we have more fun. We have more fun competing with each other. It's still hard work, but it's fun. Everyone is talking, the coaches are talking. It's like we're all friends."*
> —Jake Ricks, Auburn defensive tackle, before the Outback Bowl

The coaches were happy. The players were having fun. Now it was time to go and win a bowl game.

Van Allen Plexico
Little did they know, they'd have to win it four times!

The Auburn Tigers met the Northwestern Wildcats in the Outback Bowl in Tampa, Florida on January 1, 2010. It was the earliest game to kick off on a day full of bowl games, starting at 10 am. It was played before just under 50,000 spectators—by far the smallest crowd to watch the Tigers play in person that season.

Interestingly, this stadium was familiar to Chizik: It was the same facility where the Buccaneers of the NFL had developed the famed "Tampa 2" defense that he had studied so closely while he was coaching in nearby Orlando, at UCF.

A lot was riding on the game. It could mean an eighth win for the Tigers, but it was also a chance for the coaches to burnish their reputations, including that of the head coach—who still needed to prove himself.

In the *Montgomery Advertiser*, columnist Jay Tate noted, "If the Tigers beat Northwestern, analysts across the nation will be picking

Auburn as an SEC contender this summer. Not bad for a coach who went 5-19 at Iowa State, no?"

The task that lay before the Tigers would not be easy. Northwestern came into the bowl game at 8-4, winners of their final three games, two of which had been against Top 25-ranked teams. The Wildcats had a lot on the line as well. They hadn't won a bowl game since January 1, 1949—a wait of sixty-one years at that point. They were every bit as hungry as the Tigers. It might not be a heavyweight match, but the two middleweights competing in the Outback Bowl were about to give it their all for sixty minutes—and more.

The game began promisingly enough. Just as they had in the Iron Bowl, Auburn got out to an early, 14-0 lead. They scored on a very short play and then a very long one—both largely set up by defensive back Walter McFadden.

First McFadden intercepted Wildcat QB Mike Kafka's pass on Northwestern's 31 yard line, with no return. Kodi Burns finished off the ensuing short drive with a 1-yard touchdown run.

Northwestern came right back, passing their way down the field. They looked as if they were about to tie the game. But then McFadden intercepted Kafka again, this time in the Tigers' end zone. He returned this one 100 yards for a score.

Van Allen Plexico

The first part of the game could scarcely have gone better for Auburn. We were up 14-0, just a few minutes in.

Who at that moment would have imagined the bizarre twists and turns this game would soon be taking?

Kafka brought the Wildcats back down the field again and the third time was the charm. Kafka hit Andrew Brewer for a 39-yard touchdown.

The two teams went into the locker room at halftime with Auburn leading, 21-7. Auburn seemed firmly in control of the scoreboard, but Chizik and Roof had to be concerned that the Wildcats had moved the ball seemingly at will up and down the field, behind the strength of Kafka's throwing arm. Northwestern dominated in total yards (289-194), total plays (52-29, a stat that had to bother Malzahn), and time of possession (19:55 to 10:05). The three turnovers by the Wildcats were the difference so far. Without McFadden's two interceptions, the score likely would have been 21-14 in Northwestern's favor, if not worse.

The two teams exchanged punts and interceptions for most of the third quarter. Remarkably, with less than three minutes remaining until (what was supposed to be) the final quarter, Northwestern still had only 7 points.

That changed in a hurry.

Kafka connected with a wide-open Andrew Brewer for another touchdown, this one from 35 yards away. Then the Wildcat defense forced a three-and-out on the Tigers. On the very next play after Auburn's punt, Kafka hit Drake Dunsmore on a short screen pass that the big receiver turned into a rambling, 66-yard touchdown, shedding would-be tacklers left and right on his way to the end zone. Suddenly, what had seemed like a cakewalk for the Tigers was a tie game, 21-21, going into the final frame.

Van Allen Plexico

It's worth noting that, on Auburn's brief drive between Northwestern touchdowns, we actually saw Onterrio McCalebb play quarterback in the Wildcat formation for possibly the only time in his Auburn career. Unfortunately, the play gained only 3 yards.

Now finding themselves tied, Auburn fought back. After Todd methodically passed the Tigers down the field, Ben Tate punched in the short touchdown, putting Auburn back ahead, 28-21. Then, following a Northwestern punt, Terrell Zachery exploded for a 50-yard run that set up another short Ben Tate score.

Auburn had increased its lead to 35-21, with half of the fourth quarter gone. The Tigers would have loved to relax at this point, but seven minutes yet remained. Somehow, those seven minutes (plus overtime) would contain at least as much action as the preceding fifty-three. And it started with Ben Tate's celebration of that second touchdown.

"Ben's touchdown could have pretty much put the game away for us. But after scoring, something told him it would be a good idea to celebrate what was likely the final touchdown of his

> college career by dunking the football over the crossbar of the goalpost. His dunk drew a fifteen-yard penalty for unsportsmanlike conduct that would be assessed against us on our kickoff."
> —Gene Chizik, *All In*

Unfortunately, Northwestern had lots of time left. Kafka quickly brought them down the short field that resulted from the penalty. They scored another touchdown. The Tigers did manage to block the extra point attempt. Auburn led by 8, at 35-27, with three minutes remaining.

The lead wasn't as comfortable as it had been. Even so, the Tigers just needed to run the clock out to claim their eighth win.

They couldn't.

After a nice run by Onterio McCalebb, Ben Tate fumbled on the second play of the drive, giving the ball back to the Wildcats.

Northwestern quickly took advantage and scored again, this time on an 18-yard pass from Kafka to Sidney Stewart with a minute remaining. They completed the 2-point conversion to tie the game.

One minute remained. One minute for Auburn to try to get the ball downfield far enough to kick a potential game-winning field goal. Wes Byrum was ready, standing by on the sideline.

Then disaster struck again. The Tigers got a great return on the kickoff but fumbled, near midfield. Now it was Northwestern that had the opportunity to kick a game-winner as the clock expired.

They drove to the Auburn 27-yard line, where the Tigers stopped them with three seconds remaining. Their kicker, Stefan Demos, missed the 44-yard attempt wide right, the ball curving off toward the Tampa Bay Buccaneers' pirate ship.

With that, the game went into overtime.

And then things got *really* weird.

Auburn got the ball first and drove to the Northwestern 4 yard line, where Wes Byrum hit a short field goal to put the Tigers ahead, 38-35.

Northwestern took over and tried a halfback pass, but the defense blew it up, holding the Wildcats to a short gain.

On the second play, Kafka hit a receiver for very little yardage, but the ball came loose as Auburn's defenders tackled him. The ball bounced back up the field and into the hands of Kafka, who picked it up and was tackled. Flags flew. The referees conferred for a while and ruled that the receiver had in fact caught the ball and then fumbled, and the penalty was on Auburn's Neiko Thorpe for illegally batting the loose ball when he and some Northwestern players were all diving for it. Auburn had made a great defensive play and were somehow being penalized for it.

Then the referees got together again and reviewed the play. Oddly enough, Northwestern actually wanted the play to be called a fumble because, in that case, the ensuing penalty against Auburn would result in a first down.

After further review, the referees ruled that the receiver caught the ball and was down—thus nullifying everything that had come afterward. Thorpe's batting of the ball had never officially happened, so there was no penalty. Northwestern faced 3rd down and 1 from the Auburn 16. By this point, Northwestern's Kafka had attempted 75 passes, completing 46 of them for 522 yards—all school records.

Kafka took the snap, surged forward and, on second effort, managed to convert the first down.

With 1st and 10 at the Auburn 15, Kafka was swarmed by the blitzing defense and appeared to fumble. The ball was recovered by Auburn. If so, it meant the Tigers had won the game. The players ran onto the field, celebrating.

Then the referees reviewed the play and reversed the call. Kafka's elbow had hit the ground before the ball came out.

So the game wasn't over. Northwestern still had the ball, but way back on the Auburn 31.

The second down pass fell incomplete, but on third and 24, Kafka completed a pass down to the Tigers' 19. Stefan Demos, the Wildcat kicker, came out onto the field to attempt a 37-yard field goal that, if good, would tie the game at 38-38.

Demos missed the kick—wide right again, deflecting off the goalpost. Auburn's players ran onto the field for a second time, to celebrate what looked like a win for sure.

But there were flags on the play. One of Auburn's defenders, T'Sharvan Bell, had slid sideways on the wet grass, right into the kicker's plant leg. His back had been to the kicker by the time they had collided, but it didn't matter. Demos was hurt, and the penalty gave Northwestern a first down on the Auburn 9.

On first down, Kafka's pass was ruled incomplete. On second down, the Wildcat QB was pressured hard and chased out of bounds at the 8. On third down, Kafka couldn't find anyone open and scrambled to the 5. Now it was fourth down yet again. Northwestern sent out a backup kicker, Steve Flaherty.

> *"With the backup kicker in, we coaches had our eyes open for some kind of trick play. When we saw Northwestern line up in a kick formation that was different from the previous one, we started yelling for our players to watch for a fake field goal. I don't think the players heard us, but they still made a game-saving play."*
> —*Gene Chizik,* All In

Almost before the Tigers could get set, the Wildcats went into action, attempting a fake kick. The snap went to a running back, who ran left—but not before stealthily handing the ball to a receiver, who remained frozen for an instant, then took off to his right. As most of the action moved to the left side of the formation, following the running back, the receiver with the ball darted toward the right corner of the end zone. If he scored, Northwestern would win the game. Auburn's defenders sniffed the play out, however, and strung it out wide, toward the right sideline. Neiko Thorpe defeated his blocker and blew up the ball carrier, knocking him out of bounds just short of the goal line.

> *"I knew it was going to be a tough game and it would be hard to pull off a win. I didn't know, however, that we would basically have to win the game four times."*
> —*Gene Chizik,* All In

For the third time, the Auburn players raced out onto the field. This time, they actually had something to celebrate.

> *"Ben Tate came up to me. I don't even remember hearing what he said. 'I'm not talking to you right now,' I joked with him. 'I'm too mad at you.'"*
> —*Gene Chizik,* All In

ALL THEY DID WAS WIN

Van Allen Plexico
In terms of turnovers, it had been an ugly game. Northwestern threw 5 interceptions and lost 1 fumble. Auburn threw 2 interceptions and lost 2 fumbles. Ten turnovers! And each of them had a profound effect on the game.

The much-maligned Auburn defense had turned out to be the difference in this game. They'd given up a lot of passing yards to Kafka, but they'd also picked him off five times, running one of them back 100 yards for a touchdown. They'd also stopped the Wildcats' last-ditch fake field goal at the end of overtime to seal the win.

Van Allen Plexico
This Auburn team played in some wacky games. The West Virginia game in the rain; the Iron Bowl. But this Northwestern bowl game was insane.

John Ringer
We had been visiting relatives in Atlanta over the holidays, and we were driving home, back to Virginia. We were listening to this game on the car radio, and I just remember it going on and on and on, and there were a million times it could've ended. It could've ended here—but no! Or it could end there—but no! It happened again and again, and I remember by the end it was a very draining experience.

Van Allen Plexico
It was. By the time it was over and we had won, though, I was so excited for the team and the program. I had a great feeling for the future. I thought that if this staff could come in and win the games it had won, with very little defense, cobbling together a team—just think what they could do when we had some more players. When we had some depth.

> *"You could tell, if we just took it that extra notch up, that could be the difference in finishing games like we knew we were capable of."*

—Josh Bynes, Auburn linebacker

As for the head coach, time—and winning—could heal at least some wounds.

"Now that the game is more than a year and a half behind us and I'm mostly over what Ben did, I can point out that it wasn't even a very good dunk."
—Gene Chizik, All In

For all that the new regime on the Plains had accomplished, however, their program was still overshadowed by the one on the other side of the state. The one that was grabbing all the top recruits and all the headlines. Alabama won the national championship six days later, defeating Texas in the BCS title game. Nick Saban was on his way to being generally regarded as one of the greatest college football coaches of all time. It was against that impossible standard that Gene Chizik and his staff would continue to try to rebuild the Tigers' fortunes on the gridiron.

"(After the 2009 season) there was some optimism. They'd had a winning record after having a losing record in 2008. But there wasn't necessarily championship-winning optimism, because all of that was directed towards Tuscaloosa."
—Kevin Scarbinsky, columnist, AL dot com

Even so, there was plenty of cause for optimism on the Plains, headed into 2010.

Van Allen Plexico
I enjoyed the 2009 season a great deal. Everything just felt better somehow; fresher and newer. I give Coach Chizik full credit for rejuvenating the program and improving the attitudes of the players. In 2008 Auburn had felt like it was in decline and possibly about to pitch over the edge, into freefall. Only a few months later, there was a legitimate buzz around the program. Winning eight games was nice. Playing Georgia and Alabama so close had helped. But I have always felt it was that bowl game—

that weird, wild, wacky bowl game against Northwestern—that truly sold me on the idea that good things were on their way, and soon.

Several recruits of note joined the Tigers' roster heading into the following season:

Five-star receiver Trovon Reed, of Thibodaux, Louisiana, was the top recruit in that state. He was described by analysts as "perfect for a slot role in Auburn's passing game and could vie for a position returning kicks or punts."

Five-star offensive lineman Shon Coleman, of Olive Branch, Mississippi, eventually would grow into a dominant blocker during his time on the Plains.

Jeffrey Whitaker, of Warner Robins, Georgia, was a massive interior lineman providing depth at a position in need of bodies after losing several key players to graduation.

The Tigers' third five-star recruit that year, Michael Dyer, of Little Rock, Arkansas, was a 5-8, 201-pound running back, and the top player at his position on ESPN's charts. The number 5 overall player in the nation, according to ESPNU, he was described by them as "a rare combination of power and speed who should be able to compete for carries immediately in Ben Tate's absence."

Van Allen Plexico

Michael Dyer was one of the top players of that recruiting class. Auburn pulled off a coup to get him, with Gus Malzahn exercising his Arkansas connections there.

The Tigers came very close to assembling what some suggested could be a "Thunder and Lightning" rushing attack by attempting to add highly-touted Marcus Lattimore to the backfield, as well. Alas, it was not to be. Lattimore ended up choosing South Carolina, where he would play for Steve Spurrier. Who could've dreamed then that Auburn would end up playing against him twice that very next season?

Among many other players of note in this signing class was a 5-11, three-star defensive back from Birmingham who would go on to big things. His name was Chris Davis. We will encounter him again briefly here before we're done, but that will not be the end of his story as an Auburn Tiger. Not by a long shot.

Van Allen Plexico

I was very excited about a few of Auburn's new players coming in for 2010. Some of them would go on to be difference-makers; others would not. In January, still aglow in the happiness of the overtime bowl win, they all seemed like future All-Americans to me. In particular I was excited about five-star recruits Trovon Reed at wide receiver, Shon Coleman at offensive line and Michael Dyer at running back. It looked like Chizik and company were faring pretty well at recruiting. I was also intrigued by the 275-pound bruiser named Ladarious Philips they brought in to play fullback.

And yes, there was also the tall, powerfully-built junior college quarterback we'd signed just before the bowl game, on New Year's Eve. They were saying he'd played a little bit as a freshman at Florida, alongside Tim Tebow. Interesting, I thought. What was his name again?

- 7 -

AN ATHLETIC FREAK OF NATURE

"It all started on December 31, 2009. What a great day that was!"
—*Brian Stultz, AuburnWire, USA Today, December 31, 2019*

"His name was Cameron Newton," Gene Chizik stated in his book, *All In*, "and he was an athletic freak of nature."

That he was. And he would turn Auburn football—and all of the college football world—upside down, before the year was done.

The 2009 season had gotten fans excited and ignited hope among the Auburn Family once more. Now fans waited to see what this team and this coaching staff could do for an encore. Expectations for 2010 weren't necessarily huge, but there was a sense they could definitely improve on the 8-5 record of the year before.

It would begin, as so many things football-related do, at quarterback. Chris Todd arguably had overachieved in 2009, while demonstrating the viability and potential of Gus Malzahn's offense. Now he had graduated—but the new sheriff on the block was already in town.

"Gus and I were always on the same page with what we wanted this offense to look like and be. I looked at everything through the eyes of a defensive coach. There were a lot of things he did that were problematic for defenses. So, I felt like if we implemented that offense and recruited the right way, I thought the offense could be unbelievable. It all started with a quarterback."
—Gene Chizik

"During our conference call the other day with Coach Gene Chizik, he was talking about how important it is to find a quarterback for next year. He was saying maybe it's somebody we have here, maybe it's somebody we're going to get. He was kind of hinting that they had their eye on someone. So I talked to Coach pregame on the field and I mumbled 'Cameron Newton,' and oh boy did his eyes light up, and he said, 'Let me tell you, that is a signing. He is a big boy.' He was borderline drooling, guys, at the prospect of having him in January and schooling him under Malzahn."
—Rob Stone, ESPN broadcast of the 2009 Outback Bowl

Van Allen Plexico
I was thinking, if Chris Todd, bless him, could take us to 8 wins and a New Year's Day bowl, what might a 5-star, 250-pound quarterback do in this offense, with the tools he'll have around him?

Little did Auburn fans know at the time, the recruitment of that quarterback by Auburn and other schools would become a major story over the course of the coming year. A story so big it very nearly derailed the entire season.

But as the year 2010 dawned on the Plains, and the junior college transfer from Georgia, by way of Florida and Texas, arrived on the Plains, all anyone could see was a raw, untapped potential.

Cam Newton never had any business at tiny Blinn College in southeast Texas. He'd appeared destined to be the next big thing in Gainesville after Tim Tebow. But a string of events pushed him out the door at Florida and eventually down to the junior college ranks.

He'd come out of Westlake High School near College Park, Georgia, with tremendous promise and potential, and he'd signed up with head coach Urban Meyer and offensive coordinator Dan Mullen to play for the Florida Gators in 2007. As the story goes, he originally considered signing with Auburn, but was dissuaded by the fact that Kodi Burns was a freshman quarterback there. He assumed he'd get earlier playing time when Gators QB Tim Tebow left early for the NFL. He backed up Tebow for two years, but after Tebow decided to return to Florida for another season in 2009, Newton concluded he would be better off elsewhere, actually getting to play football. That led him to the junior college route.

Rumors followed him from his time at Florida, involving buying a laptop computer from another student that turned out to have been stolen. A year later, after he committed to Auburn, some in Gainesville even whispered that Newton was "about to get kicked out of Florida" for some unspecified act of academic dishonesty. Author Will Collier referred to that alleged incident as "BS" after doing some investigative journalism on it.

"Turned out the story was dreamed up by the Urban Meyer staff and peddled around," Collier told the AU Wishbone. "Staffers were bragging about it online. There was never an academic complaint about Cam, and that was straight from members of the UF Honor Court. Nobody would touch the story, until (muckraking sports journalist) Thayer Evans ran a blurb on a nascent and lightly-edited Fox Sports site. After that, other news outlets could (repeat the fake story by using) the 'Fox Sports online is reporting' dodge."

Newton ended up at Blinn College, where he could get on the playing field immediately. There he led the Buccaneers to the junior college national championship, attracting the attention of a few big-time college football programs.

As for the negative stories surrounding him, the laptop computer-related charges were later dropped after Newton entered a pretrial diversion program. None of the rest of it ever amounted to anything; nothing, of course, except "smoke," as the reporters loved to say. By the time he arrived at Blinn College, Cam thought he'd put all of that negativity behind him. He was ready to start his football career over.

Meanwhile, back on the Plains, the Auburn players and coaches were happy enough about the improvement they'd shown in going 8-5, but they were dreaming of bigger things.

> "The (2010) team had a chip on their shoulder. They were hungry. They didn't worry about who got the praise and the accolades. They just wanted to win. It was really something special. Anytime you have a team like that, you have to have great leadership."
> —Gus Malzahn, Auburn offensive coordinator

By 2010, Kodi Burns had seen it all as a player, and then some. From starting at quarterback, on and off, as a freshman and sophomore to playing receiver his junior year for Chizik's first Auburn team—and with four different offensive coordinators in three years—he was ready for some stability and success. And he wasn't alone.

> "We had a senior-led culture. And so when Michael Dyer and those guys got here as freshmen, they really saw how we did things, and they were in line. They were in accordance with what we did, because they understood that our goal was to win championships. This was our (seniors') last shot, and we were hungry."
> —Kodi Burns, Auburn wide receiver

Gene Chizik understood that those seniors—those hungry, hungry seniors—represented a hugely important resource for him, and for the team.

> "We knew if we were ever going to make a run, we could do it with this class, because simply by numbers alone, we had enough senior leadership in the locker room to actually make some noise. But we knew we had to recruit a difference-maker at quarterback."
> —Gene Chizik

Chizik, however, was certain that "difference-maker" would be a freshman brought into the system directly out of high school, or someone already on the roster. The thought of going out and getting a "hired gun" quarterback from a smaller school, just for a year or two, did not excite him.

> *"I...wasn't interested in bringing in a junior college quarterback. I prefer longevity at the quarterback position, and when you take on a junior college quarterback, you have to develop him quickly. You have him for only two years, and then you have to replace him already.*
> *Curtis Luper, our running backs coach, had visited Blinn (College) to take a look at a receiver, but he came back raving about the quarterback he'd seen there."*
> —Gene Chizik, All In

Chizik rebuffed Luper more than once over Newton. Then OC Gus Malzahn saw the quarterback on film and joined the chorus of true believers.

> *"Curtis Luper went to Blinn College to check out a wide receiver we were really excited about. He gets back and I ask what he was like and he says, 'Well, he's pretty good, but they've got a quarterback there that you wouldn't believe. I said, 'Hey, we're not taking a junior college quarterback.' (And he said) 'No, you need to at least take a look at the tape.'*
> *"So the next week I went to Blinn Junior College. And I'm walking down the hall and see Cam and I'm like, Whoa. So, at that point, I knew I was all-in on recruiting him. And the rest is history."*
> —Gus Malzahn, Auburn offensive coordinator

Some recalled Newton from his earlier years in the SEC. He left a lasting impression.

> *"I remember when he was at Florida. Just this incredible athlete who, it felt like, could be pretty much anything they wanted him to be at quarterback."*
> —Chris Lowe, ESPN

> *"At the time, Urban (Meyer) said he was as talented as Tebow. He was this six-foot-five kid, 240 pounds, who could run."*
> —Mark Schlabach, ESPN

Malzahn, Luper and the other coaches on the offensive side of the ball were relentless in pressing Chizik about Newton. Finally, just before Christmas, Chizik gave in and invited Newton to the Plains for an official recruiting visit.

When the big quarterback first stepped into the Auburn football building, Chizik wasn't at first sure who he was looking at. "Wow," he said at the time, "that's the best-looking defensive end I've ever seen."

At first, Chizik tried to keep Newton at arm's length during his visit. He was convinced the big quarterback wouldn't substantially help the team and might not even be a good fit. But that didn't last long, once they got to know each other a little. Before Newton's weekend was over, the coach had "fallen in love with his personality. He had a big, bright smile," Chizik said later, "and there was a quality about him that seemed to communicate Auburn potential."

After Newton finished his Auburn visit and returned home for the holidays, Chizik spoke with the players who had spent the most time with him during the visit. What did they think of him? Unanimously they declared him a good fit for the program.

That was the final piece of the puzzle for Chizik. His reservations were gone. He was on board. He gave the nod to the assistants to offer Newton a scholarship.

Little did Chizik and the Auburn staff know that, behind the scenes, things were happening—things that are still not entirely clear to this day—that could have derailed Auburn's season and everything the Tigers had been working towards. Facts remain scarce in the matter. What we do have good reason to believe is that Mississippi State was involved in shenanigans.

Dan Mullen had been Newton's offensive coordinator during his two years at Florida. As the head coach at Mississippi State, Mullen wanted Newton to sign with the Bulldogs. He understood that a player like Newton could do wonders for a moribund program like the one in Starkville. He was banking on their pre-existing relationship being enough to attract the big quarterback.

With an Auburn offer on the table, however, getting Newton on board was no longer a slam-dunk for Mississippi State.

> *"I talked to Cam at one point during (the recruiting) process and, him being an Atlanta kid, I still vividly remember him saying, 'There's nothing like Auburn football on a Saturday night in Jordan-Hare Stadium.' I remember thinking all along that Auburn was gonna get him. I know there was a connection with Mississippi State because of Mullen (having been) at Florida, and I knew that he was seriously looking at Mississippi State because of that."*
> —Chris Low, ESPN

Mullen might have thought he could sway Newton based on their previous ties. Some in the Bulldogs' camp, however, were not content to leave it solely to that old connection. Slowly at first, word began to creep out that money had entered the conversation. There was talk of Mississippi State offering—or being asked to offer—money for Cam to provide his services to the Bulldogs.

Did Mississippi State boosters approach someone in Cam's camp with a financial offer? Did someone in Cam's camp initiate a money-based conversation with representatives of Mississippi State? Were the people on the State side of this hypothetical conversation actual representatives of the university, or just unofficial boosters or fans? And, if this alleged dialogue was indeed happening—regardless of who first broached the subject—was Dan Mullen aware of it? Was he participating in it? Was Cam?

To this day, the argument rages on.

Whatever the truth of it at the time, it didn't work out for the Bulldogs. Cam—by all accounts, unaware of any of this—chose to play for the Tigers. He accepted the Auburn scholarship offer on New Year's Eve, 2009.

Meanwhile, back in Mississippi, feelings were hurt and grudges were formed.

Months later, when word of malfeasance involving Mississippi State got out, many around the country quickly jumped to the conclusion that, if Newton had chosen Auburn instead, the Tigers must have offered him even more money. "Where there's smoke, there's fire," they all cried, while making no effort to find out the truth first.

Van Allen Plexico
People around the country—cynical media members and rival fans, especially—couldn't conceive of the notion that Cam would choose to play for Auburn for a scholarship, if Mississippi State was offering him money. They couldn't accept that he wasn't even aware anyone was "shopping him" to the Bulldogs, much less that there had been no talk of money with Auburn whatsoever.

The thought that he might want to play for a program with a large group of seniors, more national visibility, an innovative offense and a chance to achieve bigger things—that never entered the equation for them.

There were indeed good reasons for Cam and his family to prefer that he play for the Tigers.

> *"Cam went to a Mississippi State home game, and there was video of him (in the crowd) waving a cowbell. And so everyone assumed, with the Dan Mullen connection, that he was going to go there. But you have to remember now, Gus Malzahn was considered a guru as an offensive coordinator. And he'd worked some almost miracles with Chris Todd and the offense the year before."*
> *—Kevin Scarbinsky, AL dot com*

In point of fact, it was never proven that Cam knew about the alleged MSU money—much less that Auburn ever offered him anything beyond a scholarship. Eventually, both he and Auburn would be officially cleared of any wrongdoing. But more on that later.

In the meantime, Newton was coming to Auburn to play quarterback. It wasn't massive national news, but securing a player of his caliber was a huge story to those who followed such things.

"Auburn was playing in the Outback Bowl against Northwestern," columnist Kevin Scarbinsky later noted, "(but) really the biggest news of the week was that Cam had committed."

> "It was the day before we played in our bowl game. I was in the hotel, and the fax came through to the hotel lobby (with Cam's signature). Our (coaching) staff knew this was a really big deal. I don't know if anybody else did. But, at the time, it was a good moment of, 'Hey, we've got a real chance next year."
> —Gus Malzahn, Auburn offensive coordinator

> "It was pandemonium. It was awesome. I mean, we were fired up. It had been a long week and we'd been practicing and were getting ready to play the game, and we made sure they had that (news about Cam signing with Auburn) on TV the next day (during the bowl game telecast)."
> —Gene Chizik

The coaches were excited to have Newton on the roster, but they weren't simply going to hand him the starting job. They made it clear to him he would have to win it. And Auburn had two quarterbacks already on scholarship, in Neil Caudle and Barrett Trotter, who'd had much more time in Malzahn's system.

> "They had been here (for a couple of) years and had the respect of the players. Then you have this new guy coming in, with all the hype. I made it very clear to Cam upfront that this was a quarterback battle, not a quarterback handout. And he was good with that."
> —Gene Chizik

> "He hit the ground running when he got on campus, he started developing good relationships with his teammates, and it was a short period of time before everybody knew he was the guy."
> —Gus Malzahn, Auburn offensive coordinator

Cam struggled at first with the timing the coaches and receivers expected from him, getting the ball to where it needed to be at the right moment. The coaches also weren't sure exactly what they had in the towering specimen. Just how well could he evade the pass rush? Could he break tackles?

Auburn didn't allow the quarterbacks to "go live" in practice, meaning Cam could not be tackled to the ground. He was essentially playing tag rather than tackle football. Defenders could tag Newton in practice well enough. But would they have successfully tackled him? You couldn't really be sure. On practice plays where Cam rolled out and scrambled, only to have the referee blow the whistle the moment a defender touched him—the coaches looked at each other and asked, "Could he have broken away for more yardage? Could that lone defender really have brought this six-foot-five specimen down?" The coaches wondered about it and debated it endlessly over the spring and summer. At the same time, Cam was working tirelessly on improving his passing, even as he took greater command of the locker room.

When the A-Day game finally arrived on April 18, capping off spring practice, a crowd of 63,217 fans jammed into Jordan-Hare Stadium, setting an attendance record for the spring game. Excitement was running high, given the way the previous season had ended: a near-miss against the national champions and a thrilling overtime win in a New Year's Day bowl game.

Another attraction drawing fans was their first chance to see Cam Newton play in person—even if it was in a glorified practice, against his own teammates on defense. He received a standing ovation when he first ran on the field to play.

Unfortunately for those fans, Cam's time in the game was extremely limited. The Tigers played four quarterbacks that day, and the other three got more exposure than Newton.

Cam played four offensive series and finished with 3 completions in 8 passing attempts, for 61 yards.

"I did all right," he told reporters afterward. "I can do better."

John Ringer

Cam didn't really do anything memorable in the A-Day game. Was that on purpose, to not show it to future opponents? Maybe. But I think he's one of those players that, until you go live with the quarterbacks and let the defense try to tackle him, you have no idea what he's really capable of. When he's just doing the regular quarterback thing, even then I think you can tell he has a great NFL-type arm and he sees the field well. But when he runs against defenses that are trying to tackle him, he makes people look bad.

Van Allen Plexico
And not only did we have Cam Newton, but little did we imagine our junior college transfer defensive lineman, Mr. Nick Fairley, would be a revelation on defense. He would be the Cam Newton of the defense. He was a monster. He was King of the Monsters in 2010. We had no idea going into the season what he would become. He came out of nowhere.

John Ringer
Fairley was a good player before that. I remember hearing from my brother that NFL guys were excited about one of the guys on our defense. My brother named about four other guys and they were noncommittal. Then he said "Nick Fairley," and the NFL guy lit up and said, "That's the guy."

Van Allen Plexico
We were also highly recruiting the two best running backs in the country, Michael Dyer and Marcus Lattimore. Gus was telling them they could come to Auburn and be Thunder and Lightning, like the two backs he had at Arkansas.

John Ringer
Darren McFadden and Felix Jones.

Van Allen Plexico
We end up with only Dyer. And this is what's amazing about the year he had: In a season when Cam Newton is getting enough carries to rewrite the record books as a runner, Dyer manages to break Bo Jackson's freshman rushing record at Auburn.

Throw in Mario Fannin and Onterio McCalebb, and you have a backfield of many weapons. And they all do something a little bit different.

When asked at the end of spring about Malzahn's hurry-up, no-huddle offense, Newton said, "I think I've got my hands around it. One hand around it. So in the summer and the last practice we do,

I'm going to try to get the second hand around it. This offense is a very complex offense, but when you get the core of it, you pretty much have it."

The other three quarterbacks who played on A-Day all had better statistical outings than Newton. Malzahn, however, cautioned against taking too much meaning from that: "I wouldn't read anything into anything."

One of the other quarterbacks, Neil Caudle, noted that "the defense wasn't throwing a whole lot at us, so we should have thrown a lot of completions."

Asked about naming a starter, Chizik replied, "We don't feel the pressure to do that right now."

Malzahn added that he would only choose a preferred starter "when we're 110 percent sure."

> *"By the end of spring (practice) you could tell Cam had started to distance himself (from the competition). Really, one thing that stood out to me was how his teammates responded to Cam. You could tell that it was going to be his team. Not just the offense but the whole team. Just the way his teammates interacted with him. It was like they knew he was going to be the guy."*
> *—Gus Malzahn, Auburn offensive coordinator*

The players were correct. Malzahn made his choice and got together with Chizik to finalize the decision. Cam Newton would lead the Auburn Tigers into battle in 2010. They would begin the new season with a starting quarterback they hadn't even known existed a few months earlier.

As the season began, the coaches still weren't sure how great the team and the offense, now under Newton's command, could be.

"Every team and every offense is different, especially if you have a new quarterback," Malzahn said later. "So we were still gathering information on the big picture. Now we knew going in we had the pieces around the quarterback to be very efficient on offense because they had a year in the system under their belt."

Cam would have to prove it on the field.

Springtime blazed into summer on the Plains, but the fall couldn't come soon enough for Auburn fans.

- 8 -

DEFINITELY DIFFERENT

"He made a couple plays with his legs in that first game, you just went, 'Whoa, this guy's definitely different.'"
—Gus Malzahn, Auburn offensive coordinator

It was with a sense of cautious optimism that Auburn fans greeted the arrival of the 2010 season. They knew they just might have something special at quarterback. They knew the offense had improved by leaps and bounds the year before, with the arrival of Gus Malzahn and his cutting-edge hurry-up, no-huddle offense.

But just how good the team could be? In late August, nobody had any idea.

Van Allen Plexico

I doubt I was realistically hoping for an SEC championship as the season began. In those days, in a 12-team SEC, I felt like we had at least an outside shot headed into every season. And we all know how Auburn's performances, season to season, are like a roller-coaster. Just because we were bad in 2008 and mediocre-to-good in 2009 didn't mean we couldn't be great in 2010. So I had a degree of hope that we could be competitive, in terms of at least getting to the SEC Championship game. I wasn't thinking anything like 2004 was possible, though, and I definitely didn't expect to compete for a national championship.

Auburn had taken a step forward from 2008 to 2009, and we had good new players coming in on both sides of the ball, plus a reliable kicking game. So I felt optimism was justified.

We hoped and felt that Cam would be a big upgrade at quarterback. And it wasn't just him. There had been so many weapons surrounding the quarterback in 2009, and most of them—other than Ben Tate—were back in 2010. They provided a big and diverse arsenal for Cam to take advantage of. You had Michael Dyer coming in as a more standard tailback, and Onterrio McCalebb returning as this unique speed-back that could run the jet sweep or just get outside and dive for the end zone pylon. We had all these receivers—a great possession guy like Darvin Adams and a speed guy like T-Zac. A utility back in Mario Fannin, who could do a lot of things, and a great receiving tight end in Philip Lutzenkirchen. And don't forget utility fullback Eric Smith.

We rightly give so much credit to the guy taking the snap and making the decisions. He deserves tons of it. But just remember—Chris Todd had also fared well with this offense the year before. And Cam had lots of places to go with the ball, if he didn't want to carry it himself. And all of those guys could make something happen when they had the ball in their hands.

So the offense looked to be in good shape. But how could a team with as porous a defense as we'd fielded in 2009 possibly compete for the SEC title? Could we improve it that much in just one offseason? Could we put together an offense that could overcome the defense's shortcomings? That seemed very unlikely.

We were hopeful that the team would be good.

Only time would tell how good.

John Ringer

For the first time in forever, Auburn was on the cutting edge of offense in college football. The 2009 season was clearly a "this is fun and has potential" season. With Gus Malzahn's offense

ALL THEY DID WAS WIN

Auburn had something that was both fun and was an equalizer with the most talented and well-coached teams in college football.

Auburn was coming off seasons of 9 wins, 5 wins, and 8 wins. What were reasonable expectations headed into 2010? The schedule was challenging with rising non-conference power Clemson in addition to the usual SEC West gauntlet. The good news was that most of the tough games were at home. With the addition of Cam Newton and some talented freshmen, it seemed reasonable to have higher hopes for 2010. But at the start those higher expectations were simply to "compete for the SEC West title" and "beat Georgia at home."

To expect much more seemed crazy, given Auburn's recent history.

Over the course of the 2010 season and just afterwards, at least two songs became associated with the Tigers' championship run. One of them was the team's official "hype video," shown on the screen inside Jordan-Hare Stadium and on YouTube, featuring DJ Khaled.

The opening lines would prove prophetic about this team:

All I do is win, win, win
No matter what

The next part of that song, however, includes the words:

Got money on my mind
I can't ever get enough.

This became somewhat problematic amid the accusations, toward the end of the season, about Cam Newton being paid to play. More on that later.

The opening portion of the song concludes with the lines:

And every time I step up in the building everybody hands go up
And they stay there,
And they say, "Yeah!"
and they stay there,
(Up, down, up, down, up, down)

'Cause all I do is win (Win), win (Win), win
And if you goin' in put your hands in the air, make 'em stay there

Whereupon the Auburn team would come onto the field as the fans went crazy.

And it all started with the first game of the 2010 season, as the 23rd-ranked Tigers opened up against the Arkansas State Red Wolves in Jordan-Hare Stadium.

September 4: Arkansas State

Van Allen Plexico

Auburn has an odd recent connection with Arkansas State: our next three head coaches after Gene Chizik all spent at least a season as head coach there. Each of them stayed there for only one year before moving on. Hugh Freeze left for Ole Miss after 2011; Gus Malzahn left there to come back to Auburn after 2012; and Bryan Harsin left there for the Boise State job after 2013.

They call Miami-Ohio the "Cradle of Coaches." It seems like the "Cradle of Auburn Coaches" is Jonesboro!

The fans weren't the only ones unsure of what this Auburn team could be, and what it could do.

> *"I remember like every first game of the year, you're pretty nervous. You don't know exactly what you have yet. I think that goes both individually as a player and as a team. The whole thing is new because you haven't done it in almost a year. You're a different player. You're a different person. The team is totally different with the turnover and having a new addition like Cam Newton."*
> *—Lee Ziemba, Auburn offensive tackle*

The fans may not have had any better of an idea of what the team could accomplish than the players did, but they were excited at its potential—and it showed before the game.

"Tiger Walk was crazy today. It was live," said safety Zac Etheridge, after the game. "The DBs, we always try to get the crowd pumped up as much as we can. It felt good to go through there with my teammates and see all the fans."

The national media understood that it was a big deal for Auburn's new quarterback to take the field for the first time.

> *"And now the moment Tiger fans have been waiting for, Tim. The arrival of Cam Newton."*
>
> *"Well, you hear the crowd, Bob. And for Cam Newton, this is about keeping your emotions in check. You know you've waited a long time to get back to big-time college football, but you've got to let the game come to you."*
> —ESPN broadcasters, 2010 Arkansas State game

Arkansas State, coached by Steve Roberts, had brought in a new offensive coordinator, and one with whom Auburn fans would later become very familiar: Hugh Freeze.

Van Allen Plexico
Just think: The offensive coordinator for Arkansas State in this game was future Auburn head coach Hugh Freeze. The offensive coordinator for Auburn in this game was future Arkansas State head coach Gus Malzahn—who would then become Auburn's head coach. That's just nuts.

Also, a personal note here: The previous two seasons, Hugh Freeze had served as the head coach of the football team at Lambuth University in Jackson, Tennessee. My uncle, Gene Davenport, was the chairman of Lambuth's Religion and Philosophy Department, and served as a professor and minister there for forty-five years. He and Hugh Freeze overlapped there by one year.

My uncle passed away in 2018. I never got to ask him if he ever interacted with Coach Freeze. Knowing both of them to the degree I do, I suspect they could've had some extremely interesting conversations.

Freeze had installed a new spread-based passing offense at Arkansas State, and it clicked against the Tigers that afternoon. While Auburn held the Red Wolves to just 43 yards rushing for the game, Freeze's passing attack rang up the Tigers defense for 278 yards through the air, on 28 completions out of 42 attempts. The quarterback completing all those passes—Arkansas State's Ryan Aplin—would later be coached by Gus Malzahn during his one-year stint as head coach of the Red Wolves.

Unfortunately for Arkansas State, the team facing them on the other side of the field that day was unveiling a new weapon—one that was about to blow the minds of fans in the stadium and everyone watching at home. It was a weapon they had no answer for. But that's no poor reflection on the Red Wolves. In 2010, nobody had an answer for it.

The weapon was Cam Newton.

Both teams scored in every quarter of the game, but Newton made the difference. He threw for 186 yards and 3 touchdowns while also rushing for 171—a school record for quarterbacks running the ball. His 71-yard touchdown run in the second quarter would turn out to be his longest touchdown run of the season. He faked a handoff, dropped back, then took off up the middle. As Rod Bramblett shouted on the radio once Cam was streaking down the field, "See you later!"

The folks in the stands and watching at home had finally gotten a glimpse of the jaw-dropping abilities of their new signal-caller, and a taste of what he brought to the team.

> "As all the fans saw, Cam is a big part of our offense. He can run the ball, he can throw the ball. The offensive line did a great job opening up holes. He is just a great part of our offense."
> —Darvin Adams, Auburn receiver

In practice, Cam had worn a "no-contact" orange jersey, meaning the defense was not allowed to tackle him to the ground. Now he was free to, shall we say, express himself fully on the football field.

"I think after that game we knew we had some playmakers that could make plays. In the spring and fall, (Cam) had an orange jersey on. You blow the whistle, and you ask yourself, 'Would they have tackled him or not?' That was the first game you could figure out he's extremely hard to handle, and he could handle the game pressure."
—Gus Malzahn, Auburn offensive coordinator, in 2020

The questions nagging the coaches since spring practice were finally answered: *No*, Cam wouldn't be tackled behind the line of scrimmage very often. *Yes*, he would break those tackles and complete the pass or make a run for a big gain.

The Tigers racked up 367 rushing yards overall, with Newton's total added to the 95 by Michael Dyer and 76 by Onterior McCalebb, among others. They finished with 608 yards of total offense, averaging 9.4 yards per play.

Van Allen Plexico

Cam's debut was pretty exciting. We didn't really know what to expect, coming in. I remember being shocked that a guy that big could break off a Bo-Jackson-style long touchdown run. It certainly made me feel even better about what might be coming up the rest of the season.

John Ringer

My family and I attended the Arkansas State game in person. It was the only time that season I would see the 2010 team play in person. We saw the whole Cam Newton package on display in this game. He was elusive, he was powerful in breaking tackles, he was accurate in throwing the ball.

When Cam took off on that long touchdown run and pulled away from everyone, we were on that side of the field. His explosion and burst in the open field were amazing. That was the moment that everyone stopped and said, "Wow!"

He also executed the new offense very well: the fakes and misdirection, reading the defense and delivering the ball in stride to receivers. In addition, at the end of the third quarter he led the entire team down the sideline towards the student section to get them fired up.

In short, Cam did it all and, with the weapons on the 2010 team, the Auburn offense looked dangerous.

Of course, at the same time, the defense allowed 26 points to Arkansas State, which was concerning.

Final Score:
(23) Auburn 52
Arkansas State 26

Beating Arkansas State was one thing. The question now was, how would Newton and the new-look Tigers fare against SEC competition?

It would be less than a week until we began to receive some answers to that question.

September 9: Mississippi State

Now ranked 21 in the AP Poll, the Tigers had only five days to recover from the Arkansas State win and get ready for a road trip to Starkville for a Thursday night ESPN game.

Van Allen Plexico

It's interesting to note that this Auburn team would end up playing a game on a Thursday, a game on a Friday, and a game on a Monday, in addition to eleven games on Saturdays. That's pretty rare. The only other year I can think of where we played on four different days of the week was 2002, when (in addition to Saturdays) they played a Thursday night game, a Wednesday bowl game, and the season opener at USC on ABC's "Monday Night Football."

This game was the staff's first visit to Starkville as Auburn coaches. They were surprised by the intensity of the crowd, even at an early-season game, played on a weekday. The cowbells probably didn't help.

"I remember it was a very hostile environment, first of all. You could just feel the electricity before the game. Of course, it went down to the very end."

ALL THEY DID WAS WIN

—Gus Malzahn, Auburn offensive coordinator

The Tigers struggled for much of the game.

Facing a much tougher defense than the week before, Cam went 11 for 19 passing for 138 yards and 2 touchdowns, while rushing for 70 yards on 18 carries. He led the team in rushing for the second week in a row. He suffered his first interception, but also caught a 22-yard pass from none other than Kodi Burns. It wouldn't be the last time Kodi threw a pass to Cam, in the state of Mississippi, that season.

Van Allen Plexico
I can remember being somewhat puzzled by Cam having so many rushing yards. I knew we had this freshman stud running back in Michael Dyer, along with the returning McCalebb—who had been fantastic as a freshman in 2009—and the old veteran, Mario Fannin, among others. With that kind of talent in the backfield, why are we running our quarterback so often? Not to mention, isn't that a bit dangerous, risking the starting QB that way when you don't have to? But then, you see how many yards he's gaining and how hardly anybody can stop him, and you just sort of shrug, and cross your fingers he stays healthy.

John Ringer
This ended up being a good Mississippi State team, and it's easy to forget that, with all the other good teams Auburn played this season. This MSU team went 9-4 and finished 15th in the AP Poll. Chris Relf was a good quarterback. Grinding out a tough win over them in Starkville, on a Thursday night early in the season, was a sign of good leadership and coaching on the Auburn team.

This 2010 version of Auburn was not yet what it would become, but in this game they began to show the grit and ability to come through in the clutch that would become what they were known for in the weeks to come.

We didn't throw the ball much, the first half of the season. We really just ran the read-option. And it wasn't just Cam running the ball at first. He was handing it off a lot.

Van Allen Plexico

We used to note that, every season with Gus as the coach, it would take him three or four games to figure out what parts of the offense worked and what parts didn't. Where all the controls were, on the high-speed sports car.

We were doing a lot of drop-back passing, and a lot of running the ball with Mario Fannin, and that was okay, but it wasn't the strength of the team.

The defense performed better against the Bulldogs than they had the week before. They held MSU quarterback Chris Relf to 110 yards passing and 26 yards rushing, while limiting their opponents overall to 117 yards on the ground. Nick Fairley began to emerge as a star on the defensive side of the ball, recovering a fumble, intercepting a pass, and making 2.5 tackles for loss and 1.5 sacks. He would be named SEC Defensive Player of the Week.

> "Nick Fairley was the best defensive player in college football in 2010. As disruptive and destructive a force as you could want on the defensive line."
> —Kevin Scarbinsky, AL dot com

> "As good as Cam was that year, Auburn does not win the national championship without Nick Fairley. From an inside position, the way he pushed the pocket, the way he wrecked plays, he was a terror."
> —Chris Low, ESPN

> "I liked him a whole lot better on Saturday than I did during the week. Going against him every day in practice, I could've sworn he was listening to our plays and he knew our plays, because he (was always) in our backfield. And I remember how mad I was, after practice a couple of times, (I told him), 'Hey, you need to stop listening to our plays.' And then I figured out, 'No, he's really that good.' He was a disruptor. He disrupted a whole lot of practices, I'll tell you that."
> —Gus Malzahn, Auburn offensive coordinator

Fairley would go on to win the 2010 Lombardi Award for the best interior lineman.

On a night when the offense didn't do a lot, the defense made the difference. They'd held the Bulldogs to just 7 points in the first half, as the Tigers led, 17-7. But MSU scored on their opening possession of the third quarter to pull within 3 points. For a long stretch of the game after that, neither team could move the ball. Finally, late in the fourth quarter, the Bulldogs drove into Auburn territory, with a chance to tie or win the game. Auburn's defense rose up and shut the Bulldogs down at the Auburn 41, closing out the win for the Tigers.

Van Allen Plexico

This game felt like something of a reality check, after the fireworks of the first week. I found myself wondering a bit if our new quarterback and offense weren't quite as spectacular as we'd been led to believe. But we knew Miss State was a good defensive team, and we'd beaten them on the road. I was excited to see what else this Auburn team could do.

"We started off on fire. But we put our defense in some binds, I'm not going to lie. It's just a sign of a good team. Our defense stepped up and did what they had to do."
—*Cam Newton, Auburn quarterback*

"I huddled up the defense right before we went out for that last drive. I said, no matter what, if the offense scores, we have to go back out there and defend, and we did that. We got pressure up front. They made good plays in the back end. Everybody went out there and played hard."
—*Nick Fairley, Auburn defensive lineman*

Final Score:
(21) Auburn 17
Mississippi State 14

Auburn jumped up to number 16 in the AP Poll after the road win at Starkville. They enjoyed a couple of extra days off, due to that game having been played on a Thursday. Nine days later, the Clemson Tigers came to town, as did ESPN College Gameday.

September 18: Clemson

Amazingly, on Gameday that morning, Lee Corso—who's long had a reputation for not liking Auburn—picked them to win. He wasn't allowed to decapitate Aubie in order to put his head on, as he did other mascots around the country, while making his pick. He had to settle for donning a football helmet as he stated, "Auburn!"

This would be the first regular-season meeting between these two old rival sets of Tigers since Clemson last visited Auburn in 1971. Auburn was on a 13-game winning streak against Clemson: The South Carolina version of the Tigers hadn't beaten their Alabama cousins since early in the Eisenhower administration: November 24, 1951.

Van Allen Plexico

This was Dabo Swinney's second full season as head coach. It didn't turn out to be a great Clemson team, finishing 6-7—and in fact I'm sort of surprised Dabo survived the season—but they were plenty good on the day. Their offensive coordinator was Billy Napier and their defensive coordinator was Kevin Steele—both names Auburn fans would become more familiar with in the coming years.

Early on, things looked bad for Auburn. Clemson scored two touchdowns and a field goal on drives of 76, 53 and 61 yards. Meanwhile, they totally shut the home-standing Tigers down on offense. Their defense had seven future NFL players on the defensive front, and it showed. Auburn finally managed to get on the scoreboard just before halftime with a 53-yard drive to set up a Wes Byrum field goal. At the half, Clemson was up, 17-3.

"It really was one of those physical games. It truly felt like one of those Georgia or Alabama games. You could tell on both sides of the ball that we all wanted it."
—Josh Bynes, Auburn linebacker

ALL THEY DID WAS WIN

Auburn took the opening possession of the second half and moved the ball deep into Clemson territory. But Cam Newton's pass was intercepted at the opponent's 1 yard line.

The next time Auburn got the ball, they capitalized, both passing and rushing effectively. McCalebb carried it in from 12 yards out to bring the Tigers to within one score.

Auburn forced a Clemson punt and then scored again, tying the game at 17, on an 8-yard pass from Newton to Darvin Adams.

Again the Tigers in blue forced Clemson to punt, and again Auburn scored a touchdown. This time it was a massive, 78-yard pass to Terrell "T-Zac" Zachery down the sideline. Just like that, Auburn had gone from down 17-0 to up 24-17.

"It was huge for me to see Cam come out (and perform) in the second half. We didn't do anything offensively in the first half, and in the second half, the third quarter, we scored 21 points. I saw a resilient, tough dude (in) Cam Newton leading the charge, and he never flinched."
—Gene Chizik

Clemson responded, however. They marched 77 yards in 8 plays and punched it in to tie the game again, 24-24.

Van Allen Plexico

The thing I remember so vividly about Clemson's offense in this game was how they effectively used all kinds of screen passes against us. It looked like the Auburn defense was running around in circles, trying to figure out where the ball was going and how to stop it. The Clemson quarterback, Kyle Parker, was having a career day against us, with all these little "dink and dunk" passes.

Of course, the Auburn defense was also slowly beating Parker to a pulp, and I think the cumulative effect hurt him late in the game. I've rarely seen a quarterback be so utterly worn down over the course of a game. He was pretty banged up by the end.

Both teams punted back and forth for the rest of regulation, and the game went into overtime.

And, somewhat reminiscent of the Outback Bowl at the end of the previous season, that's when things got a little weird.

Cam nearly connected with Darvin Adams for a touchdown to start OT, but the ball bounced off the receiver's outstretched fingers in the end zone, while he was being covered tightly by a Clemson DB. Auburn had to settle for a 39-yard Wes Byrum field goal. They led, 27-24, but now it was Clemson's turn.

> *"He is still limping around. I think as this game goes on, I think it's getting worse for Kyle Parker. I think the pain is getting more severe and he's trying to block it out because before, he was grimacing and now he has a noticeable limp out on the field."*
> —*Kirk Herbstreit, ESPN broadcast*

Brent Musberger, doing the play-by-play, referred to Parker as "a young man in agony."

As Clemson moved toward the end zone, their left guard, David Smith, suffered an injury. Play stopped for some time as he was tended to and taken off the field in a cart.

Once play began again, it looked like Clemson was going to win as Kyle Parker threw to receiver Jaron Brown, open in the end zone. But Parker, still in obvious pain, led the receiver just a tad too much, and the ball tipped off Brown's fingertips, bringing up fourth down.

Clemson's kicker came out to try to send the game into a second overtime. He made the kick, but the referees signaled a penalty. At first they pointed toward the Auburn defense, calling offsides. That would have given Clemson a first down deep in Auburn territory. But then the referees gathered together, conferred, and reversed the ruling. They indicated Clemson's center had made an illegal snap, moving the ball early. That pushed Clemson back 5 yards and they had to re-kick. This time, the field goal sailed wide left.

Somehow, miraculously, Auburn had won.

As Kyle Parker slammed his helmet to the ground, sank back on the bench and stared up at the heavens, the Auburn defenders raced to the sideline, celebrating. A dazed and confused Dabo Swinney, looking like a boxer who'd just gone fifteen rounds with a heavyweight opponent, shook Chizik's hand at midfield. A jubilant Cam Newton bounced with joy around the field before pausing to speak to Erin Andrews of ESPN. She asked him what he'd learned about his team during the game.

ALL THEY DID WAS WIN

"That this team is resilient and we're not gonna give up for nothing. We faced so much adversity but we stuck together and bonded at the end. There are some warriors on this team, and we're just gonna have to stick together and fight."
—Cam Newton, to Erin Andrews, postgame

Final Score:
(16) Auburn 27
Clemson 24

Van Allen Plexico

This was one of the most exciting and frustrating games of the season, as well as the one that I have always maintained Auburn came the closest to losing at the end. After all, none of the other close games this season came down to the opponent having the ball in their hands, trying to score to win the game on the final possession. This one did.

It's amazing to think how different things would've been if Clemson's Jaron Brown had caught that ball.

John Ringer

Clemson was only about a .500 team that year. This was Clemson just before Dabo started to get things rolling there. The next two years after this, they won 10 and 11 games with this same group.

They ran a lot of draws and screen passes against us, and our defensive line had almost no impact on the game.

Van Allen Plexico

Aside from nearly killing their quarterback before it was over. Of course, Fairley and company would be doing a good bit more of that as the season went along.

Two other notes: One, this was the only game in 2010 I didn't get to watch in person or on television as it was happening.

My wife is a graduate of Southern Illinois University, and they had a pretty decent team that year. We got tickets to see them play at home, so we made the hour-and-a-half drive down to Carbondale. I didn't own a smartphone yet, so I was trying to follow our game on her 2010-model Android phone. It wasn't working out too well because there were a lot of dead areas in cell coverage between our town and Carbondale back then.

The most frustrating moment was when play was stopped for that offensive lineman injury during overtime, and we weren't getting any updates at all. I assumed the game was over and we just didn't know the outcome. Only later did I discover the game had been stopped and there was nothing to report during all that stretch of time. I'd been pulling my hair out!

And two: The flag from this game flies at your parents' house in Auburn! I stop and look at it every time I visit.

John Ringer

Auburn had a fun tradition at the time where they had a custom flag that flew over Jordan-Hare for each home game of the season. The 2010 game flag is at my parents' house in Auburn and they only bring it out and fly it on game day weekends.

How did they end up with the game day flag from the 2010 Clemson game? It happened this way:

In 2010 my mother, Joyce Ringer, was nominated for and awarded the Pamela Sheffield Award by Auburn University.

What is this award?

"The Pamela Sheffield Award is presented annually to a woman who best embodies selfless service and commitment to Auburn University and the Auburn Family.

As the University describes it, "The award is presented to an Auburn woman—alumna, student or friend—in whose life are manifested the qualities of Pam Sheffield's dedication to Auburn: love, commitment and, above all, quality. Quantity of contribution will be considered, but quality of contribution, the daily love and care that marked Pam Sheffield's commitment will be of the essence in selecting the recipient of this award."

The award was established April 27, 1991, by the Office of the President and the Athletic Department to honor, commemorate and perpetuate the memory and good works of Pamela Wells Sheffield.

Joyce Ringer was presented the Pamela Sheffield award on the field before the 2010 Clemson game. Jay Jacobs talked to Joyce at the awards presentation and was impressed. Jacobs got the Clemson game flag after the game, asked Gene Chizik to sign it, and then presented it to Joyce Ringer. Chizik's note and signature are still visible on the flag today.

The Clemson game was in the books. The good Tigers had prevailed. Three games into the season, Cam Newton and Nick Fairley looked like All-SEC, maybe All-American players. But Auburn had struggled in games two and three, barely escaping Starkville and coming within a fingertip catch of losing to Clemson at home.
Even so, the Tigers had survived that early gauntlet undefeated, and there was no question that they looked like a much-improved team from 2009. Even so, nobody was talking about playing for championships or having a "Superman" on the field.
But that was about to change—and some of it changed very quickly, indeed.

- 9 -

SUPERMAN

"The bigger the moment, the better Cam actually got."
—Kodi Burns, Auburn receiver

After the narrow, overtime win over Clemson in game three, poll voters punished Auburn by dropping them a spot in the rankings, to 17.

On September 25 in Jordan-Hare Stadium, they faced their second opponent in a row from the state of South Carolina: Steve Spurrier's Gamecocks, who were also undefeated and who were ranked two spots higher in the polls.

It would be another close, hard-fought battle.

The Gamecocks had "the Old Ball Coach" on the sideline. Lex Luthor with a visor. A supervillain who had terrorized opposing SEC teams for years.

Fortunately, the Tigers brought their own superhero to the contest. And in this game, at home in his Fortress of Solitude, he was about to rip open his shirt and reveal that big "S" logo for the whole world to see.

September 25: South Carolina

On Auburn's opening drive, Cam Newton stepped up and made himself a star at last. He faked a handoff, broke a tackle, and rambled 54 yards down the right sideline. Seven yards from the goal line, he did something more; something transcendent: he became Superman.

> *"After winning the starting job at quarterback, it was a normal start to the 2010 season for Newton, putting up seven passing touchdowns and two rushing scores in the first three games. Then, the run against South Carolina happened. In what can only be described as a 'What in the world just happened?' moment, Newton kept his balance with his left hand, raced past the Gamecocks' defense and leapt into the end zone ... from the 7-YARD LINE! (If you want to see firsthand how amazing that is, measure seven yards and then try to leap that far.)"*
> —Brian Stultz, AuburnWire, USA Today, December 31, 2019

Van Allen Plexico

I recall hearing that Cam had actually injured his shoulder the previous season, at Blinn College, doing that same thing—diving into the end zone. Gene Chizik had warned him not to do it unless he had to, in order to get through the defense and score. After the play, Chizik asked Cam, "Did you have to?" Cam responded that he did, and Chizik let it go. But if you watch the replay, I don't think a South Carolina defender was in any position to stop him. But that's just Cam.

It was a highlight the sports shows played over and over the rest of the year, and it probably did as much for his eventual Heisman campaign as the arguably more famous LSU run.

A ton of home-made graphics popped up online after this game, showing Cam wearing a Superman cape as he soared over the goal line.

Sometimes a dramatic play like that can really ignite a team as well as a fan base.

ALL THEY DID WAS WIN

> *"I think once we played South Carolina and Cam kind of did that Superman there in the end zone, that's when everybody started looking at one another and saying we might be pretty good. We've got a chance to be really, really special."*
> —Kodi Burns, Auburn receiver

> *"This guy eats up yardage when he is toting the ball."*
> —Stan White, Auburn Network broadcast

A South Carolina team coached by Steve Spurrier was not going to roll over and give up. The Gamecocks came roaring back with three unanswered touchdowns, to take a 20-7 lead, midway through the second quarter. The extra point on the third touchdown was missed.

Auburn used a mix of offensive players to drive down the field just before halftime, giving the Gamecocks a steady dose of Newton, McCalebb and Dyer for eight straight plays, culminating in a touchdown that closed the gap a bit, making the score 20-14, South Carolina, at the half.

> *"I remember our offensive line coach, Jeff Grimes, and Coach Malzahn saying, 'We're gonna have to run the ball to get back in this game. We're gonna run the quarterback.' And that's really when the season completely changed."*
> —Ryan Pugh, Auburn center

> *"I told Gus, I don't care if we have to run this guy 20 times a game. Let's create some really good run opportunities for him. And if he carries it more than 20 times a game, it doesn't matter. He can handle it."*
> —Gene Chizik

A similar approach to running the ball led to Auburn's third TD, midway through the third quarter. Now the Tigers had taken the lead, 21-20.

That lead did not last long. The Gamecocks answered in just three plays, going 75 yards to score again and go up, 27-21.

Wes Byrum had the chance to pull the Tigers within 3 points but missed his second field goal of the game, giving the ball back to Carolina. Quarterback Stephen Garcia fumbled on the first play of the Gamecocks' drive, however, and T'Sharvan Bell recovered for the Tigers. Four plays later, Cam hit tight end Philip Lutzenkirchen for the touchdown that put the Tigers back ahead, 28-27.

"That team offensively, Philip Lutzenkirchen was a big piece of the puzzle. He presented a lot of different matchup problems."
—Gus Malzahn, Auburn offensive coordinator

After another Garcia fumble, this time on a sack by linebacker Josh Bynes, Auburn had the chance to pad their lead a bit. This time Newton hit Emory Blake for a 12 yard touchdown. Now the Tigers were up by 8 points, at 35-27.

Spurrier decided to change quarterbacks, as he often liked to do when his teams were losing. The Auburn defense responded by stepping up and intercepting backup QB Connor Shaw twice, ending the Gamecocks' chances. Auburn held on to secure their fourth win in four games so far.

Cam's final numbers were pretty eye-popping. He ended the game with 158 yards through the air, on 16 of 21 passing, with 2 touchdowns. He led all rushers again with 176 yards and 3 touchdowns on the ground.

Michael Dyer added an even 100 yards rushing, along with 55 from McCalebb. Zachery, Adams, Blake and Lutzenkirchen all had good receiving games, led by T-Zac with 49 yards on 4 catches.

The Auburn defense continued to play well against the run. They held highly-touted Marcus Lattimore—a player this coaching staff had recruited hard and lost out on to Spurrier—to just 33 yards on 14 carries.

The pass defense, however, struggled all season long—especially in the first halves of games. They tended to make the leading receiver for the opponent look like Jerry Rice in his prime. This time it was the Gamecocks' Alshon Jeffery who benefitted. He finished with 8 catches for 192 yards and 2 touchdowns. That unfortunate trend would continue.

ALL THEY DID WAS WIN

On the good side of things, an Auburn player was named SEC Offensive, Defensive, or Special Teams Player of the Week for each of the first four weeks of the season.

Van Allen Plexico
If nothing else, we now knew the Auburn Tigers were South Carolina state champs, and that we had a quarterback capable of some amazing things.

"I'd never seen a player in my life, in college football, that on third and short, fourth and short, was as automatic as Cam Newton was.
"I give Gene Chizik credit that he turned Gus Malzahn loose, and said, 'We've got a special player—let's build it around him. Let's let him do what he can do. And, boy, they did."
—Chris Low, ESPN

"Once he understood what his role was gonna be and what he needed to do, he then began to play freely. And (I realized) it's gonna be tough to beat us. I can tell you that right now."
—Kodi Burns, Auburn receiver

Final Score:
(17) Auburn 35
(15) South Carolina 27

Going into their fifth game, the Tigers cracked the top ten in the AP Poll for the first time in 2010. After three close finishes the previous three games, the now-10th-ranked Tigers welcomed Louisiana-Monroe for what everyone hoped would be a less-stressful contest.

October 2: Louisiana-Monroe

Van Allen Plexico
I'll admit that, as exciting as it was to see Cam flying around like Superman in the first four games—and especially against South Carolina—I was looking forward to a game where he

wouldn't have to run and could maybe heal himself up a little bit before the next bunch of big games. Going into this game, I specifically remember saying, "I'll bet Cam doesn't carry the ball on a designed run play the entire game." And that was pretty much what happened.

John Ringer
Cam didn't run the ball. They didn't want him to get hit when he didn't have to be, and it padded his stats a little bit, too.

He didn't need to in this game. There was nothing to be gained from him running.

I think there was one play where there was nobody open, and he ran around for like twenty seconds and was looking over at the sidelines, like, "Really?? Can I go, or—?"

On Auburn's second play of the game, Onterrio McCalebb ran 50 yards for a touchdown. Two plays later, Cam connected with Emory Blake for a 94-yard score—the longest run or pass play for a touchdown in Auburn history.

"It means a lot. I put a lot of blood, sweat and tears into it. Just to know my name—and also my grandfather's name as well—is in the history books, it means a lot to me."
—*Emory Blake, Auburn receiver*

Nick Fairley finished with 4 tackles, 3 tackles for loss and 1 sack, despite only playing in the first half.

"Nick was very talented, very quick-twitch, great footwork, strong with his hands. He really paid attention and was always polishing his craft. Nick sometimes would be walking to class, and he'd be working on his footwork. He really invested time in his craft."
—*Kenneth Carter, Auburn defensive lineman*

Cam Newton ended up with 249 yards passing on 14 of 19 attempts, and didn't try to run the ball a single time. Mario Fannin led all rushers with 89 yards on 10 carries. Barrett Trotter came in to replace Cam in the second half and the Tigers went on to record 505 yards of total offense while shutting out the Warhawks over the final three quarters.

> *"It would have been easy (to take Louisiana-Monroe lightly), especially when you're feeling yourself and you know you're a very talented team, but we also were aware that we had a target on our back. Malzahn always did a great job especially (in) reminding the offense that we're going to do what we do, and we're going to do it well to the best of our ability. That's the attitude we took into every game."*
> —Emory Blake, Auburn receiver

Final Score:
(10) Auburn 52
Louisiana-Monroe 3

The next Saturday, Auburn had a date in the Bluegrass State, for their second away game of the season. It would be their fifth game out of the first six to start at 6:00 pm or later, with kickoff at Commonwealth Stadium in Lexington set for 6:30 pm. They would have only one more kickoff later than 3:00 pm the rest of the season, until the bowl game.

October 9: at Kentucky

Auburn probably looked more impressive in the first half against Kentucky than they did in any other game until the SEC Championship. After the Wildcats took advantage of a kickoff return into Auburn territory to start the game, the Tigers responded with four scoring drives of their own and led, 24-7, in the second quarter.

The talk about the Tigers' quarterback was heating up, as well.

> *"Cam Newton is still averaging 94 yards rushing per game, despite not having a carry last week against Louisiana-Monroe."*
> *"There are whispers about a Heisman campaign."*
> —ESPN announcers

Midway through the second quarter came one of the most memorable plays of the season. Cam took the snap and dropped back to pass, but Kentucky brought pressure up the middle and had two defenders in Cam's face immediately. He retreated and rolled to his right. He was certainly about to be sacked, and all he could do was throw the ball away before he was driven out of bounds.

Except—he didn't throw it away.

As he was being spun around and was falling down, with his legs in the air in front of him, he somehow slung the football down the sideline about 25 yards, where Kodi Burns caught it in heavy traffic for a first down.

As Cam got up, Chizik smacked him on the rear end with his clipboard and shouted, "That's a helluva completion, baby!"

> "A play is never really dead when number 2 has the ball."
> —ESPN announcers

Van Allen Plexico

Honestly, at that point, I'm surprised Kentucky didn't just forfeit the game and go home. If Cam could make plays like that—and he's already driven Auburn down the field for touchdowns on the two previous possessions—what's even the point?

What I did not see coming was that Kentucky would somehow corral Cam and shut down the Auburn offense entirely in the second half, while scoring two touchdowns in the third quarter to tie the game. The ending turned out to be way more dramatic than one would have reasonably expected, given the beginning.

Kentucky added 10 points before halftime to close the deficit to 14, at 31-17.

The first half had been an absolute exhibition by Newton. He'd been unstoppable.

Kentucky didn't give up, however. They played much better defense in the second half and were able to hold the Tigers to just a single field goal all the way until the very end. They scored 2 touchdowns in the third quarter and a field goal in the fourth, tying the game late, 34-34. The two-headed Wildcat monster of Randall Cobb and Derrick Locke combined to bring Kentucky back.

ALL THEY DID WAS WIN

Van Allen Plexico

I couldn't believe Kentucky managed to tie this game up. In the first half, it absolutely looked like Cam could take whatever he wanted on nearly every play. He was running over, around and through the Wildcats defense. And then, kind of like for our opponents in the Iron Bowl that year, the script got flipped after halftime.

"We actually were like, are we gonna lose this game? To Kentucky, of all teams? You know, we've beat Clemson, LSU (later), all these teams, but—Kentucky?! Thank God for Wes Byrum again saving the day for us."
—*Josh Bynes, Auburn linebacker*

With 7:15 remaining in the game and the score tied at 34-34, Cam Newton stepped up and led the Tigers on a drive for the ages. That drive began at Auburn's 7 yard line, after an attempted trick-play kick return blew up in the Tigers' faces. It would lead to only a field goal, but that was all the points Auburn needed to win the game. It was also a drive that would drain all the life out of the game clock, such that Kentucky would have no time left to answer.

On a drive of 19 plays, nearly all of them runs by Dyer, McCalebb or himself, Newton led the Tigers relentlessly down the field to the Kentucky 7 yard line. Along the way, the Tigers converted three third downs and Newton rushed 10 times for 48 yards. Kentucky burned all of its timeouts before the drive was over, and could only watch helplessly at the end. With 2 seconds left, Wes Byrum stepped up and kicked a 24 yard field goal to win the game.

"The Cardiac Tigers continue to get it done."
—*ESPN announcer*

"Let's win the ballgame right here and not put it on our defense. We played physical and tried to limit the mistakes and just took it on down the field. I thought that was a big growing-up period for our entire offense."
—*Lee Ziemba, Auburn offensive lineman*

Gus Malzahn would later note that he used that drive as a coaching tool for his later teams, showing it to the players. "We use that as an example about what a championship drive looks like."

> *"I remember thinking to myself, 'If we are able to do what we need to do, drive this down while simultaneously eating the clock and get a walk-off field goal and walk out of this stadium with a win, that could be one of those defining moments.'"*
> —Gene Chizik

During the final, game-winning drive, Cam connected with his favorite receiving target, Darvin Adams, to convert a huge third down.

> *"Coach has enough trust in me to call a play at a certain time and I think the whole team did a great job giving Cam enough time to throw the ball, trying to make a play for the offense. The drive means a lot. It shows that we can drive the ball and take time off the clock and come out in the end and win a game."*
> —Darvin Adams, Auburn wide receiver

Cam finished up with 210 yards passing and one interception. He also led the team in rushing again, with 198 yards on 28 carries, for a 7.1 yard average, and 4 touchdowns.

Van Allen Plexico

If you stare at Cam's numbers too long, or see them week after week, you start to forget just how astonishing they are. In this game alone—a game where he was largely held in check most of the second half—he ran for 198 yards and 4 touchdowns. The *quarterback* did that, not some star running back.

Oh, and he also happened to pass the ball for another 210 yards.

And he did this week after week.

It's just insane.

ALL THEY DID WAS WIN

Mike Dyer rushed for 56 yards on 9 carries, with a long of 27 early in the game. Mario Fannin got more playing time and added 50 yards on 8 carries. Darvin Adams once again led the way among receivers with 101 yards on 5 catches.

> "Any time you win a championship, there's a process that goes with it. That game right there was one of the defining games of the year, I felt like. Just with our team coming together and the way that we won that thing at the end.
>
> "Out of all the games we played—people won't necessarily remember that one like they will others—that was an enormous game because if we don't do that and we tie or lose that game, we're not having a national championship conversation right now."
> —Gene Chizik

> "Auburn fans (after the BCS title game) likely screamed, 'War Eagle!' until their lungs gave out, and why not? But one does wonder: Did any of them think back to that October night in Lexington, when the train nearly slipped off the tracks—in the time it takes to snap your fingers?"
> —Dick Gabriel, WKYT Website, 2020

Van Allen Plexico
Allow me to answer that question, Dick.
Yes.
I was there. I watched it all happen in person. And I was scared to death. That game stuck with me the rest of the season, and it still does. I'm very well aware of how close the Tigers came to losing—and blowing everything—multiple times that year.

This was a strange game. The first half would later be reminiscent of what Alabama did to us in the first half of that year's Iron Bowl. In the second half, Kentucky did what Auburn did against Alabama—come back from an improbably large deficit. But then it becomes like the ending of the Oregon game, with one team eating up the clock while driving for a walk-off field goal to win. Fortunately, it was Auburn doing that at the end, not Kentucky.

In other very important news, this Lexington trip was the first time I ever had Raising Cane's chicken fingers, which have gone on to become a reasonable substitute for my beloved Guthrie's of Auburn chicken fingers.

Also, I left my Auburn jacket in the hotel room in Lexington. I called the hotel later and they found it and were nice enough to mail it back to me, rather than setting it on fire or throwing it in the trash. Kudos to them.

Final Score:
(8) Auburn 37
Kentucky 34

With the regular season now half-over, the Tigers stood undefeated, at 6-0.

It hadn't been easy. Three of those wins had come by just 3 points each. Those three narrow wins had all come against unranked opponents.

This did not seem like a juggernaut of a team. Not yet, anyway. And the country certainly was not sold on Auburn as a national title contender.

Next up, however, were games at home against the 12th and 6th ranked teams in the AP Poll.

It was time for Auburn to start impressing the country.

- 10 -

BREAKING THE HEX

"Guys, are you gonna ride with me? Somebody in there has to make a play."
—*Zac Etheridge, Auburn safety*

October 16: Arkansas

It was the highest-scoring non-overtime game in SEC football history.

It was a game in which Arkansas scored 43 points—and still lost by more than three touchdowns.

Read that sentence again and think about it for a second.

This was a game that made Auburn's famous high-scoring tilts with Florida State look like Tuberville's 3-2 game. Of course, no one could have predicted that before kickoff.

What was being predicted before this game was how the BCS standings would look the following week.

The BCS had their own team rankings, separate from the traditional polls and computer rankings. They represented a conglomeration of several existing ranking systems into one formula.

From that list, the top two teams would be chosen to play one another for the national championship in January.

Those official rankings were not scheduled to be released until the week after the Arkansas game. But of course ESPN couldn't help but peer into their crystal ball and try to guess what they would look like. The day before Auburn played Arkansas, ESPN unveiled their simulation of the BCS top ten.

Their mock ranking put Auburn at number 8 in the country, ahead of Alabama at 10. This represented a massive upgrade of 15 spots from where the Tigers had started the season. Just six weeks earlier, the AP had ranked them 23. But it also indicated they still were not being taken seriously as a threat to win the national title.

Auburn's opponent the following week, LSU, was at 6. Oregon meanwhile was at 2, with undefeated Boise State at 1.

Joe Tessitore of ESPN's "Heismanology" feature had his own mock ranking of the top four Heisman Trophy favorites. He placed LaMichael James, the Oregon running back, at the top of the list, ahead of Kellen Moore of Boise State, Denard Robinson of Michigan, and Terelle Pryor of Ohio State. Cam Newton was nowhere to be found, though they did put him at the top of their "Other players on the rise" list, perhaps moving up.

ESPNU's "The Experts" segment discussed the fact that, the previous time Auburn went undefeated, the Tigers did not even get to play for the national title. One analyst suggested, "What comes around goes around—maybe they get a shot (this year)." But Tom Luginbill threw a bucket of cold water on that, stating, "This is the week Auburn goes down. They've got the tenth-ranked pass defense (in the SEC) and Arkansas has the number one passing offense. Arkansas can't run the football, but they may not have to."

In the AP Poll, the Tigers had moved up to 7th in the country after the win at Kentucky. Arkansas was ranked 12. This would be the first game of the year for Auburn to be broadcast in the prestigious 2:30 pm CBS slot, with the network's A-team, Verne Lundquist and Gary Danielson, in the booth. It would not be the last.

Arkansas was coached by Bobby Petrino, the 2002 Auburn offensive coordinator under Tommy Tuberville. They were led by a much-hyped Heisman candidate in passing quarterback Ryan Mallett—a player the ESPN experts were slobbering over.

ALL THEY DID WAS WIN

The national media seemed certain that Auburn had been "lucky" so far, and that Mallett and his Razorbacks would bring a cold dose of reality to the Plains that weekend.

Van Allen Plexico

In our early days of doing columns for the *War Eagle Reader*, we referred to the "Hawg Hex," where Arkansas always ended up playing us better than we thought they should—and beating us badly in some of those years! To get to the SEC Championship Game—and maybe even farther than that—we'd need to break the Hawg Hex.

At last game time arrived. What ensued shortly afterward was a "wild and wooly shootout," to borrow Jim Fyffe's famous phrase. An offensive explosion beyond anyone's wildest dreams. Well over 100 points would be scored before this crazy, back-and-forth affair was over.

Of course, you wouldn't have guessed at the end of the first quarter that a veritable eruption of points was coming. Each team had managed only a single touchdown as the second quarter began.

But then the doors blew off.

Ryan Mallett was injured while being sacked by Nick Fairley. He was replaced by backup Tyler Wilson, who picked up right where the Heisman candidate had left off, and perhaps even surpassed him.

> *"The quarterback on that team was Ryan Mallett, and we put him out early in the game, and honestly, we were sitting back thinking, 'We're gonna kick their butt. This is gonna be a blowout. We're gonna win no matter what. And then all of a sudden, I believe his name was Wilson, came in the game. And we were like, 'Who is he? He's not nobody.' And (then)—sho' nuff! Air raid! Zoom—touchdown! Touchdown! Touchdown!"*
> —Josh Bynes, Auburn linebacker

Auburn fought back, over and over, in a game that turned into a track meet. For the longest time, it appeared as if neither offense could be stopped. Eventually, however, one side couldn't keep up. It was the Hogs that ran out of gas first.

Van Allen Plexico
This is the game I've gone back and watched the most, of any game that season. More than the Iron Bowl, more than the BCS game, more than LSU or Georgia. It's this one. Because it was an absolutely insane, pinball machine, ping pong match of a football game. It's just incredibly fun to watch—especially knowing how it comes out at the end.

The two teams combined for an astonishing 1,036 yards of total offense and 108 points.

Cam Newton rushed for 188 yards, while passing for another 140 on 10 completions in 14 pass attempts.

CBS had been hyping the duel between the star quarterbacks all week, and they did get a good battle at that position—just not between the two players they'd expected. After Mallett's concussion, backup Tyler Wilson went on to throw for 332 yards and four touchdowns against an Auburn pass defense that remained highly suspect, especially in the first halves of games.

As bad as the Auburn defense looked early in this game, however, they—and the special teams—sealed the deal late.

In the second quarter, the Tigers blocked an Arkansas punt at the Hogs 32, leading to a McCalebb touchdown. Later in the game, Zac Etheridge returned a fumble 47 yards for a score. Then Josh Bynes intercepted two passes by Wilson on back-to-back possessions, leading to Auburn scores.

Perhaps the most controversial moment occurred early in the second quarter, with Arkansas up, 14-10.

Mario Fannin took a handoff from Newton and plunged into the end zone. At first glance, it looked like a clear Auburn score.

As the play was ending, however, there was a commotion on the field. Arkansas players acted as if they had recovered a fumble outside the end zone. This was odd, as we'd all just seen Mario Fannin dive in for the clear touchdown.

Then the video replays revealed the issue: Fannin dropped the ball right after he crossed the goal line. Or—wait—right before? It was hard to be sure, because an Arkansas player was positioned right between the camera and Fannin. Whichever it was, the ball had landed outside the end zone and lay there between the 1-yard line and the goal line, before Arkansas players jumped on it.

ALL THEY DID WAS WIN

Either Fannin had scored the go-ahead touchdown or he'd given the ball to the Razorbacks. The officials reviewed the play for what seemed like hours, to try to determine which of those two wildly different possibilities actually had happened.

Van Allen Plexico
Watching the replays now, I think it's pretty obvious that Fannin fumbled before the ball crossed the line. Ultimately the points didn't matter to the outcome. At the time, however, this felt huge—as if it might determine the winner and loser of the game.

Finally the referees completed their review and declared, "The ruling on the field stands." It was an Auburn touchdown. Probably an undeserved one, but we weren't complaining at the time.

Disgusted, Hogs coach Bobby Petrino threw his play-calling clipboard on the ground. Little did he imagine then how little those six points would matter. Because this game was about to explode.

> *"It turned into a wild game, just tit for tat. It was crazy. I felt like every time we'd come off the field, we had to go back out and do it again. That was just wild."*
> *—Lee Ziemba, Auburn offensive lineman*

Arkansas actually led the game in the 4th quarter, 43-37.

Then the Auburn offense stepped up again. Newton passed to Emory Blake for a touchdown to put the Tigers back in front, 44-43. But the Auburn defense needed to do their part and somehow stop, or at least slow down, the Arkansas offense. They hadn't had much luck at that, so far.

> *"In the fourth quarter I called the whole defense (together) and asked, 'Guys, are you gonna ride with me? Somebody in there has to make a play.'"*
> *—Zac Etheridge, Auburn safety*

The defense responded. Zac Etheridge took a fumble back for a score, and Auburn led, 51-43. Then Josh Bynes made his first interception, after which Cam took it in to make the score 58-43.

Bynes intercepted his second pass on the following Arkansas drive, and Michael Dyer scored from 38 yards out to bring the final score to 65-43.

A very close, back-and-forth contest had turned into a rout, over the space of just a few minutes of play.

Van Allen Plexico

It reminded me of the 1985 Auburn-Florida State game, where the score was very close for three quarters, and suddenly at the end Auburn exploded and won by 32.

> *"After the game, AU defensive back coach Phillip Lolley, who along with defensive coordinator Ted Roof is bearing the brunt of the criticism for this year's woes in the secondary, talked about how the coaches had reacted to Wilson's stepping in for Mallett. The frustration in Lolley's voice was evident as he checked off all the different schemes and coverages Auburn had used attempting to slow Wilson and his receivers down, all to basically no avail.*
>
> *"In the end, per Lolley, the one thing that worked was having linebacker Josh Bynes back way up in the center of the field after the snap. That last call, of course, led to the two interceptions that iced the win for the Tigers.*
>
> *"After 51 minutes of shooting-match football, stopping Arkansas' lights-out offense essentially came down to one guy dropping back in the zone. Again, it was that kind of a day."*
>
> —Will Collier, AuburnSports dot com

One mystery that has endured about the 2010 Auburn Tigers is how their defense could look so bad early in games, and so devastating late in them.

Neither the coaches nor the players on the team know the answer.

> *"For whatever reason, we were a much better second half defensive team. The thing I remember about that defense was, at the most critical times, they were at their best."*
>
> —Ted Roof, Auburn defensive coordinator

ALL THEY DID WAS WIN

"I don't know what it was, but in the first half, we'd go out there and (give up) twenty points, thirty points, whatever the score might be. But in the second half, you couldn't tell us we weren't one of the best defenses in college football."
—Josh Bynes, Auburn linebacker

"That (game) was really something. Our offense played extremely well. You talk about execution. We were able to run the ball and when we threw it, we were very efficient. I just remember that game went back and forth, and our offense hung in there and just found ways.

"That year, the offense and defense would pick each other up. That was a game where the offense needed to respond, and they did. That just gave us more confidence as the season went on that, 'Hey, we're going to keep battling and we're going to work together and we're going to find a way to win.'"
—Gus Malzahn, Auburn offensive coordinator

"It was amazing. We went out there and played as a team. The offensive line was the key. Running behind them, it wasn't just me. The whole running back corps, all of them had an excellent game. So, it just wasn't me running the football, the glory goes to the whole offensive line."
—Cam Newton

"It was personal...before the game, a lot of people were predicting us to lose, but we just had to go out there and make a statement."
—Onterio McCalebb

"It was amazing what Cam did with the ball in his hands, both running and passing. We always knew he could run the ball, but Cam was starting to throw the ball that day with extreme accuracy and with unbelievable confidence.

"It was after that game, a game where we had to score 65 points to win because they were scoring and matching just about every time we scored, where I said, 'You know what, not only is

Cam one of the best players in the country, he's going to have to start getting recognized as a potential Heisman Trophy candidate.'"
—Gene Chizik

After this game, Auburn officially began to talk about Cam and Heisman in the same breath.

"I don't have the opportunity to watch everybody in America, but I can tell you this: No. 2 is one spectacular football player. And I am not one to go out on a limb, but everybody in the world sees it. It's not like I'm telling anybody anything new. He is a competitor. He wants the ball. He is humble. He keeps working. And he gives us a chance to win every week."
—Gene Chizik

In addition to individual awards, Auburn fans started to think about what this team could accomplish together. Was the biggest prize of all in play?

"It was the night I really began to gain confidence in the 2010 team and believe that maybe—just maybe—this team could go all the way."
—Walt Austin, College and Magnolia blog

John Ringer
The Arkansas game was one of the most fun football games I ever remember watching. It was just bonkers. Neither team could stop the other. And there was a point where it looked bad for us. And then we put it in another gear and just ran away from them in the fourth quarter.

Van Allen Plexico
I wasn't on board with the national title contenders talk yet, considering how we'd seemed to stumble through whole sections of the Clemson and Kentucky games, in particular. But I was getting there. The next game on the schedule was the big one for

me. That's when I would decide what I felt this team was truly capable of.

Final Score:
(7) Auburn 65
(12) Arkansas 43

Now the Tigers were past the halfway point of the season, and they were 7-0. They'd won a huge game on national television and rung up a top 12 team for 65 points. Cam Newton was officially a Heisman candidate and at least some Tigers fans were beginning to dream big dreams about how—and where—this team could end up.

Van Allen Plexico
In these last two games, Auburn's defense had given up 77 points. That sounds catastrophic. We gave up 77 points!
And yet we were still undefeated. You know why?

John Ringer
Because we had Cam Newton. And because, in those same two games, we'd scored 102 points!

Van Allen Plexico
I called Cam "the Magic Eraser," because no matter the mess our defense got us into in the first halves of games, Cam could eventually erase it. Every time.

So with that incredible Arkansas game behind us, it was time to face LSU.
Going into that game, a buzz was slowly growing around the idea of Auburn competing for the national championship.
But it would be a different award—an individual player award—that appeared to be on the table by the time the game ended.
We'd seen the "Superman moment." Now it was time for the "Heisman moment."

- 11 -

THAT HEISMAN MOMENT

"Everybody knew at that point. Over the headset, I think I told the staff, 'He just won the Heisman.'"
—Gus Malzahn, Auburn offensive coordinator

Auburn had learned in 1983 that, to play for the national championship, every game, every win, and every loss mattered. One little slip against Texas was enough to open the door for Miami to jump the Tigers at the end of that season. Such a thing surely wouldn't have happened to a 12-0 Auburn team that had beaten Texas and run the table against the hardest schedule in the country.

Auburn had learned a different lesson in 2004. Trapped behind USC and Oklahoma all season, they found out that you can't always control your own destiny, no matter what you do. They discovered that sometimes, even when all you do is win, it's still not enough.

As the 2010 season progressed and the dreams and ambitions of Auburn's players and fans grew, they understood from grim past experience that they couldn't afford a single slip. If the ultimate goals of this team were to remain as realistic objectives, they would have to go to Oxford, Mississippi and win. They would have to face the Georgia Bulldogs at home and win. They would have to go into

Bryant-Denny Stadium and win. They would have to go to the SEC Championship Game in Atlanta and win—for what would be only the second time ever. And they would have to travel out to Glendale, Arizona and beat the other top team in the country, whatever it turned out to be.

Before any of that, though, they'd have to welcome an old adversary into Jordan-Hare Stadium: the LSU Tigers.

A team that had given Auburn its only loss in 1988, likely denying that powerful Tigers team its shot at the national championship.

A team that had crushed them, 31-10, in Baton Rouge the previous year.

After the Arkansas game, John and Van were emailing one another in preparation for their column in the *War Eagle Reader* that week. (The columns from that season are collected in their book, *Season of Our Dreams*.) Van was just starting to buy into the idea that this *might* be a national champion-caliber team—and that, because they'd started the season so far down in the rankings, Auburn could get left out of the BCS title game again, as had happened in 2004.

John Ringer, after the 2010 Arkansas game, in response:

I can't go there again after 2004. It hurt too much at the time and I don't want to do that again. It is like being burned in a relationship really badly and then a similar girl starts seriously dating you. "Warning! Warning, Will Robinson!"

The other thing is that I watch this team, and we win, but I have had a hard time believing a team with this defense is the best college football team in America. That is just hard for me to accept. I haven't seen a lot of great defenses out there this year (LSU is very good on defense) but I am a defensive guy, and it is hard. (Oregon is much worse than us on defense, too.)

I truly believe the 2004 Auburn team would beat this Auburn team. That defense would stop this offense.

Can we please hold the "BCS is going to screw us" discussion until after the LSU game? I think debating it before then may invite a karmic backlash.

I watched Alabama-Ole Miss last night and I was not afraid (of either team). Bama will not be able to run the ball all over us, and without that we can outscore them. The Julio Jones injury is huge for them.

October 23: LSU

This game is most remembered for Cam Newton's "Heisman moment," but there were big plays before and after it, in an extremely close, hard-fought contest.

Auburn scored first, capping off a drive that covered 54 yards, mostly on the ground. Cam plowed his way in to make it 7-0 Auburn, early.

LSU kicked a field goal, and then Auburn did, too.

LSU closed out the first half with an impressive, 14-play, 78-yard drive culminating in a touchdown. At the half, the score was tied at 10-10. It was anybody's game.

LSU got the ball to begin the third quarter, with the chance to finally take the lead. The Auburn defense held, however, and the Bayou Bengals were forced to punt. Auburn took over at their own 9 yard line.

Two plays later, everything changed.

John Ringer

There was a ton of talent on LSU's defense. Auburn had Cam and Nick Fairley, but LSU had Patrick Peterson and a bunch of other great players on the defensive side of the ball. And that game had The Play.

The Play was a run by Cam up the middle, where he kept the ball. It looked like it was going to be a good gain, but all of a sudden he turned on the jets and ran away from everyone, including Patrick Peterson, who was the fifth pick in the NFL Draft and one of the best defensive backs in the NFL afterwards. Cam just ran away from him into the end zone. It was stunning.

The drive was a potent one from the start. After a 29-yard run by Michael Dyer and a 17-yard catch by Darvin Adams, Auburn lined up at the LSU 49, and the stage was set for history.

Cam took the snap, scrambled through oncoming traffic, steadied himself—and broke loose for one of the most remarkable scoring runs in college football history. Not only did he weave his massive form through the entire LSU defense along the way—he also had to outrun one of the fastest players in football, LSU's Patrick Peterson, to get into the end zone. Cam ended up all-but-carrying Peterson along with him as he crossed the goal line for the score.

"What an unbelievable run. That was a historical moment right there. That kind of run makes you want to strike a pose, doesn't it, Stan?"
—Rod Bramblett, Auburn Network broadcast

"Everybody knew at that point. Over the headset, I think I told the staff, 'He just won the Heisman.'"
—Gus Malzahn, Auburn offensive coordinator, in 2020

John Ringer
That was the moment where he went from "This is a fun player, an exciting player" to "This is the best player in college football."

"It was just a simple play we were calling all night. Coach Malzahn and the staff called that play numerous times, but that particular play the offensive line did their job. And I guess it was left to me to do my job. A lot of missed tackles, and I just tried to make the most of it. It's just a play that is in my job description to make."
—Cam Newton, Auburn quarterback

Van Allen Plexico
It reminded me of the old Six Million Dollar Man show on TV, where they'd make it look like he was running fast by doing the opposite—showing him in slow motion. It created a strange visual illusion where you perceived him to be moving slowly but also covering a lot of ground very quickly.

It was the same with Cam, in a way. He wouldn't look like he was running that fast. You'd watch him at first and think, "Oh, maybe he'll get 3 or 4 yards here." And then you realize he's already covered 10 yards. And then it's 20, and he's barely taken

ALL THEY DID WAS WIN

two more steps. He absolutely ate up yardage with just a few strides, seemingly in slow motion. It was incredible.

LSU wasn't dead, of course. They were only down a single score. A lot of football remained to be played, and the game was destined to be a war for sixty minutes.

> *"You play LSU for sixty minutes and your body doesn't feel like jumping around. Every time we play LSU, I walk away with bumps and bruises and everything else. That was a physical football game. They brought it. To be here right now, with this team like it is, I'll take the pain. We all will. It's worth it."*
> *—Byron Isom, Auburn offensive lineman*

LSU managed to tie the game again, about three minutes into the fourth quarter, with a 39-yard touchdown pass from Spencer Ware to Rueben Randle. With twelve minutes left in this clash of titans, the score was knotted up at 17-17.

Auburn's defense locked in the rest of the way. LSU would not score again. They would not make a first down again. They were held to a 3-and-out on their next-to-last possession, and their punt ended up at the Auburn 10.

As with Cam's "Heisman" play, it took the Tigers three plays to score. Cam ran for 16 yards on first down, then Dyer ran for 4 more. And then it was time to hand the ball to the "jet sweep" man.

John Ringer
The final nail in LSU's coffin was delivered by Onterio McCalebb.

After Cam's huge run earlier in the game, the LSU defense had focused on stopping his inside runs the rest of the way. That opened up the outside, and that's just where the speedster McCalebb headed. He took the handoff, turned the corner around the left end of the line, and flew 70 yards down the field before anyone could blink. The touchdown put the Tigers in blue ahead, 24-17, and that's how the game would end. LSU got the ball back one more time, but Auburn's defense held firm. The Tigers from Baton Rouge turned it over on downs without making a first down.

> "It took a lot for us to run that play. We put the work in. Cam's been running up the middle all day, and that set the trend for me to get to the outside.
>
> "That play was built on the offensive line, receivers, the quarterback, everybody playing their part. When I got the ball and I got to the outside, I had a crease with the receivers when I cut it up and I saw nothing but green grass. I was like, ''Ain't nobody stopping me from getting to that pylon.'
>
> "Once I got out in front of everybody, nobody was going to catch me. I was going to do whatever I could to get to that pylon."
>
> —Onterio McCalebb, in 2020

McCalebb was quick to praise the blocking on the play by receivers Terrell Zachery, Kodi Burns and Darvin Adams. "If it weren't for those guys, there wouldn't have been a 70-yarder."

> "You read about Superman in the comics, and you think about him as a kid. But to see him fall out of the heavens and land on the 50 yard line of Jordan-Hare Stadium—you can't believe it. You're like a twelve year old kid. You pinch yourself and you know you're in your forties and you know what you're seeing, but you're not quite sure what you saw. An out-of-body experience.
>
> "If you're an Auburn fan, with Cam Newton, there was an odd familiarity. What I mean is, if you were a child that happened to love Auburn, and you grew up in the Autumn afternoons of 1982 or 83, and you saw Vincent "Bo" Jackson run up the sidelines and into eternity, then you had this feeling. You thought it was gone, and would never come back. It came back when Cameron Jerrelle Newton stepped onto the sidelines at Jordan-Hare Stadium. That feeling, that spirit, that emotion. To have it twice in a lifetime? No way in the world it could happen. But it did.
>
> "He was one of those players, like Bo, that you didn't want to leave your seat, because you might be about to watch something that you would never see again.

ALL THEY DID WAS WIN

"The first time I watched Cam Newton play in person, my wife and I had seats on the fifty yard line in the upper deck. My wife is carrying my son. He's going to be born in about six months or so. The first time she felt the baby kick was when the stadium exploded when Cam Newton had that broken play and ran for a touchdown—went right through the LSU defense and scored. To me, that was a game-changer. It changed the landscape. It changed the atmosphere. It changed the universe of college football."
—Reynolds Wolf, meteorologist for the Weather Channel

Auburn piled up 440 yards rushing against LSU, a school record for most rushing yards against an SEC opponent. Even more remarkable, they did it against a defense that had been allowing just under 84 yards on the ground per game.

"We just couldn't get him down. He ran the ball with a vengeance."
—Patrick Peterson, LSU defensive back, on Cam Newton

"As the games went on, it was, 'This guy is serious.' And now people are having to take him seriously. When he has the ball in his hands, (the other team has to) hope he is going to have an off-night. But if he's not, it's going to be a long night for you. I'm just glad he's here and he's on our team. I think he's the best player in the country. He can pretty much do whatever you ask him to do, and he's a leader. You just don't find people that have all of that."
—Michael Dyer, Auburn running back

Cam Newton wasn't the only person on the Auburn sideline about whom some expected to see bigger things soon.

"Chizik is going to have to try to fend off the inevitable as more schools are going to come looking at (Gus) Malzahn to be their next head coach. You don't do the things Malzahn has done

on a game-by-game basis without BCS conference schools calling for your services."
—Brad Zimanek, Montgomery Advertiser, October 24, 2010

The three usual suspects led the way in rushing for the Tigers in blue, and every yard and every score would be needed to beat the Bengal Tigers.

Newton, as usual, led the way with 217 rushing yards on 28 carries, with 2 touchdowns. (He added 86 yards through the air.) Michael Dyer rushed for 100 yards on 15 carries, and McCalebb added 84 more on just 4 carries—including the long one that turned out to be the game winner.

Auburn's two touchdown drives in the second half covered 91 and 90 yards, in just three plays each. The first broke a 10-10 halftime tie, and the second broke a 17-17 fourth quarter tie. LSU had no answer for the final one.

> "I think the numbers speak for themselves. I just don't want to lose sight of the fact that our offensive line has become a really good offensive line. From left tackle to right tackle, those guys have played every snap now for eight games. They are beat up. They are tired. They get beat up during the game. They find a way to continue to press on."
> —Gene Chizik

The defense held LSU to just 17 points.

> "I thought we were a little bit beat up tonight going into the game defensively. I could not be more proud of our defensive staff, our defensive players. We were playing with true freshmen. We were playing with walk-ons. We were just fighting, clawing and scrapped our way to playing well today."
> —Gene Chizik

Nick Fairley wreaked havoc on the LSU offense. He recorded 2.5 sacks, 3.5 tackles for loss, 6 tackles and a quarterback hurry—all while being routinely double-teamed by the LSU offensive line.

ALL THEY DID WAS WIN

"We played real well, but there were times we didn't execute like we should. We went into halftime and said that we have to get to the quarterback if we are going to win this game. We harped on that all offseason not just for us to win but to have a successful season. So far it's worked for us."
—Nick Fairley

"LSU is an excellent team. Going into this game, we knew (it was the) number 1 offense (against the) number 1 defense. Clash of the titans. There were licks being taken, different people left and right. We knew that would be the case going into the game. And I think we were prepared for that."
—Cam Newton

(5) Auburn 24
(6) LSU 17

Van Allen Plexico

After the LSU game was when I first allowed myself to think that this team could do the impossible—that they could somehow break the curse, the incredible run of bad luck we'd known for so many years, when it came to national championships.

As soon as the LSU game ended, I looked at my family and said, "If we can beat that team, we can beat anyone on our schedule. We can win it all." I ran to the computer and started looking for BCS tickets. I got two with what looked like pretty good sight lines for $578 each, plus a ton of added fees and so forth. The final price for the two tickets was just under $1,500. Remember that number for something coming up later!

I knew where the BCS title game was being played, because Jeremy Henderson at the *War Eagle Reader* web site, among others, had already been talking about it—throwing around the word "Glendale." I mentioned that to my wife, and she noted that we probably wouldn't need a hotel because her uncle lived in the Phoenix area. That was a lifesaver. I don't know how, back at that time, we could have afforded a hotel for at least two nights, on top of airline tickets *and* game tickets that were so expensive. With the lodging tended to, we could *just* do it—though I did end up canceling my annual appearance at DragonCon later that year, because this trip had cost so much.

Also: In hindsight, this was one of the few big regular-season games where we didn't get behind early and have to come back from a crazy, double-digit deficit! That inspired confidence going forward as much as anything, I think.

In 2025, during the production of this book, the AU Wishbone conducted a Twitter poll. The following question was asked of "Auburn Twitter" people:

"During the 2010 Auburn football season, you first started thinking the Tigers could win the national championship after which game?"

Twitter allows up to four options to be offered. The four here were:
- Arkansas
- LSU
- Georgia
- Other

Arkansas, Georgia and Other each received about 8% of the vote. The LSU game was the clear winner, receiving nearly 75% of the vote.

After the win over LSU, Auburn fans believed. They believed this team could win the national championship. They believed Cam Newton could win the Heisman Trophy.

They believed these things *could* happen—that they were realistic *possibilities*.

But they'd been burned enough times in the past to understand nothing was *guaranteed*.

Four games remained in the regular season. The Tigers were determined to be Number One.

As fate would have it, that designation came a lot sooner than most expected.

- 12 -

NUMBER ONE

Following the win over LSU, the national rankings got shaken up in a big way.

Number 1 Oklahoma lost to Missouri that same day. Consequently, the Sooners vacated the top spot in the BCS poll. That place was taken not by number 2 Oregon but by previous number 4 Auburn, who jumped the Ducks, at least for that week. It was the Tigers' first time at number 1 in any major poll since early in the 1985 season.

Meanwhile, the AP Poll ranked them third.

Van Allen Plexico

I can fondly remember my family gathering around the TV each week to watch ESPN unveil the new BCS standings that season. When Oklahoma lost, we were buzzing over the likelihood that Auburn would move up to number 2. Instead we jumped all the way to first! I was over the moon.

The following week, Oregon moved to number 1 again, but we never fell below second. And that was all that mattered—being first or second. The only difference being ranked first or second made in terms of the BCS was what color jersey your team would be wearing while playing for the national championship.

As long as we weren't stuck in third anymore, I was very happy.

Also, remember that it had been Oklahoma that had blocked Auburn from playing USC in the 2004 BCS game. I'd been getting nervous about some kind of *"deja vu* all over again" with them. Getting the Sooners out of the way this early, this time around, was a relief.

In the meantime, Auburn had another game to play. After two fierce battles against ranked opponents in Jordan-Hare Stadium, the Tigers had to hit the road to play Ole Miss in Oxford.

Van Allen Plexico

Ole Miss on the road, right after Arkansas and LSU, had "trap game" written all over it. I was nervous.

The Rebels were coached by Houston Nutt, a coach who could on occasion be dangerous. And now teams were taking Auburn more seriously and looking for ways to limit Newton and his offense.

Nutt came up with a way. At least partly.

But it didn't matter.

October 30: at Ole Miss

Coming into the Auburn game, Ole Miss had dropped their two previous games and desperately wanted a win. Knocking off the new number 1 team in the country would turn their season around.

By this point in the season, undefeated Auburn was getting everyone's best shot.

The Rebels looked to be worthy challengers, at least at first. They got off to a big start, as freshman running back Jeff Scott took the handoff from quarterback Jeremiah Masoli and went 83 yards for a touchdown on the second play of the game. Scott carried the ball 66 times during the 2010 season, and this one play accounted for nearly a fifth of his total yardage for the entire year.

The Tigers were down 7-0 before Cam and his cohorts on offense had even set foot on the field, and barely before they'd even left the locker room. If Auburn was going to win, this would have to be yet another come-from-behind affair for the Tigers.

ALL THEY DID WAS WIN

Only 27 seconds had elapsed from the game clock when the Auburn offense took the field for the first time. From the beginning, it was obvious the coaches intended for Cam to throw the ball more than run it in this game. He attempted to run the ball only twice in the entire first quarter, gaining a net total of 2 yards.

Unfortunately for Ole Miss, what Cam didn't gain on the ground, he made up for through the air. And while Ole Miss was containing him, they let Michael Dyer and Onterrio McCalebb get loose for big yardage.

The Tigers responded to Ole Miss's shocking early touchdown with a pass-heavy drive that culminated in an explosive scoring play of their own. When Auburn reached the Ole Miss 20 yard line, former quarterback Kodi Burns lined up behind the center while Cam split out wide into Burns's regular receiver spot. Kodi promptly tossed a beautiful pass to the back corner of the end zone. There Cam outfought the Rebel defender and made his only receiving touchdown of the season.

> *"I promise you, we practiced that play about 10 to 15 times every single day, and (Coach Malzahn) didn't let us leave until we'd hit three or four perfect ones in a row. And we did that every single day leading up to that game. Whenever you rep the play over and over again, you have great confidence in it, and really it was expected. It wasn't a shock to Cam. It wasn't a shock to me. Because we had already had plenty of reps at that play, and we just went out there and executed the play."*
> —Kodi Burns, Auburn receiver

On Auburn's next possession, Onterio McCalebb matched Scott with a 68-yard touchdown run of his own. The Rebels scored again and kept pace with the Tigers for that quarter, such that the two teams entered the second frame tied at 14.

In the second quarter, however, Auburn pulled away, outscoring the Rebels 20-3 to hold a 34-17 lead at halftime. Along the way, defensive back Demond Washington made two big plays. First, he intercepted an Ole Miss pass at the Auburn 2 yard line to stop a scoring threat. Then, following a later Rebel field goal, Washington returned the ensuing kickoff 95 yards for a touchdown. By the end of the game, he'd set the Auburn single-season record for kickoff return yardage.

The Tigers added 10 more in the third quarter while shutting Ole Miss out, then exchanged touchdowns with the Rebels late in the game, for a final score of 51-31.

For once in the season, Newton was not the leading rusher, or even the second-leading rusher, for the Tigers. Limited to just 45 yards on the ground—after four straight games of gaining at least 170—Cam went on to pass the ball against the Rebels for 209 yards.

Dyer ran for 180 yards on 21 carries in what was his breakout game of the season. Onterio McCalebb added 99 yards on 9 carries, for an 11-yard average.

Some of the Tigers took the opportunity to poke fun at their opponents' uniforms before the day was done:

> "I remember they had some grey pajama-looking uniforms on (in) that game. They looked like pajamas. We were talking trash to their D line. We were like, 'Y'all look like you just rolled out of bed. What's wrong with y'all?'"
> —Lee Ziemba, Auburn offensive lineman

Auburn had now rushed for 300-plus yards in five straight conference games. And they'd done so using a variety of players, not just Newton. The Tigers had found more weapons when they'd needed them. They weren't entirely a one-man team on offense.

> "Everybody can't rush for 100 or 200 yards every week, so you have to work with what the defense is giving you. You have to go to the next thing. Tonight, they did a nice job of taking Cameron away in terms of the run game, and that was their plan. We had to work other avenues. I'm really proud of our plan."
> —Gene Chizik

Van Allen Plexico

Coach Chizik says what he says there, but the odd thing to me is, if you go back and watch the video of this game, Cam doesn't come out looking to run the ball. Chizik talks as if Cam was prevented from running, so they went to "Plan B" and had him throw it. Unless he was using run-pass options every play, and had to keep going with the "pass" option, I don't really see it that way. It looks to me as if he's intending to pass the ball or hand it off almost every time he takes the snap.

There was one series in the second quarter where Cam tried to run the ball three times out of four straight plays, and ended up with only a couple of yards total. After that, he went back to passing it and handing it off—though he did have a few good runs in the second half. So maybe that's what the coach is thinking about.

Whatever the case, it worked—to the tune of over 50 points. So I'm not complaining!

The offense continued to execute, albeit in perhaps a different way than in previous weeks. The defense, however, still looked suspect, especially for a title contender. The players didn't seem to see it that way, though:

> *"I feel like we just started to hit our stride. After some tough games, after some close games, it was just this level of 'OK, now we can see it.' That LSU game was such a big top-10 matchup, and I think as we shifted into going on the road for the first time having this No. 1 ranking, we knew what we had was special. We started to practice like it. We started to play like it."*
> —*Nosa Eguae, Auburn defensive lineman*

Van Allen Plexico

John had told me after the Arkansas game that he had a hard time believing a team could give up so many yards and points on defense and be a realistic national championship contender. The evidence seemed to support him. Among the more egregious defensive performances, the Tigers had given up 26 points to Arkansas State, 34 to Kentucky, 43 to Arkansas, and now 31 to Ole Miss. And that long run by Ole Miss to start the game... Man, I was not feeling great about our defense.

Sure, the Auburn *offense* was clicking, for the most part. Cam and company were simply outscoring those teams. "Score 31 on us? We'll score 51 on you! Score 43 against us? Here's 65 back at you!"

But even the most die-hard Auburn fans had to wonder how much longer this team could get away with allowing the opponent to light up the scoreboard that way.

(1) Auburn 51
Ole Miss 31

Auburn was now 9-0 with three regular-season games left to go. At least for this one week, they'd risen to number 1 in the BCS. They had a home game coming up the next week, against Chattanooga, that frankly concerned no one. Tigers players, coaches and fans surely believed it would be nothing but smooth sailing until Georgia.

They could not have been more wrong.

- 13 -

COMING SO CLOSE

"Fifty-three years of waiting, of hoping, of dreaming, of coming so close!"
—Rod Bramblett

Some teams regularly win national championships, such that it's probably not that big of a deal to them.

Some teams never come close to sniffing one, and know doing so is not realistic, so they don't think much about it.

Auburn is in the middle somewhere: The Tigers are fully capable of winning national championships, but it just hasn't happened nearly as often as it should, given the level of the Auburn program. And in so many years where the stars did all line up and a championship appeared to be there for the taking, they've been denied by way of strange sets of circumstances and turns of events.

One reason why the 2010 season was so incredibly huge for Auburn fans wasn't just because of how it ended. It was also huge because of the way three other noteworthy seasons had ended, and what the Tigers had been denied each time.

Let us pause in the story of the 2010 season, then, for just a moment, to look back at those three years, and how they contributed to making Auburn fans ravenous for something good to happen, at long last, in 2010.

The years resonate in the ears of Auburn fans everywhere:

1983.
1993.
2004.

Mention those three seasons, and true Auburn people will react with a visible mixture of pride and pain. Pride in what those teams accomplished, and pain over what they were denied, through no fault of their own.

Over the course of those three seasons, the Auburn Tigers finished a combined 35-1. Those three years include two undefeated seasons and a one-loss campaign against one of the toughest schedules in the history of the sport.

Any reasonable college football fan, if asked how many national championships any SEC team had likely won after going 35-1 over three seasons, would surely say, "At least two; maybe more."

Alas, no.

These years represent the times that Auburn people honestly believed their team had outright won a national championship—or at least deserved it—and were rudely rebuffed by the voters and polls. The university itself not officially recognizing them as championship teams and years only makes it worse.

To understand why the 2010 national championship mattered so much, we have to understand what happened those other years before it. We have to understand why, in 2010, when the situation with Cam Newton looked so bleak for a time, many Auburn fans simply shook their heads and said to themselves and to others, "You see? Something always happens."

Something *always* happens.

By 2010, Auburn fans weren't just hungry for a national championship. They were *ravenous*.

Before the end of the 2010 season, the 1957 AP national championship was the most recent title recognized by the university—that is, officially acknowledged, included in the media guides and commemorated with flags in the stadium.

ALL THEY DID WAS WIN

The university fully claims the 1957 title, but even that one is not without controversy. Auburn finished 10-0 that season but was on probation and did not participate in a postseason bowl game. Many of the widely-recognized ranking organizations at that time, however, released their final rankings *prior* to the bowl games. In their eyes, Auburn's ineligibility for postseason play didn't matter. The Tigers therefore were able to clinch the national championship in the AP Poll after defeating Alabama, 40-0, on November 30. But all of the other major selectors, including the UPI, chose 9-1 Ohio State, who defeated Oregon in the Rose Bowl on January 1. The Buckeyes had dropped their first game of the season at home to TCU before running the table the rest of the way. Even the selectors who made their final decisions prior to the bowl game went with Ohio State, with the AP being the sole dissenter.

Van Allen Plexico

One of the reasons always given for why Auburn only recognizes the 1957 national championship, and not the others we go into in this chapter, is that it was supposedly the least controversial and most widely accepted. And yet the AP was the only selector that chose Auburn that year. While I think Auburn was clearly the most deserving in 1957, I also think that's true about some of the other years we're going to talk about. And yet that's never been enough to persuade the university to officially claim any of them. I just don't get it.

After that 1957 title, Auburn put together two seasons that brought recognition as national champions from at least one selector, and a third that might have been the most deserving of all, but for a set of odd complications.

The 1983 Auburn Tigers faced a schedule that has been described as not just the toughest that season, but one of the most difficult in college football history.

After defeating Southern Mississippi on the first weekend of the season, they dropped a home game against a very powerful and third-ranked Texas Longhorns team, 20-7. From there, the Tigers simply refused to lose.

They won by 23 over the Tennessee Volunteers in Knoxville, then came home and took down Florida State in a tight contest ended by a huge interception by All-American linebacker Greg Carr. They went on the road and won at Kentucky and at Georgia Tech. They then came home to beat Mississippi State and 5th-ranked Florida in a hard-fought contest. The win over the Gators was the first of five games against ranked opponents to close out the season, with four of them in the top 10. After defeating Boomer Esiason's 7th ranked Maryland, they traveled to Athens to grind out a 13-7 win over 4th ranked Georgia, denying the conference-dominating Bulldogs a fourth consecutive SEC title. They then defeated number 19 Alabama (the lowest-ranked opponent of this stretch of games) in Legion Field.

Having won the SEC outright, the Tigers secured a berth in the Sugar Bowl, where they would face number 8 Michigan. After the win over Florida in October, Auburn had ascended to 3rd in the polls, behind only Nebraska and the Texas team that had beaten the Tigers in week 2. They could climb no higher in the polls unless one of those top two teams lost.

In an era before the BCS or any sort of playoff arrangement, teams that won their conferences were obligated to play in specific bowl games against specific opponents. The 1983 Auburn team had no choice but to face the runner-up of the Big Ten, Michigan, as that conference's winner was required to play in the Rose Bowl. Texas, winner of the Southwestern Conference, was set to face number 7 Georgia in the Cotton Bowl. The top-ranked Cornhuskers had to play in the Orange Bowl, against an at-large team.

And that, for Auburn, would ultimately be the problem: The 5th-ranked Miami Hurricanes, who played their home games in the Orange Bowl stadium, were at that time independent, with no pre-existing conference bowl ties, and therefore available as an "at-large" team. They accepted the Orange Bowl's invitation. That meant Nebraska would be facing their bowl opponent in that team's own stadium.

Going into the Sugar Bowl, Auburn's players and fans thought the path to a national championship was clear, if somewhat unlikely. The Tigers needed to defeat Michigan, obviously. Then they would require Miami to upset "team of the century" Nebraska and Georgia to upset Texas—neither of which seemed likely. Finally, they would need the voters who determined the national champion in the final polls to conclude that Auburn's ridiculously high strength-of-schedule made them, at 11-1, the most deserving of all the one-loss teams, and that they should be named national champions.

Unfortunately, the decision-making system for the AP Poll was a popularity contest among sportswriters. And those sportswriters were not paying Auburn-Michigan any attention at all.

The two bowls were being played simultaneously, late on the night of Monday, January 2. In an era before widespread remote controls, viewers tended to leave their televisions on one channel for extended periods of time. The poll voters who would be deciding the champion were tuned to Nebraska-Miami in the Orange Bowl. They scarcely knew Auburn and Michigan were playing.

At least one thing was going right for the Tigers: Earlier in the day, Georgia had accomplished their part in Auburn's longshot bid for the title. They'd miraculously defeated Texas, 10-9. The opportunity for a national championship was still there for the taking—or, at least, Auburn fans believed it was. If Miami could somehow take down Nebraska, they thought, the voters would surely promote the third-ranked Tigers up to first place in the final poll. No Auburn fan took seriously the notion that number 5 Miami could jump all the way up to first, regardless of how the Orange Bowl played out.

What Auburn fans didn't fully appreciate was how Orange Bowl viewers—including those aforementioned poll voters—were being told repeatedly by the NBC hosts, anxious for big ratings, that they were witnessing the game to decide the national championship. Occasional updates from the Sugar Bowl likely didn't cause anyone to jump up and change the channel. The Wolverines and Tigers were locked in an extremely low-scoring, old-school defensive battle, while Nebraska and Miami were rolling up and down the field on one another, in what was turning out to be an extremely close and interesting shootout. Style points were winning out over hard-nosed defense and "three yards and a cloud of dust."

Because Auburn and Michigan both ran the ball a lot, and didn't throw many passes at all, let alone incomplete ones, the clock also kept running in their game. Consequently, the Sugar Bowl ended well before the other game, where Miami was airing out passes that kept stopping the clock and prolonging the game. By the time the

Orange Bowl came down to its final minutes, even the few fans who had been watching Auburn-Michigan were now tuned in to it.

Miami won, of course—and in dramatic fashion, in the final seconds. Which meant Nebraska lost.

This was what Auburn had wanted, right?

In his post-Sugar Bowl interview, Pat Dye had given the ABC reporter a long and convoluted statement about why Auburn should be number 1, involving strength-of-schedule and the like. After the Orange Bowl, Miami's coach, Howard Schnellenberger, simply told the NBC reporters, "We're number 1. No doubt about it."

The sportswriters and other voters listened to Schnellenberger.

Auburn was not voted number 1. Miami jumped all the way up from 5th to claim the national championship.

Shockingly, Auburn was not number 2, either. Nebraska, losers of the Orange Bowl, had fallen only one spot, to 2nd, ahead of the winners of the Sugar Bowl. The Tigers remained third, in the same spot they'd occupied before the bowl games were played. A team that had been blown out in week 1 by Florida—who was later beaten by Auburn!; a team that barely escaped East Carolina in mid-season; a team that had been ranked fifth before the bowls; *that* team was the national champion, ahead of a team that had just finished 11-1 against one of the toughest schedules in college football history.

The *New York Times* computer poll—an NCAA-recognized selector, and a ranking that used actual numbers and math, rather than the opinions of random sportswriters—got it right. It chose Auburn as national champions.

Auburn officials made no effort to acknowledge or advertise that fact. They didn't want to "look like Alabama," claiming titles that were dubious in any way. For all intents and purposes, Miami was the consensus national champion. Auburn was third.

It was absurd. It was astonishing. It was soul-crushing.

It would become par for the course.

Of coming so close...

A decade later, the Tigers would be denied again.

The year was 1993. After twelve seasons, the Pat Dye era at Auburn had ended, and the Tigers had a new head coach: Terry Bowden.

ALL THEY DID WAS WIN

Terry brought a renewed sense of energy to the program. In his first couple of seasons, he got more out of the players than Dye had in the previous three years. Bowden reeled off an amazing twenty straight wins before finally suffering a tie with Georgia and then a loss to Alabama at the end of 1994. But in his first season, 1993, Terry's Tigers were perfect, finishing the season 11-0.

Unfortunately for them, the program was on probation due to NCAA violations that had taken place during the Dye years. The sanctions they faced included no appearances on television and, more crucially, no postseason play. The Coaches' Poll wouldn't even consider ranking them.

Their resume was not weak. They whipped LSU, 34-10, in Baton Rouge. They beat 4th ranked Florida, 38-35, in a shootout in Jordan-Hare on October 16. They beat Georgia by two touchdowns in Athens, before coming home to defeat the Tide, 22-14.

After that win over Alabama on November 20, the Tigers peaked at number 3 in the AP Poll. With no more games to play, however, they could only sit back and watch helplessly as other teams won games and moved ahead of them. The week after the Iron Bowl, West Virginia finished their season undefeated as well, and moved past Auburn to claim third place. On December 4, one-loss Notre Dame pushed past them as well.

Unable to participate in the SEC Championship Game, much less a bowl, the Tigers could only hope that, somehow, all the other undefeated teams would lose, leaving them the only undefeated major program left. Then they'd need to gather up the votes of a bunch of sportswriters who, because of the TV ban, probably hadn't even been able to see them play all season.

None of that seemed possible, much less likely.

But then, as the bowl games unfolded, undefeated Nebraska did lose to one-loss Florida State (coached by Terry's father, Bobby Bowden). Undefeated West Virginia got blown out by Florida, a team Auburn had beaten.

Somehow, it had all worked out again! At the conclusion of bowl season, Auburn was the only undefeated team left.

Would this be the year, at last? Would the undefeated Tigers gather enough votes to move ahead of all the teams that had suffered losses, and be crowned national champions?

No. The voters didn't care about any of that. They named one-loss FSU the champions.

Auburn, the only undefeated team left in the country, ended up not first, not second, not even third. They were ranked fourth.

Fourth.

Again, it was absurd. It was astonishing. It was soul-crushing.

It was indeed becoming par for the course.

Of coming so close…

Just over a decade later, almost unbelievably, it happened for a third time.

The 2004 Auburn Tigers were believed by many Auburn fans to be the best squad the program had ever produced—better than 1983, better than 1993, better even than 1957.

They combined a rock-solid defense, led by Quentin Groves, Travis Williams, Junior Rosegreen and Carlos Rogers, with a high-powered offense featuring Carnell "Cadillac" Williams, Ronnie Brown, Jason Campbell and a squadron of great receivers including Ben Obomanu, Devin Aromashodu and Courtney Taylor.

This team ran the table. They took on all comers and emerged unscathed. Unlike the 1993 team, they were fully eligible for the postseason. They crushed Tennessee for the second time that year in the SEC Championship Game, 38-28—a game not as close as the score indicated. Then they beat Virginia Tech in the Sugar Bowl, 16-13. In both games, the opponents scored garbage touchdowns late to make the score look closer than it was.

The problem for Auburn was, no mechanism yet existed to allow the third-ranked team to play for the championship. And Auburn had been stuck in third place all season, behind USC and Oklahoma, who had started the season ranked there and who were also undefeated.

As week after week went by, Auburn fans watched the Trojans and Sooners pull out win after win, escape after escape. It never seemed enough to cause the poll voters to move Auburn ahead of either of them, regardless of how impressive the Tigers' wins were. As the bowl games approached with a relentless inevitability, that sinking feeling—"We're going to be left out"—grew worse and worse each Saturday.

Sure enough, neither USC nor Oklahoma lost a single time, and they met in the BCS National Championship Game. The winner would be crowned champion. Auburn, in third place nearly all season, had no option but to do their best against the Hokies in the Sugar Bowl and then hope and pray something miraculous might happen.

Nothing miraculous happened. At least, not immediately.

USC crushed the Sooners, 55-19.

AP voters and the BCS awarded the national championship to USC. Following Oklahoma's disastrous showing, they fell to third and Auburn moved up to second.

Possibly the greatest team in Auburn football history had remained stuck in third place all season, and never got the opportunity, in a 2-team BCS system, to play for the title they felt they deserved.

Van Allen Plexico
I never understood the "S" in BCS.

It stood for "Series." But what series? It was one game!

The BCS did mark an improvement over the old system in one key way, however: It meant the top two teams would always play one another, rather than being locked into random bowl commitments against other teams.

That was great when there were two clear-cut top teams. But what if there were three?

One other thing: Auburn had at least moved up to second. They weren't stuck in third, behind a team that lost its bowl game, as happened in 1983. I suppose that represented progress...? Ugh.

Then, a bit later, something unexpected *did* happen: An NCAA investigation found that USC had been cheating! Their 2004 national championship was taken away. And there sat undefeated Auburn at number 2.

Ultimately, however, it amounted to salt in the wounds for the Tigers. Auburn wasn't moved up into the top spot. Instead, the 2004 BCS National Championship was simply "vacated."

Head coach Tommy Tuberville later asked the AP to move Auburn into the empty number 1 spot. The AP refused. The 2004 national championship remains vacant to this day, while 13-0

Auburn sits at second in a season where nobody officially finished number 1.

Absurd. Astonishing. Soul-crushing.

Par for the course.

These are the moments Rod Bramblett was referring to in Arizona when he said the "of coming so close" part of, "Fifty-three years of waiting, of hoping, of dreaming—of coming so close…!"

With three quarters of the 2010 regular season in the books and the team still undefeated, some Auburn fans—fans who had waited so long, and had been burned so many times—began to allow themselves the tiniest sliver of hope. Tentatively at first, they allowed themselves to dream.

Could *this* be the year?

Could it possibly be the year, at last?

Or… would something happen yet *again*?

As it turned out, *something* most definitely happened.

- 14 -

BOMBSHELL

As October came to a close and November began, the 2010 season was playing out like a dream for Auburn fans. With a record of 9-0, the Tigers appeared to be on track to play for the national championship. Their quarterback had become the odds-on Heisman Trophy favorite. Only three regular-season games remained. What—aside from the ever-present danger of a catastrophic injury or two—could possibly hamper the Tigers on their way to glory?

Little did anyone suspect that a potentially season-derailing issue had been brewing behind the scenes. Now, with the coming of the final month of Auburn's regular season, that issue had grown into a full-fledged controversy—one that was about to explode into full public view.

> *"Somewhere around the middle of the season, we got a letter from the NCAA, that they were going to launch this investigation about some improprieties that supposedly had happened with Cam and his father. It was simply the NCAA coming in and saying, 'Look, we're gonna check you out.' I was like, 'Bring it on.'"*
> *—Gene Chizik*

> *"At this point (in the season), Cam Newton is Cam Newton. He's the best player in college football. He's led Auburn to an undefeated record when no one expected Auburn to be undefeated. And then, all of a sudden, out of nowhere, this bombshell drops from ESPN that his dad, Cecil Newton, had shopped him to Mississippi State. It was a true bombshell. It shook college football in this state to a degree we hadn't seen in a long time—maybe ever. Certainly a player of that caliber being accused of being bought and paid for during the season, during an all-time great season. And now that's all in doubt."*
> —Kevin Scarbinsky, al dot com

Gene Chizik maintained from Day One that his staff had no knowledge of, or involvement in, any scheme to pay Cam Newton or his father. Chizik backed that up with a resolute determination to keep playing Cam, with zero concerns for what might happen to the Tigers' season if facts eventually showed something different.

> *"On Thursday, (November 4), two days before the (Chattanooga) game, reports started surfacing regarding Cameron's recruitment coming out of junior college. We knew we had done nothing wrong during the recruiting process. If we'd had any level of concern regarding Cameron's eligibility, we would not have put him on the field and risked forfeiting games for playing an ineligible player."*
> —Gene Chizik, **All In**

Van Allen Plexico

I will admit that Chizik's attitude, right from the jump, encouraged me. In virtually any other circumstance, in other scandals, I think the coach or the AD would have yanked Cam off the field immediately.

So my takeaway from Auburn's determination to keep playing Cam was that there were two possibilities: Either he and Auburn were totally innocent, or they knew they would be forfeiting the entirety of the season up until that point anyway, if the allegations turned out to be true, so a couple more games wouldn't matter in the big picture. Why hold Cam out and risk losing a game or two on the way to the BCS title, if it turns out to be false? Better to keep playing him, keep winning, and go "all or nothing," I think.

Details were murky when the story first broke. All that was generally said at first was that people at Mississippi State, the other school that had been heavily recruiting Newton out of junior college, were now claiming Cam's father had asked the Bulldogs for money in order to secure Cam's services. Reports differed on the amount, but it was usually somewhere between $180,000 and $200,000. The inference was that Cecil Newton, Cam's father, was "shopping" his son around, looking for the best deal. Many assumed that had to mean Auburn was involved as well, and had "outbid" Mississippi State for Cam.

Auburn maintained from the start that nothing of the sort had taken place—at least, nothing involving Auburn and nothing involving Cam. That would turn out to be the key distinction: Something may or may not have been going on between Cam's dad and the Bulldogs, but not between Cam and Auburn.

Even so, Auburn appeared on the cusp of losing its transcendent, star quarterback, with the two biggest games of the year just ahead.

Van Allen Plexico

Of course, few in the media or in the public cared about the specifics of the allegations. The common thing you heard was, "Auburn paid Cam." None of the allegations specifically mentioned Auburn or claimed Auburn had paid anybody anything. Nobody was saying Cam actually *received* anything, from Mississippi State or from Auburn. But yet there it was, going around, with the old "Where there's smoke, there's fire" as the fallback when you challenged someone with the facts.

> *"It's hard to state today just how out-of-control the rumor mill was. There were absolutely looney stories being promulgated and embellished upon, one allegedly 'informed' post at a time, on rival teams' message boards, and amplified by irresponsible media outlets like the Finebaum show and jackasses like Joe Schad and Mark Schlabach."*
> —Will Collier, reporting for AuburnSports dot com

On the Thursday of the Chattanooga game week, former MSU quarterback John Bond came forward and told reporters that one of his former teammates, Kenny Rogers, was representing Cam Newton and had asked MSU for $180,000 for Cam's commitment, back in December of the previous year.

Cecil Newton, Cam's father, told reporters that he knew Rogers but was not close with him and that Rogers did not represent Cam. "Everything is unfounded," he said. "The timing is so bad. Somebody is behind this. We'll figure out who."

Van Allen Plexico

I remember clearly when the news broke. I was with my family, about to eat supper at Red Robin. I think my wife saw it on her phone and showed it to me. The food arrived. Everyone else started eating. I read the story, read it over again, and then just sat there, staring at the floor, for a long time. I have no idea how long. I couldn't eat. I could barely breathe or move. I guess she and my kids were talking to me, but I couldn't hear them. I wanted to climb into a dark cave somewhere and never come out.

The first thing I thought was, "Oh no. Oh, no no no."

The second thing I thought was, "The dream season is over."

And the third thing I thought was, "We are Auburn. Something always happens. *Always*."

Auburn people know exactly what I mean by that. (Read the earlier chapter in this book, where we broke it down!) They understand that, up until 2010, whenever Auburn put itself in position to win a national championship—*something always happened*.

So I was in complete shock, sitting there at the table, my food getting cold in front of me. My mind was reeling, dazed, stunned. But there was a little part of me—the part that had been an Auburn Tiger since childhood—that whispered, "Yes. You *knew* this, or something like it, was coming. You *knew* it was bound to happen. You knew not to get too excited. You knew better than to let yourself believe. Because it's Auburn. It's *Auburn*. And something *always* happens."

"There were a lot of rumors out there. A lot of websites reporting a lot of misinformation that could've been very damaging to Cam Newton, to Auburn, to Gene Chizik, to Gus Malzahn, the whole program. It's the main topic on talk radio every single day. It's the main topic on message boards. Not just Auburn message boards. Alabama. Georgia. LSU. A huge narrative grew up. The problem was, there weren't facts to back it up."
—Kevin Scarbinsky, al dot com

Van Allen Plexico
"There weren't facts to back it up."
When has that ever stopped people from spreading rumors? Or believing them?

On the day of the Chattanooga game, Cam told reporters, "I didn't do anything wrong. I'm blessed to be at Auburn right now. I'm sure the smoke will settle. I'm looking forward to this game."
Jay Jacobs made Auburn's position on the matter quite clear. Neither he nor Chizik ever wavered for a second. They believed Cam had done nothing wrong, and they knew Auburn had done nothing wrong. That belief was reflected in every public statement either of them made about it.

"Any time you have any question about the eligibility of a student-athlete, regardless of what sport it is, you do not allow them to play. He will be playing."
—Jay Jacobs, Auburn athletic director

At the same time, news outlets were reporting that John Bond had recently participated in a conference call with MSU coach Dan Mullen and Florida coach Urban Meyer "to decide how to disseminate information about the investigation concerning Newton."

Van Allen Plexico
This was when the Auburn Family really turned on Mullen and Meyer—when word came out that the two of them had been

colluding with John Bond to put this garbage out there and try to sabotage Cam's career and Auburn's season.

I've never forgiven either one of them for this. I doubt I ever will.

Meanwhile, and almost forgotten amid all the hoopla, Auburn had a football game to play.

November 6: Chattanooga

Ten games in ten weeks. With Georgia looming on the horizon, followed by Alabama, Week 10 seemed like a good time for the starters to get a little rest. Fortunately, the Chattanooga Moccasins provided little challenge and allowed Auburn to get the back-ups in relatively early.

The Tigers blanked Chattanooga 27-0 in the first quarter. They added 21 more in the second quarter, *en route* to a 62-24 win. Cam Newton passed for a career-high 317 yards with four touchdown passes, all before the half. He averaged 21 yards per completion. The Tigers rolled up 624 total yards of offense, with Mario Fannin leading the way. The senior running back gained 96 yards on 12 carries, to go with Michael Dyer's 76 yards on 4 rushes.

John Ringer

Cam ran the ball 8 times in this game, and that was probably 8 times too many.

"We had an excellent week of practice in preparing for this team and Coach Malzahn and the entire offensive coaching staff prepared us for this game. We exploited the weakness of their defense. Those are the numbers that we are capable of producing."
—*Cam Newton, Auburn quarterback*

Van Allen Plexico

It's amazing how Cam and the rest of the players and coaches were able to stay focused on playing winning football, with everything swirling around the program that week. I think most teams would have seen their seasons derailed by such distractions.

(2) Auburn 62
Chattanooga 24

"This week was big. We went into the week just trying to make sure we came out of this game a better team, especially with the games we have coming up in the next few weeks. It is going to be a big part of our season. The rest we got today really helps us out. We get the mental reps instead of being out there physically. It is going to take complete focus, sacrifice and the little things to come out on top."
—*Antoine Carter*

"These next two games are going to be very big games, especially the Georgia game, for me personally. Then you have Alabama, which speaks for itself. We have to make sure we go out there and get after it every day in practice. These next two games will tell us a lot about our team."
—*Mario Fannin*

The Tigers were playing at the top of their form. The media's attention was increasingly divided, however. Auburn's 10-0 record and upcoming monster games with Georgia and Alabama were being overshadowed in the news by the continued talk surrounding Cam Newton and his father.

Ralph Russo, writing for the AP, noted that the allegations alone could impact Newton's Heisman campaign. "Nineteen of 23 voters reached by the AP on Wednesday said they will judge Newton like any contender unless he is found to have broken rules and been declared ineligible by the NCAA." But that meant four voters were dismissing him out of hand, without any evidence of wrongdoing.

Tom Keegan, writing in the Lawrence (KS) *Journal World*, added, "There is time for this to change, but at the moment, the race for the Heisman is a race for second place. He's the best player in college football."

By this point, however, the keyboard warriors around the SEC and the country had gotten a fierce grasp on the "Cam Newton bad" storyline, and were attempting to outdo one another as they piled on.

The allegations thrown out by the message board trolls quickly grew beyond "Cam was paid" into areas such as "Cam cheated while he was at Florida."

Writing for AuburnSports dot com on Tuesday, November 9, Jeffrey Lee reported that someone named Alex DeLaet was posting on the Rivals main message board about how Cam Newton "got caught cheating in class" during his time in Gainesville.

When FoxSports reported on these baseless allegations, DeLaet followed up his previous post with, "Aubs, sorry to tell you that I was right."

Others on the message board asked DeLaet how he'd known in advance about this report. He replied, "I have a very good source at UF."

Later he edited the post to remove the reference to Florida. Was he trying belatedly to protect someone? Perhaps; it turned out his brother worked in the video department of Florida's football program.

The FoxSports article, by the later-discredited writer Thayer Evans, claimed two additional instances of academic dishonesty by Newton during his tenure with the Gators.

Officials at the University of Florida refuted the claims. One source within the Florida Student Conduct Committee stated that "Nothing (about Newton) was reported, officially or unofficially (to the committee)." As Auburn columnist Will Collier later summarized, "No charges against Newton, to the first source's knowledge, were ever sent to the UF Student Conduct Committee."

Collier went on to note that "a second, independently verified source, also with detailed knowledge of the Florida student disciplinary system," disagreed with the assertions made by Evans.

Newton would have been in danger of expulsion if he had actually been charged with some form of academic dishonesty. But, Collier quoted the second source as saying, "I worked ten or twelve cases (at Florida) and I never saw anyone get expelled." This person added, "If Cameron Newton would have come before the committee, we would have known about it."

On Wednesday, November 10—three days before the Georgia game—Mississippi State released a statement that it had "reported an issue relating to its recruitment of Cameron Newton" back in January of 2010. MSU also noted that it had *not* immediately provided the

Southeastern Conference office with additional documentation concerning the matter, as had been requested. They finally handed over some material in July.

At the same time, ESPN reported that two "unnamed sources" claiming to be "recruiters" for Mississippi State were saying that Cecil Newton had asked them for "more than a scholarship" to secure Cam's commitment to the Bulldogs.

Auburn still was not mentioned in any of these reports. No new evidence came to light indicating that Cam Newton himself was directly involved.

At a press conference that Wednesday, Chizik led off with, "Cameron Newton will be playing Saturday against the Georgia Bulldogs. I want to get that off the table."

Meanwhile, the SEC offices kept silent, refusing comment on the matter.

On the Friday before the game, Kenny Rogers, the former MSU player John Bond had described as an agent for Newton, went on a Texas radio station. There he stated that he had witnessed Cecil Newton telling two Mississippi State coaches that he would need between $100,000 and $180,000 for Cam's commitment to the Bulldogs.

None of it involved Cam directly. None of it involved Auburn University.

When asked if any payments had been made, Rogers revealed his lack of actual information when he replied, "I don't have any knowledge of that. I was asked something. I passed it on. I have no knowledge of what they were going to do or not going to do."

Van Allen Plexico

This was all happening at the end of the week right before the Georgia game. It felt like the earth was opening up and swallowing us all. Auburn folks were wondering if Cam would be held out of the game, and if the Tigers could beat Georgia without him. But—what if he did play, and then the allegations were somehow proven true? Would we have to forfeit the game, and watch our potential championship season go down the drain?

It was so incredibly frustrating.

We watched and waited to see what Auburn, Jay Jacobs and Gene Chizik would decide to do, with regard to Cam playing. And we hoped they knew what they were doing.

John Ringer
It was a minute-by-minute media firestorm that week. It was constantly on ESPN, Finebaum, and all that. Is he going to play, is he not going to play, all that kind of stuff. What happens if he doesn't play, will we get him back for Alabama...?

When the players were introduced before the Georgia game on Saturday, the starting quarterback was Cam Newton.

Van Allen Plexico
The crowd went bananas, of course. But I was scared to death. I was happy he was playing, but I wasn't convinced the whole controversy was over. I was so afraid we'd come to regret playing Cam that day.

On the other hand, I felt strongly that playing Cam at quarterback was the only way we were going to beat Georgia and Alabama. If we didn't play him and we lost, none of it mattered anyway, at least in terms of football and the national championship. So we might as well play him, win the games if possible, and then deal with the fallout later.

But—how could Cam possibly play anywhere close to the best of his ability, with all these distractions going on around him?

> "Through all the speculation and all the insinuations, Cameron showed an incredible focus that few mature adults—let alone college students—could have maintained. In addition to the recruiting controversy, he was also dealing with the frenzy of media attention that goes with being favored to win the Heisman. In the midst of everything, football became Cameron's place of refuge."
> —Gene Chizik, All In

As it turned out, the controversy hardly seemed to faze him at all.

- 15 -

A BLESSED INDIVIDUAL

The Auburn-Georgia game is always huge.

In 2010, however, the Deep South's Oldest Rivalry carried extra significance.

Win this one, and the Tigers would have their tickets punched for the SEC Championship Game—regardless of what happened in the Iron Bowl.

Beyond that, it mattered in terms of a possible national championship, now being openly discussed. One loss would likely send the Tigers tumbling down the ranks of the BCS poll.

Georgia entered the game as the last unranked team Auburn would play that season. They'd struggled early, losing four in a row in September and October before rebounding to win three straight games over Tennessee, Vanderbilt and Kentucky (by a combined score of 128-45). Their record by the time of the Auburn game stood at just 5-5, but they were still a dangerous team with a great quarterback in Aaron Murray and a star receiver in A. J. Green.

Auburn started Cam Newton at quarterback, even as the alleged "pay-for-play" scandal swirled around him.

It was the third of five Auburn games to be broadcast by CBS, in their featured 2:30 pm CST time slot.

November 13: Georgia

Auburn scored on their opening drive, covering 80 yards in only 5 plays. The touchdown came on a 31-yard run by Newton, who seemingly dragged half the Georgia defense with him. The drive and the play appeared to set a winning tone for the game. Auburn fans were jubilant.

That feeling would not last long. Just as with South Carolina in week four, the Tigers would score first, and then somehow concede multiple touchdowns in return.

The Bulldogs came roaring back quickly, with quarterback Aaron Murray finding a wide-open AJ Green for a 31-yard touchdown pass. Both teams had scored from 31 yards out to start the game. Once again, the Tigers' pass defense was suspect in the first half.

It would only get worse for Auburn. Bulldogs safety Bacarri Rambo intercepted Newton and ran it back to the Tigers' 9 yard line. Murray threw for another touchdown on the very next play.

Auburn was forced to punt on the next drive, and Georgia hit back once more with another Murray-to-Green connection, this time from 40 yards out. With a minute to go in the first quarter, the Tigers were down, 21-7.

And yet it never felt like the Tigers were out of the game. The offense had clicked on the first drive, with Cam simply running over the defense. Fans patiently waited for the usual adjustment to the Auburn defense that always seemed to come after giving up early scores.

The Tigers got back in the game as the second quarter began. They moved the ball in a variety of ways, mostly on the ground, with Dyer, McCalebb and Newton all carrying it. Emory Blake made a big 26-yard catch at the Georgia 4, leading to McCalebb's touchdown run around right end.

After a series of punts by both teams, the Tigers finished off the half with another scoring drive. Again they spread the ball around, culminating in an 18-yard touchdown catch by tight end Philip Lutzenkirchen. The two teams would go into the locker room tied at 21.

At halftime, both sets of fans tried to catch their breath. Oddly enough, it seemed as if the game could easily have been a blowout for either team, yet neither was ahead.

But this Auburn team had been a second-half juggernaut for most of the year. The sense among the faithful in orange and blue was, *Georgia has taken their shot and failed to hold onto their early lead.* Now it would be the Tigers' turn.

Auburn started the second half by doing what they'd done to Alabama in 2009 after their first touchdown: an onsides kick. Wes Byrum executed it perfectly, as he almost always did.

Van Allen Plexico
Byrum was so good at that little "tap the ball and then hover over it until it goes 10 yards and then dive on it" thing, I felt like they should be running it after every touchdown. Nobody could stop it! But then later the NCAA changed the rules and it became a lot harder to execute.

John Ringer
This is the kind of strategic decision and risk that you can't use too much.

In this case the two teams could clearly move the ball and score on each other. (Each team only punted twice in this game, and Georgia did not turn the ball over.) So stealing a possession from the other team was gigantic. Auburn needed to get ahead and then hold Georgia off like a Cam Newton stiff arm. The decision to go for the onsides kick at the start of the second half was the correct decision at the time and a huge gamble by Gene Chizik. In that 2010 season he seemed to know when to roll the dice and when to trust his team to get the job done.

"We felt like we needed to take one possession away from them in the second half," Chizik later explained. "We needed to get some momentum coming out. We told our guys in the locker room at halftime, we said it's up and running and you have to get it."

"Auburn's kickoff team was one of the bigger differences in the game, with them getting the onside kick to start the half and take the lead. We were hoping to get the ball first and put them in a position to be behind. We didn't get good field position off

our kickoff returns and their kickoff team tonight was the best we've played all season."
—Mark Richt, Georgia head coach

After the onsides kick recovery, the Tigers went on another scoring drive, using all run plays to move the ball down the field. McCalebb carried it in again and the Tigers took the lead, 28-21. Georgia had run exactly one play on offense since the score was 21-14, in the Bulldogs' favor.

Georgia wasn't beaten yet. They came right back and scored again, evening it up at 28-28. So far, the Bulldogs were managing, in tennis terms, to "hold serve" with Auburn's offense.

That wouldn't last much longer.

On Auburn's next possession, the Tigers didn't attempt a pass, and they only faced third down one time—a third and 1 at the Georgia 5, which Cam converted by plowing ahead for the final yard, setting up a first-and-goal. McCalebb took it in from there for his third rushing touchdown of the day.

The score was now 35-28, Auburn. That was when Georgia "lost serve."

They couldn't manage a tying touchdown and settled for a field goal. Now down 35-31, the UGA offense could only watch as the Tigers marched relentlessly down the field again. This time Auburn mixed in some passes, with Cam throwing to Emory Blake and Darvin Adams before connecting with Philip Lutzenkirchen for the touchdown. The score was now 42-31, and Georgia didn't give the impression of a team able to stop the Tigers again.

Sure enough, Antoine Carter's sack of Aaron Murray at the Georgia 27, and Murray's resulting fumble, set the Tigers up for a short touchdown drive. It was the cherry on top of this offensive explosion. Newton carried the ball on almost every play, draining the clock before finally taking it in from the 1. With less than 3 minutes remaining in the game, the Tigers led, 49-31. That would be the final score.

Auburn had given up 31 points to Georgia, and yet still beaten the Bulldogs by 18.

(2) Auburn 49
Georgia 31

ALL THEY DID WAS WIN

Van Allen Plexico

I said all along during this game that the team that blinked—the team that had to settle for a field goal instead of a touchdown in the second half—would be the one that lost. I also said that Georgia coach Mark Richt in the second half was "bringing a knife to a gunfight," in the sense that he couldn't afford to settle for a smaller weapon (a field goal) in this battle royal. He needed to have Murray throwing the ball into the end zone on every possession. Richt blinked, Georgia "lost serve," and they lost.

Cam had rushed for 148 yards and passed for 151—just another day at the office for him, and an incredible demonstration of resolve and focus amid all the controversy. With 299 total yards of offense, one had to wonder if Newton was the only person in America *not* feeling the heat of the allegations against him.

> *"I'm a blessed individual on a blessed team. I would not have had any of the success I've had without the offensive line, the receivers and running backs around me. We have worked so hard as a team the entire season. Everybody is doing their job in the system and it is a great feeling when it all comes together."*
> —Cam Newton, Auburn quarterback

Lutzenkirchen caught two passes, both of them touchdowns. McCalebb and Dyer rushed for 71 and 60 yards, respectively. McCalebb scored three touchdowns, while Dyer broke Bo Jackson's Auburn record for most rushing yards during the game. He received a kiss on the head and his arm raised to the crowd by the 1985 Heisman winner.

Amid the joy of defeating a big rival and winning the SEC, there were a few storm clouds gathering at the end of the game. Georgia fans were beyond upset by what they saw as unnecessary roughness by the Auburn defense—and in particular one player on that defense—that had harassed them throughout the game.

John Ringer

Even though they didn't score, Georgia kept throwing the ball at the end of the game, and Nick Fairley kept hitting their quarterback.

Fairley had been a one-man wrecking crew on defense all year, he was the defensive player of the year, and Georgia couldn't block him for anything. They were losing by 18 points late in the game, and they could've run the ball and gotten out of there. But they kept having their quarterback throw the ball, and Nick Fairley kept hitting him. It got to a point where the Georgia offensive line started to cheap-shot Fairley. They just about started a riot on the field at that point. And it was entirely (Georgia coach) Mark Richt's fault. He was choosing to throw the ball and put his quarterback in that position. He could've kept more blockers in. He could've run the ball. They weren't going to win the game. But instead he kept throwing the ball, and every time they did, Nick Fairley planted their quarterback in the grass. So then the Georgia offensive linemen were piling on top of him, and it was going to get ugly.

A couple of Auburn players did get suspended: Mike Blanc and Michael Goggans, two defensive linemen. They would miss the first half of the following game, which happened to be against Alabama.

Nick Fairley had been penalized for a late hit on Georgia quarterback Aaron Murray earlier in the game. In the fourth quarter, he was blocked into Murray's knee, injuring the quarterback. Georgia players didn't care about the circumstances—they wanted revenge on Fairley.

In the final minute of the game, Bulldogs players took the opportunity to "exact some punishment" on Fairley. This was happening down in the scrum, where the referees couldn't see what was happening. But the Auburn players knew, and they rushed to Fairley's defense. Two of them—Blanc and Goggans—were caught throwing punches at the UGA players who'd been assaulting their teammate.

"Goggans was ejected for throwing a punch after Georgia's Ben Jones landed on Fairley at the end of the play and began roughing him up, video replays showed. That action led to

ALL THEY DID WAS WIN

Auburn and Georgia players arguing, and Goggans taking a swing. Replays show Georgia players left the bench—there were at least 33 Bulldogs on the field—to Auburn's 11 players immediately after the play. The Bulldogs were not penalized."
—Charles Goldberg, AL dot com

There was nothing Auburn could do about the suspensions of Blanc and Goggans.

"The suspensions are handled by the NCAA and are not subject to appeal."
—Charles Bloom, SEC spokesman, on the Monday after the Georgia game

Gene Chizik said afterward that he was "embarrassed" by the actions of Blanc and Goggans. "That's not who we are."
Richt knew the truth of what had happened, and he admitted as much after the game:

"I know our guys were highly emotionally charged, also. I'm not going to sit here and try to say their guys were doing one thing and our guys were doing another."
—Mark Richt, Georgia coach

So there was nothing to be done; the two backup linemen would not play in the first half of the Iron Bowl. Perhaps worse for Auburn, now the referees would be watching Fairley closely.

Van Allen Plexico
All of that had a tremendous impact on the next game.

John Ringer
Oh yes. There was a bunch of talk about personal foul penalties and roughing the quarterback and all that kind of stuff. So the referees would be looking for it. They were all over him in the Alabama game.

Meanwhile, the on- and off-field controversies somewhat obscured the fact that the Tigers had clinched the SEC West. Auburn's ticket to the SEC Championship Game was punched, nearly two weeks before they were to face Alabama in Tuscaloosa.

A team that had been deep in the doldrums just two years earlier was now headed to Atlanta, for a chance at the SEC title, and possibly much more.

> *"It is a great thing especially for the guys that have been here for four or five years. We experienced a 5-7 season my sophomore year and an 8-5 season with the new coaching staff last year. A lot of guys have been through three or four offensive and defensive coordinators, but with having the same staff from last year, we felt that we were going to go from good to great. We felt that we had a chance to go undefeated. Right now we are sitting at 11-0 and sitting as the SEC West champions."*
> —Josh Bynes

It meant that, as far as the SEC race was concerned, the Iron Bowl would be meaningless.

For everything else, it would be vital.

There were too many other good teams waiting to pounce—waiting to claim Auburn's spot near the top of the BCS rankings—if Auburn showed any vulnerability.

> *"We still have one more game in the regular season that we have to tackle. We have to finish strong. The Iron Bowl speaks for itself. We just have to continue to work hard just like we did to get to where we are now."*
> Cam Newton

For the moment, the "pay for play" allegations died down. The talk was of Auburn being 11-0, winning the SEC West, and heading to Tuscaloosa for the Iron Bowl.

> *"We had goals at the beginning of the year, and this (winning the SEC West) was the first goal. We were blessed to be in a position tonight where if we won, then obviously, we have a trip*

ALL THEY DID WAS WIN

to Atlanta. There was a lot of incentive out there. There was a lot on the line, and I couldn't be more proud of our team because of the way they responded and the way they just kept playing."
—*Gene Chizik*

- 16 -

BAD DIRT

The 2009 and 2010 Iron Bowls were played on Fridays, thanks to an arrangement with CBS Sports giving the game an exclusive time slot on the day after Thanksgiving. The 2009 edition had been the first played on a Friday in twenty-one years, and the 2010 version would be the last, after criticism from fans of both teams. In recent years, the Egg Bowl between Ole Miss and Mississippi State has moved into that spot on the calendar.

The temperature had reached an unseasonable 75 degrees the previous afternoon, but had dropped precipitously overnight and was down into the 50s on Friday morning. By the 1:30 pm kickoff, it had fallen into the low 40s, where it would remain throughout the game.

On the preseason first team all SEC list could be found three Alabama players, but only one Auburn player: offensive lineman Lee Ziemba. The same was true of the defense: three Alabama players, and only linebacker Josh Bynes representing the Tigers.

Van Allen Plexico
That shows again how few people expected the seasons Cam Newton and Nick Fairley produced. Imagine that neither the Heisman Trophy winner nor the Lombardi Trophy winner were preseason all-conference picks, much less All-Americans.

> *"The Tigers entered the game averaging 505.2 yards and 42.8 points per game. Newton had thrown for 21 touchdowns, run for 17 touchdowns and caught a touchdown pass. At kickoff, he was responsible for more touchdowns than 52.1 percent of all the teams in the FBS."*
> —Andy Staples, the New York Times, 2020

And so it was that, on November 26, 2010, Gene Chizik led the Auburn Tigers into Bryant-Denny Stadium. This would be his fifth Iron Bowl, and his third in that arena. He'd previously coached in three as defensive coordinator and one as head coach. He knew what he was getting into. He understood the magnitude of the game. But not all of the players did.

Or at least, they didn't until they arrived in Tuscaloosa.

> *"I went to the University of Florida. I played in rivalry games against Georgia, Miami, Florida State. I thought I knew what a rivalry game was. Until I played in the Iron Bowl."*
> —Cam Newton, 2024

Auburn's older players remembered what it had been like, coming to Bryant-Denny Stadium two years earlier, in 2008. It was a game in which the Tigers would not only lose but be shut out, 36-0. It also contributed to Tommy Tuberville's decision to step down.

After the 2008 game, when the Auburn players tried to exit the locker room and board the team buses, Alabama fans blocked them in.

"They probably had 2,000 fans who wouldn't let us out, and we finally needed security," said Auburn center Ryan Pugh. "It was really an ugly situation and a lot of us remembered that for a long time. It was just added motivation to go (back) there and win."

The crowd would be much larger this time around than it had been in 2008. Prior to the 2010 season, Alabama completed a major expansion project, enlarging the seating capacity of Bryant-Denny Stadium from 92,138 to 101,821. That meant the 2010 Iron Bowl would be witnessed live by the largest crowd in series history.

ALL THEY DID WAS WIN

By that point in the season, Auburn had played only three road games, visiting Starkville, Lexington and Oxford. The crowd at Bryant-Denny would be 30,000 larger than the biggest of those, the 70,776 at Kentucky.

The weather in Tuscaloosa that day was not just cool but dismal. The sun wouldn't emerge from the clouds until late in the second half. The stadium was shrouded in fog during pregame warmups.

To get onto the field, Auburn players had to walk through a tunnel beneath the Alabama student section.

> *"Waiting a few feet above the tunnel was the ferocious Alabama student section. Kickoff was nearly two hours away, but the students were already out in full force. Some threw beer. Some shouted profanities. Many were escorted out of the stadium well before kickoff. Police officers even moved some students back a few rows to avoid the threat of a thrown object injuring an Auburn player."*
> —Evan McCullers, Auburn Plainsman *Assistant Sports Editor, 2015*

The players were hit with bottles, cursed at, and spat upon. When Cam Newton entered the arena, the students pelted him with Monopoly money while the stadium public address system played Dusty Springfield's "Son of a Preacher Man" and the Steve Miller Band's "Take the Money and Run."

Welcome to Tuscaloosa.

"We all started laughing when we heard about the song," said Pugh. "Only in this rivalry would that happen."

"I'm next to Cam and Cam and I looked at each other and grinned. We thought it was funny," said receiver Terrell Zachery. Added senior tackle Lee Ziemba, "I thought it was pretty classless."

Alabama fans held up signs with derogatory messages. One spelled Auburn's quarterback's name, "SCAM NEWTON." It was a nickname that had caught on quickly among the fans of the Tigers' rivals, and none embraced it more than the fans of the Crimson Tide.

> *"Alabama, man. When you come into that stadium, they all know your background. They're gonna go on Google. They're*

gonna find every ounce of bad dirt, all kinds of things they can find out about you, and put it on a big old poster."
—Josh Bynes, Auburn linebacker, speaking in 2015

"I was nervous as hell, man. That's what you call a road game. I mean, you could feel the hate. Eighteen years old, walking out there thinking like that, I was looking for my mama. We'd been on the road all year, and I was thinking, 'Well, I've been in a road game (but not like this)'. That was a road game that for me personally was a 'welcome to college football.'"
—Jeffrey Whittaker, Auburn defensive tackle, speaking in 2015

Auburn had spent a week at number 1 in the BCS standings before Oregon returned to the top spot. Now the Tigers were ranked number 2 in both the AP Poll and in the BCS, 11-0 and undefeated. A trip to Atlanta for the SEC Championship Game was already locked down, following the win over Georgia. Due to road losses at South Carolina and LSU, the Crimson Tide had been eliminated from the conference title chase and could only try to play spoiler.

And they had every intention of doing just that.

Van Allen Plexico
We were undefeated and had already won the SEC West and were going to Atlanta, regardless of what happened in Bryant-Denny. They were playing the songs, they had the "Scam Newton" signs, they were waving Monopoly money in the air at Cam—it was the trap game of all trap games.

Even with a victory, a path to the BCS national championship game was not assured. On the morning of the Iron Bowl, three other teams remained undefeated: Oregon, Boise State and TCU. Auburn fans remembered what had happened just six years earlier and were taking nothing for granted. Even so, the chances of an undefeated Auburn team being left out of the title game seemed more remote this time than they had in 2004. Oregon, Boise State and TCU are good programs, but none of them are of the same historic caliber as Oklahoma and USC, the teams that had barred the Tigers' way the last time they were undefeated. The general sense was that, of those four, Auburn would be ranked no worse than second after the SEC title game, assuming the Tigers could win out.

On top of the pressure to go all the way, Auburn's players, coaches and fans also continued to operate under the murky cloud of the NCAA's investigation into Cam Newton and his father. Everyone waited for another shoe to drop in that case. Fortunately, the whole mess had receded into the background noise during Alabama week. But the Tigers had not heard the last of the controversy—not by a long shot.

Meanwhile, there was a game to play.

One game to decide if Auburn would finish the regular season undefeated, on track for the SEC Championship Game and perhaps the BCS National Championship Game, and maybe a Heisman Trophy for their quarterback along the way.

Or if they would be humiliated by an inferior opponent, and see their dream season ruined; ruined by their biggest rivals, in that team's home stadium, in front of the largest crowd ever to have watched the game in person, and a national audience on CBS.

Yes, two very different outcomes were on the line when the 2010 Iron Bowl kicked off. The Tigers came into the game firmly believing they would overwhelm the Crimson Tide, take the crowd out of the game early, and dominate their rivals from the opening kickoff.

They could not have been more wrong.

- 17 -

THE FIRST QUARTER: GETTING WHIPPED

In his opening to the Auburn Network's radio broadcast of the 2010 Iron Bowl, the late, great Rod Bramblett seemed to channel the very words of Apple Plus's Ted Lasso. He added a touch at the end from the song that had accompanied the Tigers' stadium "hype video" all year: "All I Do is Win."

> *"Two years ago we stood here and asked you to believe. Believe on a day when you really didn't have much reason to. My goodness. What a difference two years make.*
>
> *"Hello again everybody and War Eagle! I'm Rod Bramblett with Stan White and Quentin Riggins at Bryant-Denny Stadium, where over 100,000 have gathered—the largest crowd ever—to watch Auburn and Alabama play football.*
>
> *"Oh, the reasons to believe are plenty. Week in and week out we have seen them. It started with the debut of a quarterback, giving us a glimpse of what the future would hold. A challenge accepted by an offensive line. A fourth quarter drive in the bluegrass and a game-winning field goal.*

> "Oh yes. This could be something special. A Heisman-winning performance, and a statement. A statement that because we are 'All In,' Auburn is here to stay.
>
> "The largest senior class in school history and a record season for a freshman tailback, sealed with a kiss from number 34. A division champion crown. And even with all this, there are those on the outside looking in that just don't seem to believe. 'There's no way this team is prepared to handle the hostile environment they're about to face today.' But here's the thing: When you believe, there's no reason to fear. Fear has no place in the heart of a champion.
>
> "So, like two years ago, we ask you to believe.
>
> "My goodness. What a difference two years make, when all you do... is win."
>
> —Rod Bramblett, pregame radio introduction, Auburn Network broadcast

And now, as is our practice, we switch to the present-tense for the duration of the Iron Bowl. The past-tense will return on the other side.

Wes Byrum kicks off, and the Tide's great wide receiver, Julio Jones, returns to the Alabama 29 yard line, where he is tackled by Nieko Thorpe—who will go on to have a big game.

Alabama's Anthony Steen starts at right guard, in place of the injured starter, Barrett Jones, who would go on to win multiple awards by the end of his career. This substitution will matter a bit later in the game.

Alabama starts in the shotgun on first down, and Greg McElroy completes an eight-yard pass to Jones, who is immediately dropped by linebackers Josh Bynes and Eltoro Freeman.

On second and two, McElroy bootlegs to his left and passes in that same direction to Darius Hanks for a first down to the Alabama 47.

Running back Mark Ingram, the previous year's Heisman winner, lines up in the Wildcat on first down and hands the ball to the receiver in motion, Julio Jones, who then hands it to receiver Marquis Mays on the end around. Defensive back Neiko Thorpe pushes him out of bounds after 6 yards.

On second and four, McElroy gives the ball to Ingram, who rumbles to the Auburn 44, for another first down. On the radio broadcast, Stan White notes that Auburn made errors on defense that opened up space for Ingram to run.

Alabama remains in the shotgun and McElroy fires the ball out to his left to Ingram on a screen pass. Ingram carries it to the Auburn 36. Alabama is picking up around 8 yards per play on this opening drive. The Heisman winner from 2009 is shouldering the bulk of the load thus far.

Julio Jones takes a quick handoff on a sort of jet sweep action to the right side of the field, dodges Auburn defender Antoine Carter in the backfield, and runs to the Auburn 25 for another first down.

So far, the Tide have run the ball three times and passed the ball three times, and both avenues are working well for them. They've moved the ball 47 yards in just over three minutes of game time.

Switching to the offset I-formation, McElroy drops back and throws for Marquis Mays at the goal line, but the pass is broken up by Auburn DB Demond Washington. The referee throws a flag on Washington, however, putting the ball on the Auburn 10.

CBS points out that Alabama has not scored a touchdown in the first quarter against Auburn since 1996—a remarkable run of 13 years. Of course, that is about to change, and in a big way.

Back in the shotgun, McElroy gives the ball to Ingram on an inside run, and the back walks in untouched. That's his 40th career touchdown, second all-time for Alabama behind Shaun Alexander.

> *"It happened so fast, and it was our fault. Especially as a defense, we were looking at Julio running free, and we let Ingram walk into the end zone."*
> *—Jeffrey Whittaker, Auburn defensive tackle, speaking in 2015*

> *"You want to throw the first punch. You're already the underdog in that game so you come out swinging."*

—Alabama defensive lineman Damion Square, to Jon Solomon, 2011

The extra point is good, and Alabama leads 7-0 barely three minutes into the game.

Auburn 0, Alabama 7

From the sideline, Quentin Riggins notes that Auburn was hurt on that drive in part because the Tigers are missing two defenders, Michael Goggans and Mike Blanc, who were ejected at the end of the previous game against Georgia. They will not be allowed to participate until the second half. Additionally, Auburn's All-American defensive lineman, Nick Fairley, was in the locker room being treated for a nagging shoulder injury on the play where Ingram scored.

CBS notes that 18 of the last 22 Iron Bowls have been decided by 10 or fewer points.

Cade Foster kicks off for Alabama. The kick is short, and fullback Eric Smith catches it at the Auburn 20, returning it for 5 yards.

On first down, Michael Dyer runs to the right for no gain.

Alabama is called for a substitution violation prior to the second down play, moving the ball out to the 30.

Cam Newton remains in the shotgun and runs up the middle for 4 yards, bringing up third down and 1.

Stan White notes that Auburn's offense has a 53 percent conversion ratio, first in the SEC and third in the nation. They will not play like it in the first half today.

Cam moves under center and hands the ball to Dyer, who tries to power the ball up the middle but is stuffed by the Tide defense and loses 2 yards.

It's fourth down and 7 to go. Brian Shoemaker punts the ball away, pinning Alabama inside their own 20 yard line.

Trent Richardson replaces Ingram at tailback as Alabama comes out in the Pistol formation. McElroy fakes a handoff to Richardson, rolls to his left and hits the H-back, Preston Dial, for a short completion to the 31.

Stan White warns that Auburn is a "pursuing defense" and Alabama has caught them three times now with the naked bootleg, using play-action to make the defenders chase the back while a receiver comes open on the opposite side of the formation.

On the next play, Alabama scores as easy of a touchdown as any team ever has. McElroy takes the snap in the shotgun, looks downfield and finds Julio Jones wide open. Jones catches the pass and cruises 69 yards into the Auburn end zone. The extra point is good.

On the radio broadcast, Stan White is livid.

> *"That's a total missed coverage. T'Sharvan Bell and Mike McNeill right there going back and forth with each other and that's pitiful. That's just bad. You've got to have good communication right there, and they let Julio Jones—I could've run by that defense... Mike McNeill was at the safety and he let Jones just run right by him. When you're the safety, you're the last line of defense."*
> —*Stan White, Auburn Network broadcast*

Auburn 0, Alabama 14

Barely six minutes of game time have passed, and Alabama is up by two touchdowns. Auburn, meanwhile, has run four plays from scrimmage, including a punt, and failed to make a single first down.

> *"Right now the Crimson Tide is clicking on all cylinders here at home. Last year Alabama came from behind to win it. Auburn will have to do that here today, on foreign turf, if they want to have an unblemished record going to Atlanta next week."*
> —*Rod Bramblett, Auburn Network broadcast*

Nick Fairley missed three plays while having his injured shoulder checked by medical staff. Alabama scored touchdowns on *two* of those three plays.

Van Allen Plexico

How crazy is this? Two years in a row, the home team went up, 14-0, in the first quarter—and neither of those teams ultimately won those games.

Demond Washington returns the kickoff to the Auburn 32. Alabama is flagged for offsides on the kick, and 5 yards are added onto the run. Auburn sets up shop at their own 37.

Michael Dyer remains at running back, standing just behind Cam Newton, who is in the shotgun. Cam takes the snap and drops back, but is immediately pressured by an Alabama defender. He sprints to his left to escape, only to run into another Tide defender. There's nowhere to go. He's sacked inside the 30.

Facing second down and 17, Cam fakes a handoff to Dyer and is then sacked again, this time by Courtney Upshaw.

Now it's third down and 24 from the 23 yard line, and a drive that began with excellent field position has done nothing but go backwards.

Cam throws to Darvin Adams in traffic, but the ball slips through his hands, incomplete. It's fourth down again.

Shoemaker comes on to punt for the second time in two drives. Mays makes the fair catch at the Alabama 39, and now the Tide are the ones with excellent field position. The clock shows over seven minutes remaining in a first quarter that feels as if it's been an hour long so far.

Rod Bramblett points out that this really is the first time all season that we've seen Cam Newton and the Auburn offense look a little tentative. "Now, a lot of that has to do with the fact that Alabama's getting pressure (on the quarterback)," he adds.

Nick Fairley returns to the field for Auburn. McElroy throws to Jones, who stretches out and makes the first down to the Alabama 49.

Richardson takes the handoff up the middle for 2 yards, crossing over into Auburn territory. Bramblett notes that that play resulted in the least gain of anything the Tide have run all day.

Under center, McElroy hits Jones on a quick-hitter pass to the left side of the formation for another first down, inside the Auburn 40.

Richardson, the back, tries another inside run but only gains a yard. The Auburn defense is tightening up now, and are playing much better with Fairley back in the game.

CBS informs us that Alabama has 161 yards of offense so far, while Auburn is at -10. Alabama calls a timeout.

Van Allen Plexico
It's interesting to me that Alabama chose to call a timeout here. It's almost as if they can't believe they're suddenly not gaining 10 yards a play, and need to regroup.

Trent Richardson is in the Wildcat formation when the Tide lines up. He takes the snap, fakes a handoff on the jet sweep, then rushes up the middle for very little gain.

Van Allen Plexico
It's weird seeing Alabama run the jet sweep action so much. That's something Gus had Auburn doing from day one, and we were still running it years later, after he became head coach.

Now Alabama faces third and 8. It's their first third down of the game. McElroy drops back, looks downfield, and is brought down by a charging Nick Fairley. Fairley jumps up and celebrates by stomping his feet a couple of times, only to draw a penalty flag from the referee for unsportsmanlike conduct.

"Nothing looked particularly unusual or unsportsmanlike about the celebration."
—Andy Staples, the New York Times, 2020

Van Allen Plexico
This is one of the worst penalties I've ever seen. But it's not as surprising as you might think. Fairley had been heavily criticized by Georgia people after the previous game, where he'd wreaked havoc on their quarterback, Aaron Murray. Clearly the referees were watching him closely this week, and pounced on him the moment he did anything to attract their attention.
Again Stan White is furious at what he's seeing.

"Oh my goodness. Now that is a direct result of what has happened this week. That's a pitiful call right there. Absolutely pitiful. Nick Fairley got up and celebrated with his teammates. It's a referee trying to determine the outcome of a play and a game.

> "He took two steps. That is a pitiful call right there. I don't care if I get in trouble for that. That is a pitiful call. Alabama did the same thing. Exact same thing."
> —Stan White, Auburn Network broadcast

As Fairley leaves the field, Gene Chizik chews him out.

> "After that first flag, which we thought was totally bogus, we talked to him on the sideline. We said 'You can't do anything. All you can do is play. No celebration of any sort.'"
> —Gene Chizik, to Andy Staples, the New York Times, 2020

The penalty makes it fourth down and 4 from the Auburn 32. Alabama decides to go for the first down. McElroy is alone in the backfield, with four wideouts and a tight end. He's pressured effectively but somehow makes the throw to Mays, who catches the ball and drags a foot as he goes out of bounds for the first down.

Alabama, up 14-0, are just inside the Auburn 23 with 3:13 to go in the first quarter. McElroy gives the ball to Richardson on a draw play that is stopped for no gain.

Stan White is not finished excoriating the referees for the call against Fairley:

> "That was a direct result of Nick Fairley catching a lot of flack on what happened two weeks ago (against Georgia). That is a referee reading headlines and saying, 'Nick Fairley, watch out'—and he made an effort to call a penalty on him on any time he made a play. What's so frustrating about this drive is that officiating is not supposed to determine the outcome of games."
> —Stan White, Auburn Network broadcast

Van Allen Plexico

I lived in Atlanta during this season, and listened to a lot of local sports radio. After the Georgia game, the Bulldogs fans were all up in arms and outraged about how Nick Fairley had treated their poor little quarterback, whom I had nicknamed "Anne Murray." Well, none other than legendary UGA quarterback Buck Belue, hosting a sports radio show, clapped back against his own people on the air. "If Nick Fairley were playing for Georgia," he told his audience that week, "he'd be a rock star (to Georgia fans)." I absolutely believe that he was right. They hated him because he was crushing their quarterback. If he'd been doing the same thing to Cam Newton, they'd have built a statue of him.

On second and 10, McElroy hits Julio Jones for a first down to the Auburn 12 on a quick slant pass to the left. The next play, McElroy hits a wide-open Hanks in the end zone for the Tide's third touchdown of the game. The extra point is good.

Auburn 0, Alabama 21

Van Allen Plexico
This was all just unthinkable to me.
I always say that, at this point in the game, I was googling "least painful ways to kill yourself." I know that's pretty inappropriate, but it's kind of true! I had never imagined any game this season would start off like this—much less this game! The mere thought that Alabama could ruin our once-in-a-lifetime season made me sick.

John Ringer
We had my in-laws over for Thanksgiving and to watch the game. And they were Auburn fans, but they live in Alabama, and so dealing with the Alabama dominance and having hope was hard for them. So at this point no one was speaking and there was an air of desperation and tension in the room. It was a painful, stressful hour for all Auburn fans.

Van Allen Plexico
One difference here, compared to the Georgia game, is that while the Bulldogs also ran off 21 straight points against us, Auburn had scored first in that game. Cam had led the Tigers right down the field and put it in the end zone on the opening possession. So, against Georgia, we always knew we could score. It was just a matter of settling down and stopping the bleeding on defense.

In this Iron Bowl, on the other hand, for much of the game, there was absolutely no sense that Auburn's offense could move the ball at all, or score on Alabama.

> *"This would be the biggest deficit of the year for Auburn, if they're going to come back and win this game. They'll have to come from 21 down at the moment, with 1:58 to go in the first quarter. It has been complete domination by Alabama. They have executed to almost perfection here in this first quarter and the Tigers have been unable to stop Alabama as they lead by three touchdowns.*
>
> *We did see some signs on that last defensive possession for Auburn, that they were getting pressure on McElroy. Now, offensively, if they can get down and get a touchdown here, it's a brand new ballgame. But they've got to do something."*
> —Rod Bramblett, Auburn Network broadcast

After the third Alabama touchdown, the Auburn defensive players come off the field in something of a daze. Fans in orange and blue had to be wondering, "How could it have all gone so wrong, so quickly?"

Nick Fairley, who'd led the defense by example all season, making spectacular play after spectacular play, now gathered the other linemen. At the hotel the night before, after Thanksgiving dinner, the other players on the team had taken turns sharing with one another what they were thankful for. The defensive linemen, for whatever reason, had not done so.

"A couple of us went around (the night before) and said what they were thankful for," said defensive tackle Jeffrey Whitaker, looking back from a few years later. "Then we had to go into meetings or something like that. We came back that night and couldn't finish it."

Now, on the sideline of the Iron Bowl, Fairley grabbed everyone's attention and called upon them to speak up. To finish the assignment.

> *"We were just sitting there, nobody was really talking, and Nick Fairley said, 'What are y'all thankful for?' With the crowd*

screaming, us being down 21 points, us knowing that we were going to have to come back to win this game, he asked us all what we were thankful for."
—Nosa Eguae, Auburn defensive end, to Mike Herndon in 2011

"Everybody was looking (at Fairley) like, 'Listen—we'd be thankful for a touchdown right now. Nobody's trying to hear this today, man.'"
—Jeffrey Whitaker, Auburn defensive tackle, speaking in 2015

Eventually they yielded to Fairley's insistent pressure and, one after another, they spoke up.

"That was the first time I had my whole family at a game," says Whitaker. "It meant so much to me, and I'm definitely thankful for it."

When it was Fairley's turn, what did he say?

"He just talked about the guys around him," says Eguae. "Guys like him who were up for all these postseason awards, picked to be the number one pick, he didn't talk about that. He didn't talk about the great season he was having. He talked about guys playing next to him, his friends on the football team and how he's cherishing the moment. It was deep."

Whitaker concludes the story: "At the end of the deal, (Fairley) just said, 'Let's go on and play ball. Let the chips fall where they may.'"

Perhaps doing the "thankful" mental exercise calmed the players. Maybe it refocused them. One way or another, though, they wouldn't allow another touchdown the rest of the game.

Meanwhile, out on the field, Demond Washington takes the Alabama kickoff to the Auburn 25.

On first down, Newton fakes a handoff to Onterio McCalebb and dives ahead for 1 yard.

On second down, Cam pitches the ball to McCalebb on an option run to the right, and the back is swarmed over for a 2-yard loss.

Van Allen Plexico
Absolutely nothing was working.

I was wondering, "Has Alabama figured something out? Something nobody else, all season long, figured out?"

I remembered hearing Bill "Brother" Oliver on a radio talk show earlier that week. He had been defensive coordinator for both Alabama and Auburn during the 1990s and was considered something of a defensive guru. A caller asked him, if he were in charge of Alabama's defense, how he would go about stopping Cam Newton and the Auburn offense. Oliver replied in vague terms, but the gist of it was keeping Cam in the pocket, taking away his running lanes, and finding a defensive player that could "spy" him (play him man-to-man, like in basketball, following him everywhere and ignoring everything else).

The problem was that most teams didn't have players on defense physically capable of "spying" Cam Newton.

Alabama did.

So maybe they HAD figured something out.

So now I looked across to the other side of the field, and to one Gus Malzahn.

"Okay, Gus," I thought to myself. "The ball is in your court now. Come up with something that will get the offense moving again—and do it fast!"

After two bad plays, it's third down and 11, and the situation is looking dire. Cam is swarmed after the snap and scrambles into an all-out Alabama blitz. He appears to find a hole—it's the first time all day he's had some daylight ahead of him—but he's then brought down by the ankles by a Tide defender behind him. He's gained only 3 yards.

That brings up another fourth down and long. On the Auburn sideline, Chizik and Malzahn have their headsets off and are conferring. They appear remarkably calm and composed, given the situation.

> *"Cam Newton ran off the field and you can tell he's frustrated."*
>
> *"One of the few times this year Auburn's offensive line is getting whipped."*
>
> *—Stan White and Rod Bramblett, Auburn Network broadcast*

Shoemaker lines up to punt the ball again, but the quarter ends before the snap.

> *"To tell you the truth, looking back on it, Auburn made a bunch of mistakes (on defense). They had a blown coverage. We had a few decent drives, but they had several mistakes that we were able to capitalize on. That obviously allowed us to distance ourselves in the first quarter."*
> —Greg McElroy, Alabama quarterback, speaking in 2015

> *"For us older guys, it felt like* deja vu *all over again from '08. I'm walking around on the sideline saying, 'Just keep fighting, just keep fighting.'"*
> —Zac Etheridge, Auburn safety

At the end of the first quarter in Tuscaloosa, the score is:

Auburn 0, Alabama 21

It is the absolute nightmare scenario. Getting blown out. And not just in any game, but in the last game of the regular season, against our biggest rival, while also possibly knocking us out of the BCS National Championship Game.

If Alabama were this much better than Auburn on the day, how could the Tigers ever hope to turn things around? Could their offense, which had struggled to generate any positive yardage at all, score at least 22 points? Could they do that while simultaneously shutting down a Tide offense that had scored 21 on them in just 15 minutes?

Was such a thing even possible?

The Tigers had three quarters remaining to try to figure that out.

- 18 -

THE SECOND QUARTER: AN AWFUL BEAUTIFUL THING

"What I consider the key play of the game occurred the next time Alabama's offense was on the field."
—Gene Chizik, All In

One quarter into the game, Auburn trails by three touchdowns and has thus far failed to even convert a first down.

If there was ever an Auburn team that could come back from such a deficit, one has to believe it is this one—a team that has been scoring over 40 points per game, and that has come from behind in nearly every game this season. They trailed 17-0 to Clemson, 20-7 to South Carolina, 7-0 to Kentucky, 43-37 to Arkansas, 7-0 to Ole Miss, and 21-7 to Georgia. (Oddly, LSU was the one big-time opponent that season whom the Tigers never trailed.)

In each of those games, however, the Auburn offense showed signs of life early. They just had to get into gear and start moving the ball, and then the points came in buckets.

Against Alabama, through an entire quarter, they had shown no signs of life whatsoever. As the defense continued to hemorrhage points, nothing indicated the offense would be able to score, much less catch up or take the lead.

> "Auburn has just done nothing offensively. Eight total yards on the day. Yet to pick up a first down. Actually minus-eight. Excuse me. And Alabama, 183 yards of total offense, 156 of that through the air, and have dominated the first quarter of play. They got a call, obviously, that helped them keep that last drive alive. But the first two drives, Alabama simply executed to perfection. Now Auburn has to kick it away again and, as good as Auburn has been offensively this year, they can't afford to fall behind any more than this."
>
> "Auburn has weathered this storm, but I don't know how much more of this storm you can weather."
> —Rod Bramblett and Stan White, Auburn Network broadcast

When the first quarter ended, Auburn faced fourth and 8 from their own 28. Now Ryan Shoemaker punts to the Alabama 27. Marquis Mays gets a nice return, but a flag on the play signals a block in the back against the Tide. Alabama starts out at their own 17.

Rod Bramblett mentions that a light drizzle has started falling as the second quarter gets underway.

Darius Hanks catches a wide-open screen pass to the right sideline for 7 yards. McElroy is now a remarkable 11 for 11 passing. Any pressure Auburn is getting on him seems inconsequential.

Mark Ingram carries to the right side of the formation for a short gain, up to the 26. Bramblett notes that while he went out of bounds at the 25, the referees gave him an extra yard.

On third and 1, Ingram lines up in the Wildcat again. He takes the shotgun snap, fakes the handoff on the jet sweep, and plunges forward for the first down.

On first and 10 on their own 30, McElroy scrambles for 10 yards and another first down before Neiko Thorpe takes him down.

On the radio, Rod and Stan are getting as frustrated as the rest of us.

> "Alabama continues to gobble up yardage."
> —Rod Bramblett, Auburn Network broadcast

> *"We were overconfident at the start. In my head, I'm thinking if it goes to 28-0, it's a wrap."*
> —*Mike Blanc, Auburn defensive lineman; one of two who were suspended for the first half*

CBS shows us that Alabama is averaging 9.0 yards per play, while Auburn is averaging -0.9. Not just zero point nine, but *negative* zero point nine.

The network's color analyst, Gary Danielsen, proves prophetic with his next utterance—and with the timing of it.

> *"If they're gonna come back, Cam Newton is gonna win the Heisman. Might as well vote right after this game. If they come back, you don't have to wait any longer."*
>
> *"They have some trail to trod before that happens."*
> —*Gary Danielsen and Verne Lundquist, CBS broadcast*

Once again Alabama has a first down, with 12:42 to go before halftime. McElroy goes under center and dumps a quick pass to Ingram, who catches it just past the line of scrimmage and takes off. He immediately slips the attempted tackle of linebacker Eltoro Freeman. He then proceeds to weave his way down the field, almost untouched. Strong safety Zac Etheridge dives at him and doesn't make the tackle, but does knock him slightly off his stride, slowing him for a couple of steps. Ingram's path ahead, however, remains clear.

And this is where we came in, at the start of this book.

Ingram is on his way to a touchdown. He's already past the Auburn 35 yard line by the time Etheridge dives and fails to tackle him. There's nothing in front of him but green grass.

And yet, somehow, defensive lineman Antoine Carter hasn't given up on the play. When Ingram caught the short pass, Carter was deep in the backfield, being successfully blocked out of the play by the Alabama offensive line, nowhere near the action. But he was able to disengage from his blocker even as Eltoro Freeman slowed Ingram down at the line of scrimmage. Because of that, Carter could take off in Ingram's wake almost immediately. Now he's running down the field, hustling to just keep up with Ingram but well behind him the entire time. He's doing this despite having zero chance to catch up to the Alabama back. Or, at least, zero chance unless something slows Ingram down, even for just a moment.

But then something does slow Ingram down. That something is a diving Zac Etheridge.

> *"Instead of tracking the hip, I overran it a little bit."*
> —Zac Etheridge, Auburn safety

Etheridge doesn't make the tackle, but he does cause Ingram to react, sidestepping the safety. In doing so, he stumbles. For a moment it looks like he's going to fall down, but he manages to right himself as he crosses the Auburn 25. Just as he's back upright, however, Antoine Carter finally catches up to him. Carter grasps for Ingram with his left hand and simultaneously swings his right fist at the ball, cradled in the crook of Ingram's arm.

Again: A football is shaped funny, and it tends to bounce funny. The one thing it does not do is roll in a straight line, like a bowling ball.

The ball comes out of Ingram's grasp, flies through the air, lands at about the 7, and rolls in a straight line, like a bowling ball. Straight into and through the end zone.

> *"The thing just went on a beeline. It was a straight roll, like a volleyball."*
> —Gene Chizik

If the ball had gone out of bounds at any point before the goal line, it would've remained in Alabama's possession. The fact that it did not is simply astounding—and is perhaps the difference between a win and a loss; between a good season and a great one; between an SEC championship season and a national championship season.

> *"I couldn't believe the ball had tightroped the sideline without going out. Nine times out of ten, the ball would have bounced out of bounds somewhere before the goal line and Alabama would have kept possession inside our twenty."*
> —Gene Chizik, All In

Auburn defenders dive for the ball as it crosses the back line of the end zone. It doesn't matter. Whether they down it in the end zone or let it roll across the back line, either way it's the same result: a touchback. Same as a kickoff. Auburn's ball.

The Tigers were mere yards and split seconds away from, in all probability, being down 28-0, early in the second quarter. Could any team have come back from such a deficit? Especially when their opponents had just landed yet another body blow on them?

Fortunately, we will never know.

"If Alabama had gone up four touchdowns on us at their place, that would've been a steep hill for us to climb," noted Chizik later. "That play changed lives."

Instead of trailing by four scores, it's Auburn's ball at their 20, with an eternity of game time remaining.

Even more astoundingly, it hadn't happened to a turnover-prone back. Quite the opposite, in fact. It was only the Heisman winner's *second fumble ever*, in over 550 career rushing attempts. "I was stumbling," Ingram told reporters later. "I was trying to get my balance. When I got my balance, he hit it out. Great play."

As Carter, a 6-foot-4, 256-pound defensive end, chased down Ingram, he heard the voice of his position coach, Tracy Rocker, speaking his mantra in his head: "Don't ever quit."

"That play is an eye opener every time I think about it," he told reporter Jon Solomon. "How much can be accomplished just by not quitting."

Five years later, Carter added, "It was all pursuit drill and hustle. That changed the momentum. I think that play gave the team a lot of hope, gave the fans a lot of energy, and we went on from there."

> *"The play that they make, that they absolutely do not win the national championship without, is the hustle play of the year, by Antoine Carter."*
> —Chris Low, ESPN

"If the football that was once carried by Mark Ingram had done what physics usually demands on that chilly, drizzly Friday afternoon in Tuscaloosa, Ala., then we probably wouldn't remember much about this game," observed Andy Staples in the *New York*

Times in 2020. "It wouldn't have a name (The Camback). Auburn people wouldn't tell their children and their grandchildren about the moment when all hope was lost and Antoine Carter just kept running. For them, Black Friday 2010 would be the darkest Friday—the day Alabama spoiled a potential national title run. Nationwide, it might be a footnote to the story of Chip Kelly's first national title at Oregon."

> *"It's so crazy how everything happened because the ball literally went straight down the sideline when it should have gone out of bounds. You could just see the whole momentum change on just that one play."*
> —Zac Etheridge, Auburn safety, 2011

> *"That play changed lives."*
> —Gene Chizik, to Andy Staples, 2020

> *"It was an awful beautiful thing that it did roll like that.*
> *"You see so many times where guys will turn and watch plays and then they'll say 'Oh my gosh, that guy missed a tackle or this guy broke out.' Then they'll start running. By the time they do, it's too late and they miss it by six inches. Well, Antoine didn't do that. As a result of that, some wonderful things happened."*
> —Ted Roof, Auburn defensive coordinator

"Antoine Carter's play was probably by far the biggest play ever in the Iron Bowl, besides the Kick Six," noted Tigers linebacker Josh Bynes, looking back in 2015. "That play was pivotal, because you never know. What if he scores a touchdown? It may not have been a championship season."

> *"We just needed a spark. We just needed it to bounce our way."*
> —Ryan Pugh, Auburn center

> *"Without that fumble, it's possible nothing that came later would have mattered. It was the spark that produced a chain reaction that would lead to one of the greatest comebacks in*

college football history. A bounce had finally gone Auburn's way, and that opened the floodgates."
—Andy Staples, the New York Times, 2020

"When that happened, we said, 'All right, (Alabama have) had enough. When that play happened, that was when everybody was like, 'Okay, we're going to win this game. We're gonna win it."
—Jeffrey Whittaker, Auburn defensive tackle, speaking in 2015

John Ringer
There were two big plays that happened in this game for Auburn. One was the individual play that turned the game around. The forced fumble by our defensive end. They were up 21-0 and about to score again, and Antoine Carter forced a fumble. And forced it on Mark Ingram, who never fumbled. It was the turning point of the game.

The other play involved Alabama's best receiver, Julio Jones. The Auburn defense couldn't cover Julio Jones if our lives depended on it. You can talk about all the big passes we were giving up, but that was against much lesser receivers than him. In the first half, he did whatever he wanted against our defense. That was a big reason why they kept scoring. But in an effort to make sure they won the game, Nick Saban let him return kickoffs in this game, which they never did otherwise. It was Saban going the extra mile to make sure they beat us.

Julio Jones returned the second half kickoff and got injured on that play and was never the same. I don't know how much he played in the second half, but he was a non-factor from that point forward. It was one of those big decisions over the years that blew up in Saban's face.

Auburn does a quick huddle as play resumes, then the players hurry out to their spots. Cam Newton is alone in the backfield, with four receivers arrayed in an odd formation to his left and one to his right. He takes the snap and tosses the ball to Emory Blake, the hindmost of the four on the right—and Blake drops it.

Second down: this time, Cam completes the pass. Terrell Zachery catches the wide screen and gets to the 29.

Cam runs up the middle to the 32. It is Auburn's first successful first down conversion of the day.

Auburn is in the hurry-up now. Gus Malzahn likes to run the ball up the middle immediately after a successful first down conversion. Cam gives the ball to Dyer, who manages three yards.

A quick "half-huddle," and then Auburn attempts a reverse, but the Alabama defense blows it up for a 5-yard loss, pushing Auburn back to its own 30.

CBS notes that Auburn trailed in seven of its eleven wins so far this year. But they never trailed by as much as 21.

On third and 12, Cam fakes a handoff, avoids the rush, and throws a quick pass to a wide-open Zachery—who drops the ball.

Two drops of easy passes on this drive have brought the Tigers to another fourth down. To make matters worse, Ryan Shoemaker then gets off one of his worst punts ever, barely making it to midfield.

Alabama has mitigated the damage of Ingram's fumble and now they have the ball back, just across the midfield line.

Van Allen Plexico
This part of the game was absolutely agonizing. After the brief euphoria of the Ingram fumble, it felt like we were right back in trouble again. Had the Antoine Carter play been just a temporary stay of execution?

Richardson runs to the right for 5 yards.

> *"The luxury Alabama has now is they can line up in an Ace formation and run the ball left and right and just run the clock. And that's exactly what they want to do. They have executed their game plan to perfection—get (the score) up early, get Cam Newton off the field and keep him confused, and just pound it a little bit. I look for them to do that—pound it, pound it, play-action fake, and take a shot deep."*
> —Stan White, Auburn Network broadcast

McElroy fakes the handoff and rolls to his left, but Nosa Eguae is all over him, forcing him to throw the ball out of bounds just as the big lineman smashes into him.

Now it's third down and 5 to go. McElroy manages to avoid a massive blitz by Auburn's defense and hits Julio Jones at the Auburn 30. Jones takes off down the sideline. Neiko Thorpe dives for him and misses. Here comes 28-0 after all, it looks like.

Yet somehow he does not score. Mike McNeill catches him and brings him down at the Auburn 3 yard line—another forgotten moment that would prove to be huge in this game.

Alabama fans in the stands are in a frenzy now, cheering and hugging and high-fiving. They know they missed an easy opportunity to run up a fourth touchdown on the Tigers mere moments earlier, but here they are, knocking on the door again.

Van Allen Plexico

You know that, in their minds, the Alabama fans in the stands had long-since moved this game into the "Win" column. Now they were all relishing the continued beat-down and wondering just how many points they would score on Auburn. At this point in the game, with over nine minutes remaining until halftime, they could easily have been up 35-0. Nobody—nobody in the history of college football—would be coming back against this Alabama team in this stadium with that score on the scoreboard.

And, at this point in the game, Alabama didn't look like they were slowing down any time soon. It wasn't like Auburn's 14-0 lead in the previous Iron Bowl, where we did it with smoke and mirrors and you knew it was just a matter of time until the Tide corrected their course and got rolling. Auburn had done next to nothing so far, especially on offense, to provide any indication things were ever going to change.

CBS notes that the total net yardage in the game to this point is: Julio Jones 162, the entire Auburn offense 2.

The Auburn offense's greatest accomplishments to this point have been gaining one first down and getting their yardage total into the positive range before halftime. They are at least no longer going backwards.

Alabama lines up just inside the Auburn 3 yard line, first and goal. McElroy is under center, with Richardson the lone back behind him. McElroy takes the snap and floats an easy pass to the wide-open running back as he crosses the goal line. It will be the easiest touchdown for Alabama of the day.

Inexplicably, with no Auburn player within three yards of him, Richardson drops the ball.

> *"That's just a catch and toss to a little kid. You don't know why it happens. You're just glad it happens. That whole year we were blessed."*
> —Zac Etheridge, Auburn safety, to Jon Solomon in 2011

Van Allen Plexico

If the Ingram fumble through the end zone marked the moment Auburn stopped the bleeding, this seems to be the moment the momentum slowly began to shift.

In the moment, it wasn't perceptible. Nobody watching the game at the time, seeing Richardson fail to catch the pass, would have said, "Oh yeah, now this is Auburn's game, baby!" Nobody was thinking that. It was second down and goal to go at the Auburn 3. You had to think Alabama would come right back with a power run up the middle and Ingram would take it in for the score. But they don't.

When you go back and watch the game again now, this drive feels like the last time in the entire game that Alabama's offense really had the upper hand. Something fundamental shifts here. I don't know exactly what it is, but something changes when Richardson drops the ball. If he catches that little pass, maybe the shift doesn't happen—or maybe it doesn't matter if it does, since they'd be up, 28-0.

In fact, it's remarkable how many times the score of this game was *almost* 28-0. But it never quite happened.

It doesn't happen here. Richardson drops the ball. And everything starts to change.

On second down and goal to go, Richardson takes the snap in the Wildcat formation and runs right, but the Auburn defense stops him for no gain.

On third down and goal to go, Alabama brings more receivers onto the field and McElroy lines up in the shotgun. He throws to the right side of the end zone but the ball falls incomplete as Mike McNeill effectively covers Hanks.

Alabama kicks the short field goal and goes up 24-0 with eight minutes to go in the first half.

Auburn 0, Alabama 24

After all the amazing output by the Alabama offense... After all the struggles by the Auburn defense... and after the terrible play by the Auburn offense, who had earned exactly one first down so far... After all of that, somehow Alabama still only led by a score of 24-0.

Was 24-0 Alabama ideal? Certainly not.

Was it the best-case scenario for that point in the game, given the way the two teams were playing? Very likely, yes.

Van Allen Plexico
Make a note as well, here: It was a mistake by the Auburn special teams—a bad punt from deep in their own territory—that set Alabama up at midfield to start that drive. That will not be the only time Alabama benefits from a bad play in Auburn's punt-related special teams game.

From the Auburn sideline, Quentin Riggins reports that OC Gus Malzahn has been preaching to the Auburn offense to be patient. Cam isn't being patient and isn't setting his feet when he throws. Riggins notes that Malzahn says they need to run more screens and draws to attempt to counteract Alabama's heavy blitzing, especially on second and long.

Auburn's Onterio McCalebb returns the kickoff to the 20.

With 7:56 to go in the half, Auburn comes back out on the field. Cam keeps the ball and runs into the center of the formation, then has to struggle and fight to gain 5 yards.

Next he gives it to Dyer, who runs to the right side of the formation for no gain. The running game is simply not there today.

On third and 5 from the 25, Newton pump-fakes to the running back in the flat to his left. He then resets and fires the ball downfield to Kodi Burns, who fights his way to the 45 for a first down—their second of the game.

Auburn is in the hurry-up again, and Dyer carries for 5 yards before being smashed by an Alabama defender. Alabama is penalized for a substitution violation and accepts the penalty, making it first and 5 near midfield.

Saban was furious about the call, and let everyone in the stadium know it.

> *"The head coach for the University of Alabama was 10 yards out on the field, doing a whole heck of a lot more than Nick Fairley did when he sacked Greg McElroy, and there was nothing done about that."*
> —Rod Bramblett, Auburn Network broadcast

In the most promising drive of the day so far, Auburn has a first and 5 at their own 49 yard line. Newton takes the snap and rolls to his left, looking for a receiver, but fails to find one. He's dropped for a loss by Courtney Upshaw at the Auburn 45.

Because of the penalty, it's just second and 8. CBS shows a graphic saying that Alabama has run 17 plays in Auburn's territory, while the Tigers have yet to cross the 50.

Cam stands in the shotgun, Dyer behind him and to his right. He fakes a handoff to the left, rolls to his right, and fires the ball to a sliding Darvin Adams, who makes the first down at the Alabama 37 with 5:56 to go in the half. Alabama players protest that the pass was incomplete, but the referees do not stop play.

Auburn now appears to have a first down in the Tide's territory for the first time today. But, with these officials, appearances can be deceiving—as the Tigers are about to find out.

Cam lines up in the shotgun with Dyer behind him and to his left and fullback Eric Smith ahead and to the right. Cam takes the snap and hands the ball to Dyer, who blasts through the line for what should be a long gain—and then the referees blow the whistle and decide to review the previous play.

On the radio broadcast, Rod and Stan agree that the pass was not actually caught by Adams. That will make it third down and 7—despite the fact that Auburn had already snapped the ball before the referees decided to review the play. (There's disagreement between the officials and Nick Saban about the proper placement of the ball after the replay, resulting in Auburn somehow gaining a yard from their previous spot. CBS, meanwhile, shows the down and distance to be third and 9, which is clearly at odds with the reality on the field.)

Facing another do-or-die, drive-prolonging play, Kodi Burns comes through again. How far we have come from the agonizing meeting at the start of the 2009 season, when Burns stood up and told the team he didn't want them divided over Chris Todd being named starting quarterback. Now Burns is a valued member of the receiving corps. As the ferocious Alabama blitz closes in on Newton, he throws the ball over the middle. Burns makes the catch for a gain of 13 yards, to the Alabama 40, for a first down.

The Tigers instantly go back into hurry-up mode. As they always did in Malzahn's offense, they follow a big first down with a no-huddle run up the middle. Usually they don't get much from it, but here Michael Dyer surges ahead for four, to the Alabama 36. Just over five and a half minutes remain before halftime.

Newton takes the second-down snap and starts forward a step, then ducks back into the pocket and throws the ball long down the left sideline. There awaits a streaking Emory Blake, two steps ahead of two Alabama defenders. Blake juggles the ball before securing it, a mere instant before the Alabama player catches him and grabs at his arm. If the Tide defender had caught him half a step earlier, he likely would have dislodged the ball, which would've fallen incomplete. Blake had just enough time to secure his grip before being hit. Touchdown Auburn!

Van Allen Plexico
Something very important also happened as Emory Blake is catching that pass, but it won't become apparent until the third quarter. Keep that in mind!

> *"Any time you can get a drive started off a third down and keep it going off of third down, it really helps the team, gives them confidence. We went down and scored, and it changed the game."*
> —*Kodi Burns, Auburn receiver, speaking in 2015*

Wes Byrum's extra point is good. The Tigers are finally on the board, with 5:28 remaining in the half.

Auburn 7, Alabama 24

Byrum kicks off for only the second time on the day. The kick is returned by Julio Jones to the Alabama 23.

On first down, McElroy's pass is tipped at the line and could easily have been intercepted, but it falls harmlessly to the ground.

On second down, tight end Preston Dial catches a short pass and is instantly brought down. Meanwhile, Auburn's pressure gets to McElroy, driving him into the turf as he throws the ball.

Alabama makes a first down on the next play, with McElroy hitting Hanks for 9 yards.

From the 35, Alabama runs a screen pass to Julio Jones, who breaks loose and gets all the way to the Auburn 41.

"Not one single time has Auburn been able to stop Alabama on offense today," notes Rod Bramblett, apparently forgetting the Ingram fumble forced by Carter. "Three touchdowns and a field goal, and once again Alabama is moving it after Auburn scored a touchdown."

On first and 10 from the Auburn 41, McElroy dumps it to Ingram on a quick screen. Ingram picks his way through the Auburn secondary for 17 more yards.

Stan White is still upset with the Auburn defense.

> *"That's just bad defense right there, is all there is to it. Alabama's doing a good job of executing, but it's just bad defense as well, to allow a running back to not be touched until he's 12 to 14 yards downfield."*
> *—Stan White, Auburn Network broadcast*

At the Auburn 24 now, Alabama takes a timeout to consider their plans with 2:41 to go.

CBS shows us that McElroy is now 17 for 21 passing, for 318 yards—a career high—and 2 touchdowns, with no interceptions. They also show us the McElroy family celebrating in the stands.

Alabama runs a wide screen pass to Ingram, who is knocked out of bounds inside the Auburn 20.

McElroy's second down pass is complete to Dial for 11 yards, to the Auburn 8 yard line.

On first and goal, Ingram takes a pitch and runs to his right, but is brought down for a short gain. At the end of the play, the ball is knocked loose. That could have been another miraculous moment for the Tigers, if they had been able to recover Ingram's second fumble of the day. Unfortunately, an Alabama lineman is able to dive on top of it.

Auburn calls a timeout, with 1:02 remaining in the half. In the stands, McElroy's sister is dancing and singing in the stands as the Tide fans around her celebrate.

Despite the short gain and recovered fumble, Alabama is still in goal-to-go territory, knocking on the door once again. Auburn was narrowly able to hold them to a field goal the last time they penetrated this deeply, but that took a dropped wide-open pass by their running back. They didn't get the big play when Ingram fumbled this time, but they're going to need some kind of fortuitous turn of events to avoid going down 31-7 just before halftime.

And they get it. Not a miracle, though. A miracle is a gift. This turn of events is earned. It's created by the play of the Auburn defense—and particularly by Nick Fairley, making his presence known at last.

It's still second and goal at the Auburn 8. McElroy is under center, with Ingram as the only back behind him. A touchdown here, just on the cusp of halftime, and the game is over.

McElroy takes the snap and drops back a step, into the pocket, looking to pass. Ingram moves forward to protect him.

Fairley smashes his way through the Alabama line and arrives in the backfield before any of that can matter. There is no pocket. And Ingram is about to get destroyed.

An Alabama lineman hanging off of him, the big Auburn defender collides with both Ingram and McElroy simultaneously. Like some deranged Sasquatch, Fairley momentarily has all three Alabama players in his grasp. As he smacks McElroy in the face, the football comes out of the quarterback's hand and seems to float in midair for a moment, before dropping to the turf behind them. McElroy is too busy being mangled by Fairley to pay any attention to where the ball has ended up. The lineman and the running back are turned away from the line of scrimmage, facing toward Fairley and the ruins of what once was their quarterback. Fairley is the only one of the four looking ahead, towards the end zone.

And towards where the ball has landed on the grass.

> *"With no celebration to occupy his mind (because of the earlier admonishment about it from Chizik), Fairley was the first player to notice the ball on the ground. He hadn't heard a whistle, but he saw no one else moving toward it. 'Something had to be going on,' Fairley said that day."*
> —Andy Staples, the New York Times, 2020

None of the other offensive or defensive players are close by. The defensive backs are downfield, covering the receivers. The other linemen from both teams are locked up with one another. Only Fairley, of all twenty-two players on the field, seems to have situational awareness.

As the three dazed Alabama players stand there—or lie there—in shock, Fairley literally crawls on his hands and knees around them and pounces on the ball.

First down Auburn.

> *"Mark Richt, the Georgia coach, said 'He's as close to Warren Sapp as I've seen.'"*
> —Gary Danielsen, CBS Sports broadcast, on Nick Fairley

Van Allen Plexico

We noted at the beginning of the game that Alabama's star right guard was injured and couldn't play. He was replaced by the backup, Steen. Guess who Fairley was matched up against at the start of that play?

Auburn has dodged another bullet. And Alabama's offense won't look right the rest of the game. In one play, Nick Fairley has broken it.

On first down from their own 12, Newton looks downfield and throws to Darvin Adams on the right sideline to the 32, with 49 seconds to go in the half.

Another first down, and Mario Fannin comes in at running back. Newton throws to Adams on the right sideline again, and Adams eventually catches it, but was still bobbling it before it went out of bounds. Stan White protests repeatedly that the play should be reviewed, because it was a catch, but the referees do not choose to do so.

Newton gives the ball to McCalebb on a wraparound draw on second down, for no gain.

Cam is sacked by Courtney Upshaw on third down. There are eleven seconds to go.

With a timeout on the field, CBS shows replays of the earlier play that prove Darvin Adams did catch the ball. Stan White is apoplectic over the fact that the referees did not even look at the replay. He is not the only one.

At 4th and 18, Shoemaker comes on to punt. He sends it down to the 33 of Alabama, ending the half.

> *"To be honest, the way Alabama played in the first half of this football game, Auburn could be down by a lot more than 17. Auburn will get the ball first in the second half, trailing Alabama 24-7."*
>
> —Rod Bramblett, Auburn Network broadcast

- 19 -

HALFTIME: LET'S GO, LET'S GO, LET'S GO

"McElroy and Julio Jones were brilliant in the first half."
—Verne Lundquist, CBS

As Chizik heads for the locker room, CBS reporter Tracy Wolfson asks him, "Coach, this is the first time we've really seen Cam Newton struggle to move the ball. What's been the problem so far?"

"Well, I just think our whole football team right now, we need to settle down and play," Chizik replies. "We had a little bit of success there, later in the half. We've got to settle down, we've got to figure out what adjustments we need to make. Defensively we're giving up too many big plays. We've got to go get it figured out."

"You mentioned the big plays on defense," Wolfson says. "We talked before the game about containing Julio Jones, and you said that would be key. So what do you need to do in the second half?"

"We're going to have to find some ways to double him, to play hard on him up front and play somebody deep over the top," Chizik says. "We've got to get him under control and we've got to tackle better."

Van Allen Plexico

Watching the game again, I continue to be amazed at how cool and calm and collected Gene Chizik always is—even as it looks like the season is collapsing underneath him here in Tuscaloosa. When he talks with Wolfson there, you might well think Auburn is leading by 3 rather than trailing by 17, with their national championship hopes on the line.

I can see how his low-key, even-tempered approach would work well with a group of experienced players—so many of them seniors—like this team possessed.

I can also see how things could go bad quickly, a couple of years later on. Maybe that approach doesn't work quite as well with a younger crop of inexperienced guys. I don't know.

In virtually any other season, with any other quarterback than Cam Newton and any other defensive player than Nick Fairley, a 17-point deficit at halftime in Bryant-Denny Stadium would seem insurmountable.

But the Tigers have stopped the bleeding on defense, for the most part, and shown a few signs of life on offense.

As Auburn's players head down the tunnel to the locker room, the CBS cameras show Nick Fairley wearing a broad smile on his face.

> *"Everyone else in the Auburn locker room knew why Fairley was smiling. Earlier in the season, the Tigers had erased fourth-quarter deficits against Clemson, South Carolina and Arkansas. They had been tied with LSU until five minutes remained. They had fallen behind 21-7 to Georgia in the first quarter and won 49-31."*
>
> —Andy Staples, the New York Times, 2020

A normal team might well have felt the hill that still towered before them was too much to climb. To try to come back against one of the top teams in college football, in their own stadium, when all the pressure was on you? To have dug yourself such a deep hole in the first half—a hole that easily could have been much, much deeper—and then try to climb out of it, and in only two quarters? No, a normal team might have dismissed the possibility entirely.

ALL THEY DID WAS WIN

But this was not a "normal" team. This was no ordinary team. This was a team that had come from behind time and again. For every single first quarter that they could be blamed for allowing themselves to fall behind, there was a second half where they locked down on defense and exerted their will on offense. They knew—all of the players knew, and from firsthand experience across weeks and weeks of SEC football—that this hill *could* be climbed.

More than that—they knew they *would* climb it.

They weren't happy about the situation. But they were not intimidated by it, either.

> *"We honestly didn't even sweat that much at halftime. We were furious. If I remember correctly, at halftime, we said, 'We're gonna come back and win.'"*
> —Josh Bynes, Auburn linebacker

Cam Newton was too much of a fiery competitor to roll over and take what Alabama had been dishing out for much longer.

> *"We scored right before the half, we went in and, you know, everybody was saying, 'Oh, (let's make some) halftime adjustments.' But really it was our players, and it was Cam. He was going person by person, calling them out."*
> —Gus Malzahn, Auburn offensive coordinator

> *"Inside Auburn's locker room at halftime, the coaches let the players talk to one another. With the exception of Newton, who had joined the team that January, most of Auburn's key contributors had been together between three and five years. They'd seen their coach get fired. They'd beaten Alabama and been crushed by Alabama. They knew they couldn't play worse than they had in the first quarter, and if the offense could pop the type of big plays it had all season, the score could get closer."*
> —Andy Staples, the New York Times, 2020

It surely helped that they had faced deficits like this before, and it didn't hurt that they now found themselves in that situation against their biggest rival. It added extra fuel to their fire. As Ryan Pugh put it, "We didn't come this far, to lose this one. Lose a different one, but don't lose this one."

The Auburn players understood that they faced a very good bunch of players in crimson; players that had just run circles around them for most of the first 30 minutes of the game.

But there are groups of players, and there are *teams*.

> "Obviously Bama had way more talent than we had on that team. But we had a team chemistry and an understanding of each other. The game was easy, because we all played as one."
> —Zac Etheridge, Auburn safety, to Andy Staples, 2020

> "We had confidence. And we knew we couldn't let all those comebacks we'd had during the season go to waste. Especially against Alabama. And in what better forum to do that, than in Bryant-Denny Stadium?"
> —Josh Bynes, Auburn linebacker

Chizik challenged them to show the world that what they'd done in the first half was not an accurate representation of who they were.

> "I told them, 'What we presented to the world in the first half is a joke. It's laughable. And that's what's happening right now. Everybody's laughing. But—I said 'But'—'If you go out there, and you play with urgency, you execute the offensive and defensive (plays) the way they were designed—it's not rocket science—we'll come back and we'll shock the world. And we did.
> From that point on, the demeanor, the body language, and the presence of the sideline completely changed. The game was a completely different story in the second half. And that was the difference in the game."
> —Gene Chizik

Gene Chizik and the other coaches made few adjustments or other statements to the players. Before the team went back out on the field, however, he told them, "Get the ball, take it down and score, make it a 10-point game, and we'll change this thing. It's that simple. So let's go. Let's go play. Let's go. Let's go."

- 20 -

THE THIRD QUARTER: RIGHT WHERE THEY WANT TO BE

"At halftime, we felt (Alabama) had played the best half of their lives and they've got nothing left."
—Kodi Burns, Auburn receiver, to Jon Solomon, 2011

Auburn, lucky to be down "only" 24-7 and not much worse, receives the kick to start the second half.

CBS posts a graphic showing that McElroy finished the first half with 335 yards on 19 of 23 passing. Newton, meanwhile, has been averaging 303 yards passing, but today has only 87. Much of that came on one play, the touchdown to Emory Blake. And in terms of rushing, an Auburn unit that averages 308 yards per game (third in the NCAA) is still trapped in the negative zone, with -10.

The Alabama crowd is loud and excited. They are primed and ready to see these upstarts from the Plains finished off, their perfect season ruined.

Auburn needs to take charge from the get-go. They need to find a path forward for the offense; an approach that moves the ball and makes first downs. They do not need to play like they did at the start of the first half, and give up more points. Above all else, they need something good to happen, and quickly.

As the crowd roars their favorite cheer—the one beginning with "RTR"—Cade Foster kicks off. Demond Washington catches the ball at the 10 and returns it to the 31 yard line.

Rod Bramblett reports that the rain has stopped, but it's still overcast—with the stadium lights on—and "it's just cold."

Donta Hightower blitzes and brings down Cam Newton for a 1 yard loss on first down.

Van Allen Plexico

Not the start to the second half we were hoping for. Not by any means.

On second down, however, something happens.

Ontario McCalebb stands to Cam's right. At the snap, Cam runs to his right and fakes the handoff to the back, then looks downfield and unloads, throwing deep in the direction of the left sideline. Terrell Zachery runs under the ball to try for the catch, being chased by freshman defensive back Dee Milliner. Alabama's all-star safety, Mark Barron, is there as well, waiting. The question doesn't appear to be, "Will T-Zac catch it?" The question looks to be, "Which of the two Alabama DBs will make the interception?"

Except, neither does.

Milliner is too slow and doesn't arrive in time. Barron seems unable to jump up to attack the ball. Zachery is the only one in position and able to catch it, and he snatches it out of the air, then stiff-arms Barron into the turf. Now he's off to the races, Milliner half a step behind him the entire way. The defensive back dives for T-Zac's legs at the 10, but Zachery avoids that last-gasp tackle attempt and crosses the goal line for the touchdown.

The Tigers have just traveled seventy yards in two plays. As Stan White shouts: *"Now we've got a ballgame!"*

Coming to the sideline, Cam Newton goes up to Gus Malzahn and simply states, "We're going to beat 'em now."

Auburn 14, Alabama 24

That 21-point lead has become a 17-point lead and now a 10-point lead.

Alabama fans in the stands and watching at home are getting antsy.

As for how Mark Barron was unable to make the play on the ball, it turns out he had injured himself earlier in the game. When Emory Blake caught the first Auburn touchdown, Barron was pursuing him. Blake juggled the ball momentarily before bringing it in. Barron saw that and reached out, trying to slap the ball away. When he did so, he tore the pectoral muscle in his right arm.

> *"Even at halftime, (Barron) said, 'Put a patch on it, I'm OK.' And he continued to play in the second half and actually had the opportunity to make a play that he'd probably made nine out of ten times if he wasn't hurt. But he couldn't make it. That's when we realized maybe something more was wrong with him."*
> *—Nick Saban, to Jon Solomon, 2011*

The Tigers weren't expecting Barron to even be involved in Terrell Zachery's touchdown play. They expected he would be covering the tight end instead. "T-Zach was supposed to be wide open," Kodi Burns later told Jon Solomon, "but Mark Barron read it really well."

Unfortunately for Barron, once he got to Zachery, he couldn't do anything about the catch.

"I couldn't lift my arm. I couldn't get my arm up. I probably would want to take that play back if I could."

> *"It was an incredible effort by (Barron) to play with that injury and he was still fairly effective. We didn't really decide to go at him more, but we were aware of it so you may not shy away from him as much if he was healthy."*
> *—Rhett Lashlee, Auburn graduate assistant, to Jon Solomon*

> *"Now it's time for that defense to step up as well."*
> *—Rod Bramblett, Auburn Network broadcast*

Less than a minute into the second half, the Tigers have pulled the game to within 10 points.

CBS is feeling the momentum swinging. They post a graphic showing "Comeback Wins Under Gene Chizik." In addition to the 2009 West Virginia "Rain Game," they list three games from the current season: The Tigers trailed Clemson, 17-0; they trailed South Carolina, 20-7; and they trailed Georgia, 21-7. Auburn came back to win all of those games, scoring 27, 35 and 49 points, respectively. The graphic also notes that Auburn has a 4-2 record when trailing by 10+ points under Gene Chizik.

Wes Byrum's kickoff is short, bouncing out of bounds at the 3. Bramblett notes this may have been the first time all season that a Byrum kickoff went out of bounds. It's a violation and it gives Alabama great field position, starting at their 40.

Now Alabama does what Bramblett and White have been suggesting they have wanted to do: run the ball and run the clock. McElroy gives it to Ingram from the single-back set, and he powers ahead for 5 yards. The problem for Alabama is, Auburn's run defense has been stout all season and all game long.

On second down, Alabama sticks to the same formation but McElroy throws a quick out pass. The receiver, Mays, doesn't turn around and the ball is nearly intercepted.

Now facing third and 5, McElroy completes the pass over the middle, but Mike McNeill arrives in a hurry and with bad intentions, smashing the receiver to the turf. This brings up fourth down and 1.

Alabama lines up to go for it, with the ball on their own 49 yard line. McElroy dives into the scrum and gets the first down.

Bramblett notes that Auburn's two defensive linemen who weren't allowed to play in the first half, Blanc and Goggans, are now available. That should help with depth and stopping the run, the rest of the way.

From just across midfield, Ingram gets the handoff and slips down as he crosses the 50, for a gain of a yard.

On second down, Trent Richardson catches a quick dump pass behind the line of scrimmage, turns upfield—and slips as well. Eltoro Freeman brings him down before he can recover his footing. The turf of Bryant-Denny Stadium is apparently rooting for Auburn. The play loses 2 yards, bringing up third down and 10 from midfield.

ALL THEY DID WAS WIN

It is the longest third down yardage Alabama has faced in the game. The Tide coaches consider the situation and call a timeout.

When play resumes, McElroy takes the snap from the shotgun. Auburn brings enormous pressure up the middle. McElroy knows where he wants the ball to go all along, staring down his receiver on the left side. He lets it go and the ball hits Alabama's Darius Hanks in the numbers—but the pass is broken up by T'Sharvan Bell.

Fourth down. Alabama has to punt, for the first time all day. Again: we are well into the third quarter, and this is the *very first time* Alabama has had to punt today.

Quindarius Carr makes a fair catch at the Auburn 18.

Van Allen Plexico

I have long maintained that making a fair catch—or really any kind of fielding of a punt—is one of the worst moments for a team in a football game. Think about it. All eleven players on your defense have just worked extremely hard to stop the other team's offense from making a first down. You've done it—you've stopped them, and done so outside of field goal range. (Otherwise, the opponent would be attempting a field goal.) You've forced them to punt. And after all that, you send one little guy out there to catch the ball and try to run it back a few yards. The one thing you don't want him to do is drop it or touch it and lose control of it, and let the punting team recover it. If he does, he's nullified the accomplishments your defense has just made. He's done the equivalent of fumbling the ball. But it's even worse than that. In effect he's given up the equivalent of a long pass completion to the opponents. They take possession of the ball way down there, rather than where they were when they punted. It's a disaster all around. And it all comes back to whether that one little guy can look up in the air and find the ball and catch it, while eleven players on the other team are bearing down on him with a head of steam from running some forty or fifty yards directly at him.

I've always said: If I were a coach, I'd *never* put a punt returner on the field. I'd just let the ball bounce where it wanted to. For me, the dangers of trying to catch it outweigh the benefits.

We will see a good example of this coming up later in the game, unfortunately.

235

Stan White notes that Alabama's goal on defense is to prevent Cam Newton from getting past the line of scrimmage. So he expects some quick screens and other plays that can take some of the pressure off of Newton. Quentin Riggins adds that Alabama is copying how Clemson played defense against this Auburn team, "slow-playing" the defensive ends and containing Cam in the pocket. "That's why Marcel Darius seems like he's all over Cam Newton, and the sweeps and reverses aren't there. Not yet."

Cam defies Alabama's plans and runs up the middle for 6 yards on first down.

On second down, Cam gives to Onterio McCalebb running right. This time, the blocking is there, and McCalebb gains 16 yards before finally being forced out of bounds at the Auburn 39. Kodi Burns helps by getting a great block on the Tide defensive back out wide. Mark Barron, the injured Alabama safety, is the defender who gets McCalebb out of bounds, and you can tell that his arm is still bothering him. He can't wrap the back up and instead just sort of slings him over the sideline.

Michael Dyer tries to find an opening on the left side of the formation on first down, but there's nothing there and he's stopped after only a yard gain.

The second down short pass to fullback Eric Smith is broken up by two Alabama defenders.

Auburn is 3 of 8 on third down so far today. They're about to be 3 of 9. Cam drops back and suddenly pressure is all over him. He retreats deeper into Auburn's end of the field and avoids Marcel Darius, then lets it go downfield. Darvin Adams nearly brings the pass in at the Alabama 45, but the ball goes off his hands and falls incomplete. Fourth down.

Ryan Shoemaker punts the ball to Alabama. Marquis Mays fair catches it at the Tide's 24.

On first down for Alabama, McElroy fakes the handoff to Ingram, then settles into the pocket and looks, and looks, and looks downfield. He takes too long. The Auburn defense, led by Michael Goggans, closes in on him and sacks him for a 1-yard loss.

On second down, Julio Jones catches a wide screen pass at the right sideline and through sheer ability fights his way to the 28. Now it's third and 7.

McElroy drops back and throws a deep pass to nobody. He has to let it go quickly because the Auburn defense is again converging on him, and he takes a hard shot to the chest from linebacker Josh Bynes just as he lets the ball go.

Just as Auburn's pass rush took a slow but inevitable toll on the Clemson quarterback, grinding him down to a nub before overtime arrived, they're doing the same thing to McElroy.

A penalty flag signals an illegal man downfield for Alabama, but Auburn declines it. Alabama has to punt. This is Auburn's first three-and-out of the game.

The Tide's punter barely gets the kick away, and Carr makes another fair catch, this time at the Auburn 25.

Van Allen Plexico

First Auburn couldn't stop Alabama, then Alabama gave up two long touchdown passes to Auburn. Now the game has settled into a sort of stalemate.

Newton begins this series by faking a handoff to McCalebb, who is running left to right across the formation in a sweep action. Cam surges forward on the quarterback counter draw for 9 yards, looking more like his usual self now.

On second and 1, McCalebb this time motions from right to left. Cam takes the snap and again fakes the handoff to him, but then steps back and tosses the ball to him anyway. The speedy back catches it at the 38 and runs down the left sideline to the 49.

Van Allen Plexico

I love this play. I believe we ran it several times in the second half. Earlier, when Cam would try to run wide or would give the ball to one of the backs on a sweep action, the Alabama defensive ends would be right there to blow it up. The wrinkle the offense adds here, which works to perfection, is to have Cam fake the handoff on the sweep. When the defensive ends see that Cam still has the ball, they let the running back go, and close in on the quarterback—only for Cam to then throw it (sometimes over their heads!) to the back, who's now wide open.

Newton rushes for 3 yards on first down, crossing midfield. Gus Malzahn is going crazy, signaling to the offense to hurry up and run the next play before Alabama can get set or adjust.

From the Alabama 48, Newton hands the ball to McCalebb, who flips it to Terrell Zachery on the reverse. Alabama swallows him up before he can get more than a couple of yards downfield.

But Alabama is flagged for another substitution violation. So now we know what Gus was shouting about, and why he wanted the ball snapped so quickly. The penalty moves the ball to the Alabama 43, making it second down and 2.

McCalebb takes the handoff from Newton and dashes to the outside. Now the Auburn run game is finding space to operate. McCalebb gets loose. He carries the ball to the Alabama 32 and notches another first down.

If it worked once, maybe it will work again! Cam hands the ball to McCalebb, who again runs around left end, and suddenly the vaunted Alabama run defense that disrupted everything the Tigers attempted in the first half is nowhere to be found. McCalebb is off to the races, making it all the way to the 13 yard line before being knocked out of bounds.

> *"Gus Malzahn has seen something. That's twice in a row they've done that. McCalebb was able to cut it up inside and get another first down. Auburn's in the red zone for the first time tonight."*
> *—Stan White, Auburn Network*

CBS informs us in a graphic that McCalebb is averaging 8.8 yards per carry this season, which is the best in the entire NCAA.

Van Allen Plexico

Onterrio McCalebb was such a great weapon when he could operate in space. From 2009-2011, he piled up yards and dominated at yards per attempt. Then, in his senior year, new offensive coordinator Scot Loeffler tried to make him into a "feature" tailback, running him up the middle and into the teeth of the defensive front, and it didn't really work at all. McCalebb needed to operate within schemes that gave him room to get free and use that raw speed and elusiveness. Gus Malzahn was very good at creating such conditions for him. Scot Loeffler was not.

Newton runs a quarterback draw and, with some good blocking ahead of him, makes his way to the 8 yard line on first down. Cam is grinning when he gets up. He looks confident that he knows how this drive is going to end. Meanwhile, Gary Danielsen points out that Auburn ran that play with only ten men on the field.

With Mario Fannin and Eric Smith now in the backfield, Newton rolls to the right and finds a wide-open Fannin at the Alabama 5. Fannin catches it, turns upfield and picks his way to the 1 yard line. First and goal.

Van Allen Plexico

Mario Fannin makes a nice play here, to put the Tigers in scoring position. I'd like to take that opportunity to say a couple of nice things about him.

He'd played extensively even as a freshman in 2007, providing some much-needed punch to that final Al Borges-coordinated offense. In fact, he got more carries (84) and gained more yards (448) that season than in his subsequent three years of playing for the Tigers. And he was almost as good of a receiver as he was a running back, gaining nearly 1,000 yards through the air, over the course of his college career.

Somewhere along the way, though, he injured his shoulder. He was never quite the same afterward. If a defender hit him the wrong way, there was a fair chance he'd lose control of the football and fumble it.

Consequently, John and I always used to hold our collective breath and chew our fingernails when he would catch or carry the ball. That was because you never knew what was going to happen next. He could make a great play, or he could turn the ball over.

It was great to see him actively contributing to this team as a senior, even with the other excellent backs on the roster.

Auburn has driven down to just outside the Alabama goal line. Everyone in Bryant-Denny Stadium knows what is going to happen on the next play. It is all too predictable, yet absolutely unstoppable.

Cam takes the snap in the shotgun, fakes to Fannin running to the left, and simply bulldozes his way into the end zone, blasting Alabama defenders out of the way as he goes.

The kick is good, and Auburn somehow has pulled within 3 points of the Tide. A game that looked on its way to being a humiliating blowout has turned into something entirely different.

Auburn 21, Alabama 24

Two interesting milestones accompany that touchdown. It is the first rushing touchdown allowed by the Alabama defense in Bryant-Denny all season long, and it is Cam Newton's 18th rushing touchdown, breaking the single-season record previously held by Bo Jackson and Cadillac Williams.

Quentin Riggins points out that Auburn, on that series, used an unbalanced offensive line with senior offensive tackle Lee Ziemba on the same side of the formation as Alabama's star linebacker CJ Moseley. Clearly, it was effective.

CBS displays a graphic showing that Cam Newton has, thus far in the season, rushed 221 times for 1,310 yards, for a 5.9 yard average, with 18 touchdowns. They compare that with Bo Jackson's 1985 statistics, in which he rushed 278 times for 1,786 yards, with a 6.4 yard average and 17 touchdowns. They point out that Bo won the Heisman that season.

Those numbers are indeed compelling, and on their strength alone, Cam should be in the Heisman conversation. What they fail to note, though, is that Cam is the quarterback, not a running back. When he's not rushing for all those yards and touchdowns, he's passing for even more.

The stadium is still packed and rowdy despite Auburn's comeback. The clock shows 4:25 remaining in the third quarter. Clearly the Alabama fans expect their team to get back into the groove it was in earlier.

Wes Byrum sends a low, line-drive kickoff down the middle of the field, right between the two Alabama returners. Neither reacts, each apparently waiting for the other to move, and the ball skitters through the end zone for a touchback. The Tide will start play at their own 20 yard line—a drastic improvement for Auburn from the previous kickoff that resulted in Alabama starting at their 40.

Alabama comes out in the pure I-formation for the first time today. McElroy gives it to Richardson, who is stood up and driven back by a host of defenders in white.

McElroy takes the second down snap from the shotgun and throws downfield. Julio Jones has no play on the ball as two Auburn defenders arrive at the same instant as the ball, which is nearly intercepted. Josh Bynes lays a lick on Jones, causing him to exhibit what Stan White calls "alligator arms."

CBS informs us that while Alabama dominated total yardage in the first half, 379-87, the script has completely flipped after halftime. For the second half, it shows Auburn with 161 yards to Alabama's 15.

Facing third down and 9, Trent Richardson catches a short screen pass in the right flat and can't find any running room at all. After circling around for a few steps, he's swarmed over by half the Auburn defense. In three plays, Alabama has gained at most 3 yards. They have to punt again.

Now all of the momentum is solidly on Auburn's side, and the Tigers trail by just 3 points.

Both of those things are about to change on the next play.

Quindarius Carr does not call for a fair catch. The punt drops into his arms at the Auburn 35, but an Alabama defender is already bearing down on him. Carr manages to evade that man, but no sooner does he start upfield again than a second Tide player smashes into him, head on. Carr is knocked backwards, the ball tumbling from his grasp before he hits the turf. T'Sharvan Bell makes a valiant attempt to recover the fumble but Alabama has him outnumbered and they pile on top of the ball. Courtney Upshaw recovers it for the Tide at the Auburn 27. It is the first turnover of the game.

Van Allen Plexico

This is exactly what I was talking about earlier. It is a potentially game-changing play. Auburn had fought back to within 3 points, the defense had stuffed the Tide for a three-and-out, everything is going Auburn's way—and then this one mistake by Carr undoes all the good the defense accomplished and breathes new life into Alabama.

If Carr had just gotten out of the way and let the ball hit the ground, the Tigers might have had to start a little deeper, but they would have possession of the ball!

Grinning Alabama fans high-five one another in the stands.

"There's no excuse for it. That's all that can be said. Quindarius Carr took a lick. He's fair caught them—he fair caught the last one that was a bomb that he shouldn't have fair caught—but that one he should have fair caught. (A defender) was bearing down on him. He got away from the first would-be tackler and took a nasty lick, but you know what? There's no excuse for it. You cannot have turnovers on the special teams, period. Auburn was right back in the game, poised to take the lead, and then a turnover."
—Stan White, Auburn Network broadcast

With a fresh set of downs, Alabama puts McElroy in the shotgun again and he passes to his left to Julio Jones, who is knocked out of bounds by Thorpe at the Auburn 13.

On the next play, Jones makes another catch just inside the Auburn ten and is tackled at the 7.

Now it's second down and 5, and Alabama pulls the backup right guard, Anthony Steen, who has been playing in place of the injured starter, Barrett Jones. In his place comes tackle Alfred McCullough.

McElroy throws to Jones again inside the 5, but Neiko Thorpe manages to knock the ball away.

Van Allen Plexico
Neiko Thorpe was never one of my favorite players. He seemed to get burned a lot in coverage. But give him credit here. There's no question he plays the game of his life in this Iron Bowl. He's all over the place, making plays.

On third and 5 at the 7, McElroy passes the ball into the end zone only for Demond Washington to knock it away. But flags are thrown all over the field. At first it looks like just pass interference on Washington, but the referee announces that, before the ball was snapped, Alabama committed a false start. That means the play was dead from the beginning, so the interference never actually happened. Unfortunately, that also means it's not fourth down. Alabama is backed up five yards but gets another shot, this time from the 12. They can make a first down without scoring, if they reach the 2.

CBS points out that Alabama has committed 6 red-zone turnovers this season, the most of any team in the SEC. Two of those have come in this game.

Third down and 10: McElroy has an eternity to throw as he scrambles to the left side of the formation, pursued by Antoine Carter, but he can't find anyone open. Finally Eltoro Freeman comes up and puts a lick on him, knocking him out of bounds back at the 15. Now it really is fourth down.

McElroy continues to get pounded.

Alabama settles for a 32-yard field goal by Jeremy Shelley that just sneaks inside the left upright with 1:05 remaining in the third quarter.

Rod and Stan continue to talk about how much of a victory that series was for the Auburn defense, holding Alabama to just 3 points when the fumbled punt had seemed to give all of the momentum right back to them. It's the third time in the game that Alabama has been held without a touchdown while inside Auburn's 10 yard line.

Washington takes the kickoff at the 5 and brings it out to the Auburn 33.

> *"Auburn has done exactly what they wanted to do, Rod. With less than a minute to go in the third quarter, they've cut this lead from 24-nothing down to a 6-point lead. They're right where they want to be with the ball on the 33 yard line."*
> *—Stan White, Auburn Network broadcast*

CBS notes that Nick Fairley now has 4 tackles, 2 sacks and 1 forced fumble.

Cam takes the snap on first down, fakes the handoff to McCalebb on the left-to-right motion sweep, and dances his way ahead for 4 yards.

243

Van Allen Plexico

It looks at this point as if the coaches have decided that McCalebb gives them a better option at running back in this particular game than Michael Dyer or Mario Fannin. He's been in a lot over the last few series. The Alabama defense has to respect his speed, which opens things up a bit for Cam when he runs straight ahead.

Malzahn motions frantically for the offense to hurry up.

Now Auburn runs the inverse of the previous play. Cam fakes the handoff to McCalebb, takes a step forward, then tosses it out to McCalebb in the flat. This is the second or third time they've run it, and it's giving Alabama fits. They are struggling to decide whether to chase the running back away from the formation or close in on Newton in the center. Cam is working it like an option run attack, reading what the defense does and then choosing to keep it or throw it to McCalebb. The quick back runs to the Auburn 46 for a first down before being knocked out of bounds by cornerback Dre Kirkpatrick.

Now the Tigers do send in Michael Dyer, who pounds the ball up the middle for 3 yards. With that, the third quarter comes to an end. Auburn has outscored Alabama 14-3 since halftime, and are right back in the game. But Alabama still clings to the lead.

Auburn 21, Alabama 27

- 21 -

THE FOURTH QUARTER: FIVE DELAY

Auburn starts off the final frame of the game with a reverse play that is all Gus Malzahn.

It's third down and 3 at the Alabama 47. Auburn does a quick or "sugar" huddle, then Newton lines up in the shotgun with fullback Eric Smith to his immediate left and two receivers just beyond him. The receiver farthest away from Newton is so deep in the slot, he's actually standing a step behind the quarterback. Newton fakes the handoff to Smith running right, then gives it to McCalebb, who is suddenly running the sweep behind Smith. Meanwhile the deep receiver fakes catching a pass on the opposite side of the formation. Rod Bramblett refers to it as a "Statue of Liberty," meaning the quarterback stands still while trying to deceive the defense.

It doesn't yield tremendous returns. McCalebb runs for just over 3 yards before being brought down by multiple Alabama defenders who weren't fooled.

Van Allen Plexico

This is prime Gus. This is what I both love and hate about him, sometimes. You can just see him drawing this up with salt and pepper shakers at Waffle House, and it probably looked good there. Like it would spring McCalebb for thirty yards down the sideline. But these overly complex plays of his rarely work for more than a couple of yards, because they take a long time to develop and have a lot of moving parts. And sometimes, having a lot of moving parts slows down the offense even more than it does the defense.

With the not-quite-4 yards gained from all that effort, the Tigers find themselves facing third down and 3 at the Alabama 47. Auburn is just 3 of 9 on third downs on the day.

Auburn lines up with McCalebb to Newton's immediate left and a slot receiver back deep again beyond him. This time, upon taking the snap, Cam fakes to McCalebb moving right, then passes to Emory Blake, the slot receiver, on a quick screen. No fewer than four Alabama defenders meet him at the line of scrimmage and bring him down for no gain.

Gus Malzahn's screen-pass schemes on this drive have not worked. Auburn faces fourth down and 3.

Malzahn and Chizik confer briefly, then Auburn calls a timeout to consider whether or not to go for it.

During the timeout, Chizik and the assistants huddle up to discuss their options.

Coming out of the timeout, Auburn lines up in the shotgun with McCalebb standing to Newton's right and two receivers on either side of the formation—two out wide and two in the slot. Cam starts to motion for the snap, then pauses and most of the Auburn players look to the sideline. Upon receiving new instructions, presumably after Gus has taken a look at the defense, the entire offense shifts. The slot receivers—one of them is Philip Lutzenkirchen, the tight end—move in closer to the ball, curving around in what looks like a punt-protect formation. McCalebb steps forward and joins them in the blocking scheme. The outer two receivers remain where they were. Now alone in the backfield, Newton appears to be preparing to punt.

"It looks like they're gonna pooch kick it," Bramblett observes. "This could be a short punt," guesses Verne Lundquist, on the CBS broadcast.

ALL THEY DID WAS WIN

Alabama's defense hurries to react and adjust to the sudden change in formation. Tide players move this way and that, pointing and shouting at one another. They end up with eight defenders crowding the line of scrimmage while two remain covering the wideouts and one is deep at safety position in the center of the field.

> *"The Tigers had run (this) package on fourth-and-short several times that season. If the defense played tight on the receivers, coaches would signal for Newton to punt the ball. With no return man, Auburn could pin its opponent deep in its own territory. But if the defense showed a softer look, coaches would tell Newton to try to find a receiver at the first-down marker.*
>
> *Just before the snap, several of Auburn's players motioned inside to show a look that screamed 'PUNT.' But when Newton looked to his left, he saw (Alabama defensive back Dee) Milliner playing four yards off receiver Darvin Adams. That's when Newton got the green light to throw."*
>
> —Andy Staples, the New York Times, 2020

On the snap, the four linemen and one safety charge forward but the three linebackers freeze, standing at the first down line. This has created an interesting situation: Auburn has eight players blocking five oncoming defenders, so Newton should have plenty of protection. The three linebackers are left standing there with nothing to do. And the two cornerbacks find themselves in single coverage on Auburn's two receivers—both of whom take off in mirror image down the sidelines opposite one another.

Cam drops back two steps, looks to his left, and fires a pass ahead and to the left sideline, in the direction of Darvin Adams.

Adams has run nine yards down the left side of the field and then cut sharply toward the boundary. The ball is there as he turns and looks back, and he makes the catch just before going out of bounds. The Alabama defender flails helplessly at him but can do nothing. First down, Auburn. It's the play they tried to run against Georgia and failed to execute properly.

Van Allen Plexico

Gus definitely believes in his plays and, if they don't work once, he'll just run them again and figure they'll get it right this time. Regardless of how high the stakes are.

With regard to this play, I'm reminded of what Steve Spurrier said after the 1994 Auburn-Florida game in Gainesville. Auburn had faced a fourth down in Florida territory, late in the game, and Pat Nix made the completion for the first down to Thomas Bailey. Spurrier said he knew the game was over when the Tigers made that first down. This play had a similar feel, like Auburn was relentlessly marching toward the go-ahead touchdown. If Alabama couldn't stop them on that fourth down, how and when would they ever stop them?

On the Alabama sideline, Nick Saban looks increasingly uncomfortable. He's hunched up, arms crossed, jabbering into his headset microphone, while Kirby Smart shouts at the defense.

As soon as the first down is signaled by the referees, Malzahn immediately begins signaling for the offense to line up and run the next play. After a horrendous start to the game, Cam Newton is now 11-18 passing for 206 yards and 2 touchdowns. He's also run for a touchdown.

Now it's first and 10. Newton takes the snap, fakes the handoff to McCalebb, then uses him as a lead blocker as he cruises around right end and makes his way down to the 26 yard line, gaining 12 yards. What had previously been an airtight containment of the edges by the Alabama defense has become a leaky paper sack.

Michael Dyer substitutes in for McCalebb and Newton gives him the ball. He cuts to his right and then upfield. In the first half, plays like this were getting blown up in the backfield. Now they're breaking open for big Auburn gains. Dyer runs to the Alabama 13 before being pushed out of bounds. It's another first down.

Still in the hurry-up, Auburn is clicking on all cylinders, and the Crimson Tide seems to have no answer for it.

As soon as the ball is positioned at the 13, Newton calls for the snap again. He gives to Dyer, who plunges up the middle for 3 more yards, to the Alabama 10.

Still moving at ludicrous speed, Cam takes the snap and immediately throws it out wide to Emory Blake in the left flat.

There's not an Alabama defender within five yards of him, but by the time he gathers the ball in and crosses the line of scrimmage, they're converging on him. He fights his way to the 7 before being tackled by CJ Moseley. It's third down and 4.

CBS notes that Auburn made zero first downs in the first quarter but has 15 since then. Alabama made 11 in the first quarter but only 9 since then.

Cam calls out instructions as the players move into position for the next play. He appears utterly calm and collected—which is astonishing, given the situation on the field and on the scoreboard.

The clock reads 12:10 to go in the game. Auburn still trails by 6 points. The Tigers are now situated on the far left hashmark, with one receiver lined up on the far side, one on the short side, and one—Blake—in the slot, to Newton's left. Ontario McCalebb stands to Cam's right. Philip Lutzenkirchen is in at tight end, on the right end of the line.

> "After Chizik came to Auburn from Iowa State prior to the 2009 season, he asked Malzahn to add a red zone tight end throwback pass to the offense. Such plays — where most of the offense goes in one direction and the tight end floats in the other direction toward the end zone — had driven Chizik crazy as a defensive coordinator.
>
> "Malzahn added the play, which the Tigers called Five Delay. Each week, coaches would attach the pass to a different run look. That week, they had attached it to a quarterback sweep to the right. During games that season, Chizik would get on the headset and remind his offensive staff: 'Remember Five Delay, especially when this is a nut-cutter—especially when this game is on the line.' But the timing hadn't seemed right.
>
> "As the Tigers faced the goal line, Malzahn and company signaled in Five Delay."
>
> —Andy Staples, the New York Times, 2020

Center Ryan Pugh would later say the play rarely worked in practice. Gene Chizik believed it was because the defensive scout teams they'd run it against were not as overly aggressive as the defenses the team would face in real games on Saturdays.

Alabama may even suspect it is coming. According to Pugh, Hightower shouts to CJ Moseley to watch Lutzenkirchen once the ball is snapped, to make sure he isn't up to something. Moseley is a freshman, though. Perhaps that contributes to his not successfully keeping track of the tight end.

As Newton takes the snap, the slot receiver—Emory Blake—is in motion from left to right. He and the back—Mario Fannin—both run to the right side of the formation. Cam fakes the handoff to Blake on the sweep, even as Fannin blocks Alabama's blitzing linebacker, Courtney Upshaw, taking him completely out of the play.

Newton ducks down, as if he can somehow lower his six-foot, five-inch frame to the point that the defense can't see him anymore. That done, he starts to drop back and rolls slightly to his right.

As all of this is happening, the tight end, Lutzenkirchen, casually slips away from his blocking duties. Blake will move to pick up the block on his defender, but ends up not needing to. The tight end drifts diagonally across the formation and downfield, to a point just inside the 5 yard line. There he turns back and looks toward his quarterback.

The pass rush is converging on Newton deep in the backfield, surely believing they have him dead to rights. But the fact of the matter is, it's already too late for them. He gently lofts a pass back to his left and toward the end zone. The ball travels over their heads, against the grain of the entire play—and there is Lutzenkirchen, facing towards the quarterback, waiting for it.

Three Alabama defenders realize what is happening and race to try to stop the big tight end, but there's no way they can get there in time. Lutzy makes the easy catch, whirls around and strides into the end zone. In celebration, he executes what will later be described as a sort of deranged River Dance, his legs swinging wide left and right.

> *"I've been getting so much grief for that (celebration). It's just one of those things where I was so excited, I really didn't know what I was doing."*
> —Philip Lutzenkirchen, Auburn tight end

> *"Philip snuck out the backside, and there was born the Lutzy (dance). That's how it happened."*
> —Gene Chizik

ALL THEY DID WAS WIN

"Coach Malzahn was saying, 'They'll be playing this touchdown for your grandchildren someday and then... oh, wow, look at that.'"
—Lee Ziemba, Auburn offensive tackle

Auburn players and coaches celebrate. Alabama players on the field shout and exclaim at one another, clearly upset—in particular Hightower, who chews Moseley out for not blowing up the play he'd seen coming. On the Tide sideline, an exasperated Kirby Smart, the Alabama defensive coordinator, has both his hands and his eyebrows up, as if saying, "I have no idea how that happened!" Saban stands next to him, doing a slow burn. As Smart continues to try to defend what just happened, Saban turns and walks away.

Cam Newton looks up at the sky and smiles. Speaking in 2018, Newton said that, at that moment, the fog that had hung over Bryant-Denny all day vanished. "It was as if the whole sky had parted open. The sky was like an Auburn orange and blue. Honest to God."

- 22 -

THE FOURTH QUARTER: KEEP THE PRESSURE ON

Following the touchdown on Five Delay, Wes Byrum's extra point is good, and Auburn leads the game for the first time. That was Lutzenkirchen's twelfth catch of the year, and five have gone for touchdowns.

Auburn 28, Alabama 27

"It was 24-0. 24-0! And Auburn has outscored Alabama 28-3 since that point. A long time left in this, and Auburn has to keep the pressure on and on."
—Stan White, Auburn Network broadcast.

CBS presents a slide show of "Auburn's Close Calls This Season," showing the deciding plays against Mississippi State, Clemson, South Carolina, Kentucky and Arkansas. They add that Auburn is 3-0 this season when trailing by 10+ points.

Van Allen Plexico
They are also undefeated when *not* trailing by 10+ points.

Byrum kicks off and Julio Jones brings it out to the 32. One of Alabama's primary weapons, he injures himself slipping down on the grass during the return and does not come back out with the offense on this drive.

The Alabama crowd is behaving very differently than they have been the entire game before now. They're standing still, subdued, and quiet. They've just watched a 24-point lead evaporate before their eyes. With nearly twelve minutes remaining in the game, they're trailing for the first time. Perhaps they are wondering if their offense can get going again and bring them back. And perhaps they're wondering how much worse it can get for them.

CBS displays a chart of the last four Alabama drives. They've started at their own 40, 24, 20, and the Auburn 27. No drive lasted more than seven plays and none resulted in more than 12 yards gained. The first three ended in punts, and the fourth didn't result in a first down, either—it simply started so deep in Auburn territory, because of the Auburn fumble, that they were able to kick a field goal without making a first down.

McElroy lines up in the pistol formation with Richardson the single setback behind him. Richardson takes the handoff and manages to gain 7 yards, but they are 7 very tough yards.

On second down, the Tide sticks with the same formation and Richardson picks his way to the 42 for a first down.

On the next play, McElroy drops back to pass but is swarmed before he can find a receiver downfield. He scrambles forward, evades Nick Fairley—who momentarily grabs his ankle—and stumbles before tossing the ball ahead, shovel-pass style. As he does so, Eltoro Freeman delivers him a solid blow. Meanwhile Richardson catches the ball and trudges across the midfield stripe before he's brought down.

McElroy is slow to get up, and the tight end, Dial, has to help him. The Auburn pass rush has been getting to him all day long. Usually he's gotten rid of the ball just before being hit, but there's little question it's taking a physical toll on him. CBS informs us that he's been sacked four times, hurried twelve times and knocked down ten more times. He's looking more and more like the Clemson quarterback in the fourth quarter.

It's second down and 1, and Alabama continues to stick with the pistol formation. Auburn brings a linebacker forward in position to blitz and is crowding the line with five players. Richardson takes another handoff and runs to his right, trying to use his blockers to find a crease and get the first down. He comes up just short, as Eltoro Freeman and Josh Bynes lay the lumber to him.

Van Allen Plexico
Eltoro Freeman delivers some brutal hits in this game, especially to McElroy. I doubt Alabama's players were in a hurry to ever see him again afterward.

On third and inches, Alabama struggles to get lined up properly. Failing, they have to call their second time out of the half.

Nine minutes remain in the game as the Alabama offense borrows a page from Gus Malzahn's playbook and suddenly hurries up to the line. McElroy takes the snap and surges forward on the quarterback sneak for what looks like a first down. But there are flags on the play. The referee signals that Alabama committed an illegal shift before the snap. Not all the players were set when they snapped the ball. And this after burning their next-to-last time out to prepare for the play.

On the sideline, Nick Saban looks fit to be tied. On the field, McElroy is clearly furious.

Now it's third and 5, instead of third and inches. Operating under center, McElroy rolls out to his right and barely evades Nick Fairley's pressure before passing to Mays. The receiver is tackled immediately but stretches out, gaining the 5 yards they'd lost on the penalty back. Now there are inches to go again, but this time it's fourth down. The ball is on the Auburn 47, positioned on the right hashmark, just to the side of the big Alabama midfield logo. All it will take is a field goal to put the Crimson Tide back in front again, and they're getting close to kicking range.

CBS notes that both teams have been perfect on fourth down conversions, with Auburn 1 for 1 and Alabama 2 for 2.

Again the Tide offense hurries up to the line for a quick snap to McElroy, who is operating under center. Auburn's defense crowds the line, ready. McElroy takes the snap and tries to lunge forward, but he is instantly met by a host of Tigers defenders, pushing him back. Eltoro Freeman comes out of the pile with the ball, but the officials seem to think he grabbed it after the play was dead. The spot, as it has been all day long, is extremely generous toward the home team, giving them at least a yard they didn't earn, and Alabama has the first down.

Now at the Auburn 46 yard line, Alabama pitches the ball to Mark Ingram on the toss sweep to the left. At first it looks like he'll make some serious yardage, but he is quickly cut down by Demond Washington for a gain of only 4 yards.

On second and 6, the Tide goes back to the pistol formation, with a tight end on each end of the offensive line, and now with Ingram at tailback in place of Richardson. The big back takes the handoff and rumbles to the left side of the play for a gain of 12 yards and another first down. Stan White points out that Womack, the Alabama pulling guard, jumped before the snap but wasn't called for the penalty.

Alabama is on the Auburn 34, at the outer edge of field goal range. In the first half, it was the Tide's passing game that gave the Tigers fits. Now it appears their running game is coming to life.

Still in the pistol, Ingram takes the handoff and runs to the short side of the field again. What's been working is that they're running to the opposite side of the formation from where Nick Fairley is lined up, and handing the ball off from the Pistol very quickly, before Fairley can get into the backfield. They're pulling the tackle on the side of the field the action is moving toward, and having him step outside of the tight end on that side of the formation, providing an extra blocker wide.

But this time, as the tackle relocates to the left of the tight end, he totally misses his block. Auburn's defenders easily penetrate the line, meeting Ingram four yards behind the line of scrimmage. Eltoro Freeman harasses the running back for a moment but Ingram gets away—only to be met by Neiko Thorpe, who stands him up until Dee Ford arrives on the scene. Together they hustle him out of bounds for a loss of 3 yards.

Bramblett notes that it's second down and 13. (CBS claims it is second and 12, but that's not correct. It's not the first time their situational stat boxes have been wrong today.) McElroy is in the shotgun formation as the clock dips below six minutes remaining in the game. This drive is chewing up a lot of time, and keeping Auburn's defense on the field. Earlier it appeared that, even if the

Tide scored here, Auburn would have plenty of time to come back on offense and reclaim the lead. Now that supposition is being brought into question. Can Alabama essentially eat up the entire fourth quarter with this one drive, scoring too late for Auburn to have a chance to answer?

This titanic game is far from over, and Alabama is moving into scoring position.

- 23 -

THE FOURTH QUARTER: NEWTON'S LAW

Auburn dodges a bullet on second down.

McElroy throws deep downfield, aiming for Kevin Norwood, but Demond Washington comes over his back and knocks the ball away, incomplete. Norwood gestures to the referees for a flag for interference. That would put the ball on Auburn's 22, within easy range of a go-ahead field goal.

The rest of the Alabama players and fans clearly want a penalty called—"I was waiting for it," Bramblett interjects—but no flags fly. Stan White argues that the ball was not only behind Norwood but too high to be caught. It's third down and 13 from the Auburn 37.

Van Allen Plexico
We've come a long way from Bear Bryant eyeing the ref, and then that flag instantly flying.

CBS notes that Alabama has passed the ball 37 times so far in the game, while running it 29 times. It seems as if most of those runs have happened on this drive, which has gone on for an eternity.

Alabama barely gets the play off in time. McElroy rolls to his left, wanting to throw deep, looking, looking…

Van Allen Plexico
Alabama was having good success with their pistol-based run game for most of this drive. What killed them was the tackle of Ingram for a loss on first down. It put them behind the sticks. Instead of being able to line up and pound away with Ingram and Richardson, they've had to go back to McElroy surveying the field and throwing the ball, and that plays right into Auburn's hands. Now Nick Fairley and his associates have more of an opportunity to "tee off" and get to him. And that's what happens here.

Alabama is in the shotgun, spread out wide. Auburn puts seven players up tight on the line of scrimmage, showing blitz. Fairley is on the left side of the interior of the defensive line. Safety T'Sharvan Bell has replaced a linebacker and has moved up to Fairley's left, crowding the line. Antoine Carter is standing at the right end of the line. Pressure will be coming, and it will be coming hard and fast.

McElroy takes the snap and moves to his left, away from Fairley. But meanwhile T'Sharvan Bell looks like he's been shot out of a cannon. Because that side of the Alabama line has to respect Fairley's menacing presence opposite them, they don't react anywhere near fast enough to stop Bell. He has streaked past them and into the backfield before McElroy has taken his second step into the pocket. All the rest of the Alabama blockers are to the left of the quarterback, effectively removed from the play.

One lone Alabama player chases Bell and actually manages to dive at his feet, slowing him for an instant, as McElroy steps up and away from him. But then the quarterback makes the mistake of hesitating as he searches downfield for an open receiver. Meanwhile the Tide linemen are still engaged with the Auburn defenders and are clueless as to what is happening right behind them. The player who tried to block Bell is on the ground where he fell, also out of the play. It's just McElroy and Bell now, one on one.

McElroy, wanting to throw the ball, waits a split second too long, and Bell is upon him. The Auburn safety first latches onto the quarterback's arm to keep him from passing, then wraps both arms around his waist and swings around behind him, throwing all of his weight and momentum into the move.

McElroy keeps the ball cocked in his arm and keeps looking for a place to throw it, but it is far too late now. Bell has a firm hold of his arm. He couldn't throw the ball if a receiver were standing five yards in front of him. He's still in that passing posture when Bell smashes him head-first to the turf. As Bell jumps up and runs toward his teammates to celebrate, McElroy lies there in the fetal position, unmoving, the ball resting on the ground beside him.

> *"Here comes pressure. McElroy is going down! T'Sharvan Bell slams McElroy down at the 40, and McElroy is hurt."*
>
> *"Oh, that's his right shoulder, and I'll tell you what, being a quarterback, I know how he feels. Alabama separated my shoulder in 1992. He got slammed down pretty hard right on it."*
>
> *"Fifth sack of the day for this Auburn defense."*
>
> *—Rod Bramblett and Stan White, Auburn Network broadcast*

Trainers hover over McElroy for a couple of minutes before helping him off the field. He's clearly woozy and barely able to walk in a straight line. Stan notes that clearly it wasn't just a shoulder injury. "I'm not sure his bell didn't get rung." (By Bell!)

He's thrown for nearly 400 yards but has been sacked five times.

With 5:36 to go in the game, Alabama faces a fourth down and 16.

Sideline reporter Quentin Riggins raises the question of what Nick Saban's best option is now. "Do you bring your backup quarterback in, *a la* Pat Nix and Stan White?"

Van Allen Plexico

Riggins is referring to the 1993 Iron Bowl, and the play sometimes known as "Nix-to-Sanders I." White, the starting quarterback, was injured on third down, just on the Alabama side of the 50 yard line. Instead of punting or attempting a long field goal, Auburn head coach Terry Bowden sent backup Pat Nix in for the fourth down play—and Nix threw a touchdown strike to Frank Sanders.

(Nix-to-Sanders II was the winning touchdown pass the same two players pulled off at the end of the following season's

Auburn-Florida game in Gainesville, when the Gators were ranked number 1 in the country.)

Riggins points out that the only other option for the Tide is "to punt and play defense, knowing your defense has not stopped Auburn the last couple of drives. Tough decision for Nick Saban."

Alabama lines up in punt formation.

"Quendarius has already fumbled one today," Rod notes. "Maybe Alabama hopes that'll happen again."

The Tigers get a lucky break here. The Alabama punt travels 13 yards and goes out of bounds. Instead of having to begin the drive at their own goal line, Auburn will have it at their 27. Nick Saban tears off his headset and screams at the punter as he comes off the field.

On first down, Cam runs up the middle for a yard. The clock goes below five minutes remaining.

Newton stands alone in an empty backfield on second down, with two receivers to the right and one to the left. The Tigers show an unbalanced line with a tight end and receiver—Kodi Burns—positioned on the right end of the offensive line. Cam takes the snap and runs across the 30 before being brought down at the Auburn 32.

It's third and 5 for Auburn, with the clock ticking below four minutes to go. Rod notes that Auburn is only 4 for 11 on third down on the day.

Newton has McCalebb behind him at running back and Eric Smith to his right at fullback, just behind the tight end, Lutzenkirchen. Before the snap, McCalebb motions up next to Newton. Cam takes the snap and puts the ball in McCalebb's stomach as the back runs to the left. It's an option play, with the quarterback now having to read the defense—particularly the defensive end—and decide whether to let McCalebb go with it or pull it back and run it himself.

It looks like McCalebb would easily have the first down and maybe more, given his great speed, as he heads toward the sideline. But Newton has already pulled the ball back and now he surges upfield. He gets just enough of a block from Smith to dive across the first down line.

Except for one thing: The spot, as has happened every single time today, is incredibly unfavorable for Auburn. The Tigers are inches short.

Stan White is melting down over the terrible spot. But there's nothing to be done. It's fourth down, on their own end of the field. With the ball at the Tigers' 37 and the game—and the season—on the line, they're going for it.

Van Allen Plexico

By this point in the game, I wasn't concerned Cam wouldn't get the first down. I was concerned the referees would then step in, mark the spot a yard further back, and give the ball to Alabama.

Auburn does the quick huddle one more time, and then the Tigers come to the line with Newton in the shotgun. Three blockers are arrayed around him in the backfield. He takes the snap and simply dives over the entire offensive and defensive lines, rolling off of them and easily converting.

Ryan Pugh, Auburn's center, later told Jon Solomon of AL dot com that he was afraid he would pass out, waiting to snap the ball. Newton was trying to run the clock and delayed as long as he could before lifting his leg to signal for the snap. The wait was an excruciating twelve seconds. "As the blood rushed through Pugh's head," Solomon reported, "(Pugh) worried that the snap wouldn't come soon enough to avoid his keeling over and creating a fourth and 6."

"It's one of those small plays in a huge game most people don't even think about," Pugh told Solomon. He added that he spoke with Gus Malzahn after the game: "He said he was freaking out and it was the longest 20 seconds of his life. I told him, 'Hey, I was just worried I didn't pass out.' He joked (that) it's good to know we have our priorities in life."

With less than three minutes to go, Auburn has a first down.

Cam keeps it again on the next play but is dropped for a loss, back to the 36. He appears to hurt his knee on the play, and Auburn calls timeout with 2:35 remaining. Other than to take a knee at the end, he will not carry the ball again in this game.

It's second and 12 and Alabama is out of timeouts. Newton hands the ball to McCalebb, who races for the left sideline, where he is tackled after a gain of 3. Now the Tigers face a third down and 9 at their own 40.

In total yards this half, Auburn has 241, while Alabama has 67. What an incredible turnaround.

The Tigers run the play clock down to one second before calling their second timeout. Now the clock shows 1:47 to go. Between Alabama's long drive that resulted in nothing, and this Auburn possession, the fourth quarter has simply evaporated. The Auburn offense huddles up with Gus Malzahn as a still-serene Gene Chizik strolls along the sideline, the very picture of composure.

Quentin Riggins states that Auburn should run a bootleg or a counter with Cam, but by all means keep the ball on the ground and keep the clock running.

The Tigers lineup for this critical third down with another unbalanced line. The wide side of the field is to the right, and Auburn has Lutzenkirchen and Eric Smith there, giving them four blockers to the right of the center. McCalebb motions toward Newton just before the snap, and again Cam runs the read option. This time he lets the back have it, and McCalebb races to the outside. Two Alabama defenders fight through blocks to try to meet him at the line of scrimmage. He's fast, but so are the Tide players, and one of them corrals him for a 1-yard loss.

Ryan Shoemaker jogs out onto the field. Auburn will have to give the ball back to Alabama.

As the play clock runs down to 1 second, Chizik calls Auburn's final timeout.

Alabama is preparing to send in freshman backup quarterback AJ McCarron. CBS helpfully shows a moment from the Tide's game with Mississippi State on November 13, in which the young quarterback had done something to provoke Nick Saban's ire. Saban chews him up one side and down the other as the two walk along the sideline, and at one point the coach even smacks McCarron on the rear end—hard!

McCalebb, apparently hurt on the previous play, hobbles off the field. Between him and Cam being dinged, this game cannot end soon enough for Auburn.

The punt isn't great, but Marquis Mays lets it bounce once in front of him, then snatches it out of the air at the Alabama 19 before getting buried there by Auburn's coverage unit. There are 51 seconds to go.

ALL THEY DID WAS WIN

"It was effective. It wasn't pretty, but it was effective."
—Stan White, Auburn Network broadcast

On first down, McCarron is pressured by Nick Fairley and has to pass before he wants to. The ball goes off the hands of Julio Jones, who is being covered by Neiko Thorpe.

On second and 10, McCarron has plenty of time to throw, but his pass ends up in the hands of T'Sharvan Bell at the 47. Unfortunately for the Tigers, Bell drops the ball as he crashes to the ground. Receiver Kevin Norwood, suddenly finding himself the defensive back on the play, does his part to break it up, and it's incomplete.

Now it's third and 10, and only 39 seconds remain. Again McCarron has all day to throw, but his short pass to Norwood bounces off the receiver's chest and falls incomplete.

Van Allen Plexico

How different this Alabama passing game looks now, compared to the first half. Or is it the Auburn defense? Or a combination of both?

I'm still not sure.

Fourth down and 10 for Alabama, with 35 seconds to go. They're still at their own 19 yard line.

McCarron throws toward Julio Jones on the left sideline, but Neiko Thorpe breaks it up. Auburn takes over.

Van Allen Plexico

This is by far the best game I ever remember Neiko Thorpe having. He's covered well, he's made tackles, and he hasn't gotten burned. At least, not in the second half.

"Auburn is gonna win," shouts Rod Bramblett on the radio broadcast. "Auburn is gonna win!"

"That is your ballgame, folks," agrees Stan White. "One of the biggest comebacks in Iron Bowl history, in Auburn history. Twenty-four to nothing! And 28-27 is going to be your final score. This Auburn football team would not be denied. Came to Tuscaloosa, riding this train on to Atlanta next week, with a possible stop in Glendale, Arizona, my friend."

Down on the field, Cam Newton smiles that broad smile, brings his hand to his mouth, kisses it, and gazes up at the heavens momentarily. Then he takes the snap, takes a knee, and that's the game.

Auburn 28, Alabama 27

> *"There it is. For the eighth time in eleven years!"*
> *"And the Alabama players don't go out to shake hands. They run back to the locker room."*
> *"For the eighth time in eleven meetings, Auburn defeats Alabama. And today, inside the walls of Bryant's court, Newton's law reigns supreme. Tigers 28, Alabama 27. A 27-point deficit erased. And Auburn finishes the regular season twelve and oh, and they go to Atlanta to play for a chance to go to Glendale, Arizona. An unbelievable comeback."*
> —Rod Bramblett and Stan White, Auburn Network broadcast

CBS shows Cam's final stats: 13 for 20 passing for 216 yards; 3 passing TDs with no interceptions; 39 rushing yards and 1 rushing TD. In the post-game crowd, he hugs Marcel Dareus and other Alabama players, then pulls off his helmet and races to the stands, celebrating with the Auburn crowd.

"It doesn't get much better than that," gushed Kodi Burns afterward. "To be able to go to Alabama, to be down 24-0 against one of the better defensive teams that has ever played college football, was something special.

"You have to have a lot of different things that go your way, and it did that night. But at the same time we never gave up. We never stopped believing. We always knew that we could come back and really get it done."

Gene Chizik later sums up the remarkable nature of what Auburn had accomplished that season, in terms of coming back. "It was our eighth come-from-behind win of the season," he notes, "and the fourth time we had won after trailing by at least 10 points."

It is the third Iron Bowl in a row where one team led, 14-0. It is the second in a row in which the team that led by that score *lost* the game.

Van Allen Plexico

This Auburn team, in this game, demonstrated the ultimate level of resilience and belief in themselves. Nearly anyone else would've given up once the score became 24-0. But they never did. They kept fighting, kept scratching and clawing, and made huge play after huge play, over and over, until they finally took the lead, and then held it.

And that last part is bigger than people remember. After Auburn scored to take the lead at 28-27, nearly *twelve minutes* remained in the game. That had been enough time for Alabama to score three touchdowns in the first half.

Alabama had plenty of time to come back again, and they only needed a field goal to regain the lead. But Auburn's defense totally shut them down and out the rest of the game. If not for the dropped punt return, Alabama would've been shut out for the entire second half. What a turnaround.

The Auburn Tigers had come into Bryant-Denny Stadium at its most insanely hostile. They had gone toe to toe with Nick Saban and his whole slew of 4- and 5-star players all over the field and up and down the depth chart. They had dug themselves a massive hole, early on. And some way, somehow, they had won.

Scoring Summary

Q	Time	Team	Description	AUB	BAMA
1	11:34	BAMA	Mark Ingram 9 yard run (Shelley kick)	0	7
	8:39	BAMA	Julio Jones 68 yard pass from McElroy (Shelley kick)	0	14
	1:58	BAMA	Darius Hanks 12 pass from McElroy (Shelley kick)	0	21
2	8:01	BAMA	Jeremy Shelley 20 yard field goal	0	24
	5:08	AUB	Emory Blake 36 yard pass Newton (Byrum kick)	7	24
3	14:04	AUB	Terrell Zachery 70 yard pass Newton (Byrum kick)	14	24
	4:25	AUB	Cam Newton 1 yard run (Byrum kick)	21	24
	1:05	BAMA	Jeremy Shelley 32 yard field goal	21	27
4	11:55	AUB	P Lutzenkirchen 7 yard pass Newton (Byrum kick)	28	27

	AUB	BAMA
First Downs	17	23
Rush-Yds-TDs	41-108-1	30-69-1
Cmp-Att-Yd	13-20-216	27-41-377
TD-Int	3-0	2-0
Total Yards	324	446
Fumbles-Lost	2-1	2-2
Turnovers	1	2
Penalties-Yards	2-30	7-40

Alabama ran 10 more plays than Auburn did: 71 plays for Alabama to 61 plays for Auburn.

Alabama ran the ball 30 times and passed it 41 times.
Auburn ran the ball 41 times and passed it 20 times.

ALL THEY DID WAS WIN

Alabama had more penalties for more yards, and turned the ball over twice (the Ingram fumble and the McElroy sack and fumble), compared to once for Auburn (the dropped punt return).

Team Stats	AUB	BAMA
1st Downs	17	23
3rd down efficiency	4-13	4-13
4th down efficiency	2-2	2-3
Total Yards	324	446
Passing	242	400
Comp/Att	13/20	27/41
Yards per pass	10.8	9.2
Interceptions thrown	0	0
Rushing	108	69
Rushing Attempts	41	30
Yards per rush	2.6	2.3
Penalties	2-30	7-40
Turnovers	1	2
Fumbles lost	1	2
Interceptions thrown	0	0

Passing

Player	C/ATT	YDS	AVG	TD	INT	QBR
Newton	13/20	216	10.8	3	0	85.4
McElroy	27/37	377	10.2	2	0	76.5

None of the quarterbacks who played in the game threw an interception.

Newton ended up throwing for more touchdowns (3) than McElroy (2); something that did not seem likely in the first half.

Newton also ended up being the second-leading rusher in the game, despite gaining only 39 yards and going backwards much of the first half. Onterio McCalebb was the game's leading rusher, with 50 yards on 8 carries.

Auburn Rushing

Player	Att	Yds	Avg	TD
Cam Newton	22	39	1.8	1
Michael Dyer	9	27	3.0	0
Onterio McCalebb	8	50	6.3	0
Terrell Zachery	1	-5	-5.0	0

Alabama Rushing

Player	Att	Yds	Avg	TD
Mark Ingram	10	36	3.6	1
Trent Richardson	10	24	2.4	0
Greg McElroy	8	-10	-1.3	0
Julio Jones	1	12	12.0	0
Marquis Maze	1	7	7.0	0

Auburn Receiving

Player	Rec	Yds	Avg	TD
Emory Blake	3	39	13.0	1
Terrell Zachery	2	79	39.5	1
Kodi Burns	2	32	16.0	0
Darvin Adams	2	29	14.5	0
Onterio McCalebb	2	24	12.0	0
Philip Lutzenkirchen	1	7	7.0	1
Mario Fannin	1	6	6.0	0

Alabama Receiving

Player	Rec	Yds	Avg	TD
Julio Jones	10	199	19.9	1
Darius Hanks	5	39	7.8	1
Mark Ingram	4	91	22.8	0
Preston Dial	3	26	8.7	0
Trent Richardson	3	9	3.0	0
Marquis Maze	2	13	6.5	0

- 24 -

POSTGAME:
WE HUNG OUR HATS ON THAT

Auburn had won the Iron Bowl. The Tigers had completed a perfect regular season. They'd won the SEC West. They'd beaten Alabama in Tuscaloosa. And they'd managed the biggest come-from-behind win in Iron Bowl history.

The Tigers' defense had yielded a troubling 377 yards of passing to Greg McElroy and the Alabama offense, with Julio Jones alone accounting for 199 of that output. But they'd held Alabama's vaunted running backs to just 69 yards on 30 carries, for an average of barely 2 yards per carry. Once they had adjusted to the Tide's passing game and nullified it, Alabama was not going to score again—unless Auburn turned the ball over deep in their own territory. They did, just one time, and it was not enough to give Alabama the win.

The Auburn offense took forever to get going, but once it did—just before halftime—they were able to score exactly enough points to win the game.

Evan McCullers, the Auburn *Plainsman* Assistant Sports Editor, noted when looking back on the game from five years later that the Auburn players "celebrated in different ways. (Cam) Newton ran around the field with his hand over his mouth, having silenced anyone still critical of his on-the-field performance. Nosa Eguae ran to the stands, where he saw two Auburn fans who had been harassed for their fandom during the game. He thanked the fans for their support and hugged them. (Antoine) Carter tried to run the Auburn flag around the field, but the idea was shot down by the Auburn coaches."

Van Allen Plexico
It was never entirely clear to me what Cam was trying to convey when he put his hand over his mouth while he was running around celebrating after this game. My first thought was that he felt he'd been stifled and silenced by Auburn coaches or administrators in the days before the game—not allowed to speak to the media.

Meanwhile, the meaning and magnitude of this win was just beginning to sink in to the men in white uniforms on the field.

"As players, you realize what it means to the people of this state," observed Kodi Burns in 2015. "You realize what it means to the people who have played before you. It's bigger than me. It's bigger than Cam Newton. It's bigger than Bo Jackson. It's bigger than anyone that's played there. It's about the people who love Auburn. It's about the family and what winning that game means to those people."

Van Allen Plexico
When the game ended, all I remember feeling was an enormous sense of relief. Unlike most years, I wasn't thinking of that game purely as the Iron Bowl, on its own—as in, "Let's beat Alabama and win the Iron Bowl!" That year, they had a couple of losses already and were out of the running for any championships, while we were undefeated. Going in, I was thinking of this game as part of something bigger: another stepping stone on the path to the BCS championship.

But of course, it was still Alabama on the other side. So it was never going to be that simple.

When things went sour, almost immediately, I felt utterly sick. Disgusted, depressed, despondent. I always joke now that I was googling "Least painful ways to kill yourself," but that's not miles away from the truth!

By the end, when we'd taken the lead at last and held on to win, all I felt was relief. Not excitement, not joy, not running around screaming, like we all did at the end of a few other Iron Bowls I could mention. Just cold sweat, and relief. A sense that the universe was back on track. Our hopes and dreams still remained achievable. They hadn't been destroyed—and hadn't been ruined by the absolute worst bunch of people that could have ruined them.

Everything was still on the table for us.

In 2010, Gus Malzahn was still using the hurry-up, no-huddle scheme he'd been employing for years. The offense didn't substitute players in and out every play, so they could snap the ball as soon as the referee set it and blew the whistle. This meant the offense took much less time between plays, moved faster overall, and consequently ran more plays over the course of the game. Malzahn was convinced that the team that was able to run more plays in a game usually won.

Malzahn wanted his offense lined up and ready to snap the ball the instant the referee marked it ready for play. This meant he didn't substitute players on offense as often as most teams do. If the offense doesn't swap players in and out between plays, the defense isn't allowed to, either. Malzahn wanted to wear the defense out, get them confused, and catch them in bad matchups with his offensive players.

A downside to not subbing in new offensive players, however, was that he couldn't have one of those new players bring the play call to the quarterback when he subbed in. Malzahn needed another method—and a very fast one—to get the signals for the next play to the quarterback and the rest of the offense on the field. He therefore created a board with color-coded letters and numbers on the sideline, operated by one of the backup quarterbacks, in a process almost like flipping the digits on an old clock radio. The numbers were visible to anyone who cared to look, but you would have to know what each number and color meant, to take advantage of it. Auburn had used this system for all of 2009 and 2010, up through the Iron Bowl.

This raised a question: Could Alabama have figured out Auburn's offensive play-calling signals? Did the Tide defense know what was coming, before the ball was snapped?

It seemed one possible explanation for the struggles the Tigers had faced on offense in the first half. Auburn had rushed for -10 yards through the second quarter before vastly improving to 118 yards in the second half. CBS analyst Gary Danielson noted early in the game, "It seems like they're in the huddle half the time."

Receiver Terrell Zachery later said Auburn did make a few changes at halftime. "Teams were reading our signals all year. So we just made adjustments in the second half. We had more than one play for each signal. That was routine."

When asked about it years later, graduate assistant Rhett Lashlee replied that he was sure Alabama had figured out a few of the calls, and Auburn did make some changes because of that, "but we didn't overhaul like crazy. I never felt they knew everything and that's why we were struggling (early in the game). They had a good plan and just executed."

Asked the same question, Auburn center Ryan Pugh responded, "There are a lot of stories from that game that haven't been publicized. I could be the one to break the silence, but I don't want to yet."

Said college football analyst Andy Staples, "Whatever the truth, Alabama's defense played (in the first half) like it knew the plays."

Alabama linebacker Dont'a Hightower had a different explanation for why the two halves were so different. "It felt like (after halftime) we stopped keying on the things that we were able to and we feel like we beat ourselves."

Just as dramatically as the Auburn offense corrected itself at halftime, the Tigers' defense came to life in the second half after sleepwalking through the first. Said Gene Chizik, "We blew coverages (to start the game). We played the absolute worst defensive half of football known to man, and I felt very fortunate that we were only down three scores."

By all rights, Alabama should have won the game. Not just because they so outplayed Auburn early in the game, but because of the disparity in the levels of talent between the two rosters. Certainly college football writer and podcaster Andy Staples felt that way, when writing about the game a decade later:

> "Looking back, this game feels like a mismatch even though Auburn had future Heisman Trophy winner and NFL MVP Newton running the offense and future first-rounder Nick Fairley on the other side of the ball. Besides Newton, Auburn's other offensive starters combined for exactly one career NFL start. Meanwhile, ten Alabama contributors from that game... were all still playing meaningful NFL snaps (ten years later)."
> —Andy Staples, 2020

As for Nick Saban, he looked back on the game a few months later with his customary level of snark and sarcasm:

> "Since things went bad, I think it was a horrible job of coaching, if you want to know the truth about it. It's just like everything else. When it goes good—the same guy coached the first half as the second half. So whatever happened in the first half, I guess we all did great. Whatever happened in the second half, we really did bad."
> —Nick Saban, to Jon Solomon, 2011

> "After you come back from 24 points (down) and you're able to pretty much shut down an offense like Alabama's—which was prolific, which had three first-rounders—we hung our hats on that. We worked so hard. Guys would start being accountable. So when you made a mistake, you watched film, you learned from your mistake and you didn't make the mistake again.
> "Going into the SEC championship, we were able to go out there and play good defense. Going into the BCS championship, we were able to go out there and play good defense. It goes back to the Alabama game."
> —Nosa Eguae, Auburn defensive end, 2011

In an article in the *Montgomery Advertiser* in 2020, Josh Vitale talks about some of the superstition-based things Auburn fans did during the game to try to affect the outcome. He mentions one of the

Tiger Hosts who, after the third Alabama touchdown, fled to a restroom stall inside Bryant-Denny Stadium and prayed.

> *"So many Auburn fans have a similar story from that day. Some shed their coats despite the cold and rain in order to display their lucky shirt or jersey more prominently during the second half. Those watching at home switched seats or even rooms in order to change the mojo. Nearly every one of those Auburn fans will tell you that what they did played some part in that miracle."*
> —Josh Vitale, Montgomery Advertiser, 2020

Van Allen Plexico

I tell this story every semester in one of the college courses I teach, when we talk about the concept of superstition. I tell them that I've never considered myself superstitious at all.

But!

In the spirit of truthfulness, I then add that I'd worn my navy blue Dameyune Craig number 16 Auburn jersey over a white t-shirt every week of the season in 2010—and consequently, we were undefeated after eleven games, and headed for the national championship. And then I made the terrible mistake of going with an orange undershirt for the Iron Bowl, under the misguided notion that it would somehow help the team. *Of course* it didn't help—it broke up what had been working all those weeks! It's so obvious in hindsight! And so, after Alabama scored to go up 24-0, I raced into the bedroom, tore off that orange t-shirt, put on a white one, and put the jersey back on over it. And *of course* Auburn then proceeded to win the game.

I always say, "Cam Newton deserves at least half the credit for the win. But clearly *I* deserve the other half, for changing shirts."

Against seven tough SEC opponents, the Auburn offense had scored the following:

Opponent:	Auburn scored:
South Carolina	35
Kentucky	37
Arkansas	65

ALL THEY DID WAS WIN

LSU	24
Ole Miss	51
Georgia	49
Alabama	28

That's a total of 289 points in just seven conference games.

It's over 41 points per game.

That is an absolutely astonishing number, and one that deserves to be remembered forever.

And in their next game, they'd outdo all of those totals but one.

- 25 -

FREAKISH AS USUAL

"There's no vindication in my world. That's not how I live."
—Gene Chizik

Following their Iron Bowl win, the Auburn Tigers jumped back ahead of Oregon to reclaim the number 1 spot in the BCS rankings. The Ducks had held that spot for the previous four weeks.

Auburn had a week to prepare for the SEC Championship Game. It would be a rematch with Steve Spurrier's South Carolina, a team that had somehow emerged as the best of a bad group. At 5-3 in the SEC, South Carolina was the only nationally-ranked Eastern Division team, and the only one with a winning conference record—as hard as that is to imagine. Meanwhile, in the Western Division, only one team—Ole Miss—was unranked and had a losing record. This was truly a season of domination by the Western side of the conference.

Van Allen Plexico

The SEC West was so much better than the East that season. Without the conference divisions, Auburn would've had to play the team with the second-best conference record overall, and that would've meant a rematch with Arkansas. They and LSU both finished the regular season at 6-2 in the SEC—both better than South Carolina's 5-3—but Arkansas beat LSU head-to-head in their final game of the season.

I remembered that crazy Arkansas game back in October all too well. Let's just say I was very glad to be having a second helping of chicken rather than pork in the Georgia Dome.

Coach Chizik felt good about their opponents as well. "We were confident about the rematch," he wrote in his book, *All In*. "We had gone back and studied film of the previous game enough times to see that we could have won by two or three touchdowns if we hadn't made so many mistakes. We reevaluated everything we'd done in that game and came up with our best expectations for what South Carolina would try to do against us."

Despite the distractions, the Tigers were remarkably focused on the task before them. Linebacker Josh Bynes noted, "The only thing we have to do is take care of what we're supposed to do this week. We know what's going to happen after that. In order to get there, we have to play that one game. If we take this opponent lightly or we play that kind of game where we give them the SEC championship, then we won't get there."

Safety Zac Etheridge was asked why Auburn's defense was playing so much better in the second half of games. Opponents converted only 23 percent of third downs in the fourth quarter and overtime, with scoring 40 percent lower in the second half as well.

> *"All the coaches talk about finishing. That's something we didn't do last year. Obviously this year we have been focused on finishing games. Once we get a feel for what teams are doing, what their game plan is, we play a lot faster and we just finish the game."*
> —Zac Etheridge, Auburn safety

Van Allen Plexico

It was fortunate for the defense that Auburn had Cam Newton and all those other weapons on offense. They could afford to go down multiple touchdowns in the first half of games and still come back and win after the defense finally did "get a feel" for the other team.

ALL THEY DID WAS WIN

On Monday, quarterback Cam Newton and offensive lineman Lee Ziemba were named to the AFCA Coaches' All-America Team. Auburn was one of only four teams with multiple players on the 25-man team. They were the first Auburn players to make the team since offensive lineman Ben Grubbs in 2006.

Also on Monday, the University of Alabama announced it had fired the part-time employee who had played "Son of a Preacher Man" and "Take the Money and Run" during Auburn's warmups in Bryant-Denny Stadium the previous Friday. A university spokeswoman said any songs and videos played in the stadium had to be approved by the athletic department, and the unnamed staffer had not cleared those songs.

Van Allen Plexico
You'll note Alabama fired the anonymous staffer for violating the rule about playing anything without pre-clearance, but they didn't mention anything by way of an apology to Cam or to Auburn, or that it was just wrong regardless of the rules about getting pre-approval.

The next day, reports surfaced in the *Tuscaloosa News* that a full-time employee had played a central role in the playing of the music after all. Justin Brandt, director of Crimson Tide Productions, declined comment when asked by reporters if he had approved the playing of the songs and was shifting blame to a part-timer. An investigation by Alabama was said to be ongoing.

Also on Tuesday, Chizik was asked by a reporter if being "12-0 and two wins away from a national championship provides a measure of vindication" after the negative reactions by some in the Auburn community to his hiring. Chizik replied, "There's no vindication in my world. That's not how I live. That's not what's important to me. What's important to me is that, as the head coach of Auburn, I give our football team and fans a chance to win every week, and we do the best job as coaches that we can. It says something."

Steve Spurrier was asked about how his team, by winning the Championship Game, might "ruin the league's chance to win a fifth straight national title." His response: "Oh, we don't worry about that.

We worry about South Carolina, our state, our team. And we're trying to win our first conference championship."

Unfortunately, after a couple of weeks of mostly silence on the "pay-for-play" allegations, the NCAA began the week by dropping the other shoe.

On Monday, November 29, the NCAA notified Auburn that they had determined Cecil Newton, Cam's father, along with Kenny Rogers, had approached Mississippi State with a monetary request in return for Cam's commitment.

The NCAA identified Rogers as "an owner of a (player) scouting service," and determined he was acting as an agent for Cam—something impermissible under NCAA rules of eligibility.

> *"On Monday the NCAA ruled that a violation of amateurism rules had occurred. Schools are required to declare ineligible any player found out of compliance with NCAA rules, so we followed proper procedures and declared Cameron ineligible. However, we immediately filed an appeal with the NCAA."*
> —Gene Chizik, All In

Auburn had no choice but to immediately declare Cam ineligible to play in the SEC Championship Game. If the allegations were true, Cam's college football career was over—probably along with Auburn's chances of winning the national championship.

Van Allen Plexico

It was like, "Oh, no—not this again." It seemed even worse than what we'd been hearing and going through prior to the Georgia game. No sooner do we seemingly settle the issue and refocus our attention on football than here comes the "Cam Newton violations" talk again.

Looking back on that time now, Will Collier explains why Auburn officials and coaches never seemed particularly panicked, despite nearly everyone else freaking out:

> "The same night the story broke on ESPN... every single person I'd ever met (was) texting or emailing me with some variation on 'WTF?' when I heard from a friend in Auburn.
>
> "The gist was, 'This is not a new story. We've known about it since early in the year. It's not an Auburn story. It's a Mississippi State story. We did our due diligence at the time Cam was signed, and we have been completely transparent to both the SEC and NCAA. It's not going to be a problem.'
>
> "I would try to explain that to people who were panicking, with little success. It wasn't concrete enough to write about professionally, but I'd gotten enough of the background to be reasonably confident that Auburn wasn't about to go the way of SMU.
>
> "The Thursday night before the Georgia game... the NCAA investigators were in the Auburn athletic department interviewing Cam and his parents, prior to making a final determination on his eligibility.
>
> "Shortly after those interviews, I heard from a friend inside the AD: 'We're fine. He's eligible. No violations. Everybody needs to chill out.'
>
> "Again, this was not something that I could report on as a piece of journalism, or even in an opinion column, without breaking a confidence. The best I could do was tell people, 'Auburn is fine. Cam is fine. Stop driving yourself crazy over this and get your game face back on.'
>
> "And, in the end, that turned out to be that."
>
> —Will Collier, 2025

No one in the Auburn athletic department or administration believed their university had done anything wrong in regard to Cam's recruitment. And they weren't going down without a fight.

On Tuesday the university appealed the ruling, laying out their arguments for why he should be ruled eligible.

Van Allen Plexico

From Tuesday night until Wednesday afternoon, we all waited, holding our breath. Could Barrett Trotter quarterback the Tigers to a win in Atlanta? If he did, could he beat Oregon in the BCS title game? Did we really want to find out the hard way?

And after all the amazing, miraculous escapes Cam had pulled off on the field that season, could he pull off one more great escape—this time from the clutches of the NCAA?

It turned out he could.

On Wednesday afternoon, the NCAA accepted Auburn's arguments and reinstated Newton's eligibility. Investigators found that Cecil Newton and Kenny Rogers "worked together to actively market the student-athlete as part of a pay-for-play scenario," but concluded that Cam was not aware of the scheme and had not participated in it. He couldn't lose his eligibility over something he had nothing to do with. He was in the clear.

A joint Auburn-NCAA document released as part of a Freedom of Information Act filing in 2011 stated that, "Despite numerous media reports suggesting Newton himself has engaged in wrongdoing, the facts clearly demonstrate Newton has done nothing wrong."

Auburn went on to say, "There is no information suggesting that Rogers had similar discussions about a cash inducement with any other institution (besides Mississippi State), either directly or indirectly." The document also stated that Auburn "had no contact with Rogers while recruiting Newton and was in no way involved with offering or considering an offer of any recruiting inducement."

Van Allen Plexico

It's worth noting that Cam was cleared because the NCAA decided he wasn't aware of what his father and Rogers were up to, with regard to demanding money from Mississippi State—but at no point did the NCAA implicate *Auburn* at all. There was never any insinuation that Auburn University or its representatives paid or even offered the Newtons anything beyond a scholarship. If that had ever been alleged, it would have been stated publicly as part of this ruling.

> *"Based on the information available to the reinstatement staff at this time, we do not have sufficient evidence that Cam Newton was aware of this activity, which led to his reinstatement. From a student-athlete reinstatement*

> *perspective, Auburn University met its obligation under NCAA bylaw 14.11.1. Under this threshold, the student-athlete has not participated while ineligible."*
> —*Kevin Lennon, NCAA vice-president*

Van Allen Plexico
That last sentence was huge, as well. If Cam had been found in violation of the rules, Auburn would've had to play without him in the final two games of the season, *and* they might have had to give up every previous win in 2010. In other words, forfeit the entire season.

> *"The conduct of Cam Newton's father and Rogers is unacceptable and has no place in the SEC or in intercollegiate athletics. The actions taken by Auburn University and Mississippi State University make it clear this behavior will not be tolerated in the SEC."*
> —*Mike Slive, SEC Commissioner*

Van Allen Plexico
Slive actually tossed out a compliment to Auburn—and to Mississippi State, somehow—over how both schools had handled the situation. Their "actions" in response to the allegations "make it clear this behavior will not be tolerated in the SEC."

How anyone could compliment Mississippi State over their handling of the issue is beyond me. They colluded with somebody—maybe Cecil Newton, maybe not; I think the jury is still out on that, to be honest—and when they didn't get Cam, they tried to turn him in and hurt Auburn as collateral damage in the process. If anybody had ended up with a "lack of institutional control" penalty resulting from this mess, I think it should've been them!

> *"After a solid month of accusations, innuendo, and media feeding frenzy, the final result was... nothing. No change. Minus a period of a few hours between Monday and Wednesday, Newton was and remains an eligible player at Auburn.*

> "The NCAA also affirmed that Newton had been eligible for Auburn's prior 12 games in 2010, putting the oft-speculated possibility of forfeits and/or vacations of those games, all victories, off the table.
>
> "In other words, all is the same as it ever was. Auburn remains undefeated, Newton remains the starting quarterback, and a month's worth of non-stop 'reporting' accomplished nothing other than driving up the ratings for the Auburn-Georgia game.
>
> "Kind of makes you wonder what all the fuss was about, doesn't it?"
> —Will Collier, columnist, AuburnSports dot com

The situation now settled, the Auburn players and coaches were more than ready to turn their attention to the SEC Championship Game. "I'm glad to get that all behind us," Chizik told the media, "because we're focused on one thing, and that's winning the game in Atlanta."

On the Friday before the game, the *Montgomery Advertiser* reported that "the NCAA's decision to affirm Cam Newton's eligibility wasn't popular on a national scale."

To this, Collier in his column noted, "Nobody at Auburn was asked for anything in return for Newton's signature, and nobody provided anything for it. On the basis of that, Auburn ought to be punished… why? Because that would make you feel better?"

Clearly the head of the NCAA was concerned with this public perception. He issued a statement:

> "We recognize that many people are outraged at the notion that a parent or anyone else could 'shop around' a student-athlete and there would possibly not be repercussions. I'm committed to further clarifying and strengthening our recruiting and amateurism rules so they promote appropriate behavior by students, parents, coaches and third parties. We will work aggressively with our members to amend our bylaws so that this type of behavior is not a part of intercollegiate athletics."
> —Mark Emmert, NCAA president

ALL THEY DID WAS WIN

Van Allen Plexico

First, just think about what Emmert is saying here. He's arguing that people are "outraged" that Cam and Auburn suffered no "repercussions"—for something the NCAA admitted neither of them actually did!

Second, yes, the decision was definitely not popular around the country and on the radio and TV talk shows. As if that should matter in a case of rules and facts rather than opinions and hot air.

Nearly everyone had bought into the "where there's smoke, there's fire" argument. I remember, at the time this was happening, defending Cam constantly. I was arguing with my friends from around the country who all had strong opinions about him—almost all of them negative. Nearly all of them believed he was guilty and was getting away with some crime.

I asked them, "What if I called up your favorite school's athletic department, represented myself to be the father or agent of a star player they are recruiting, and asked for money? Should that player now be disqualified, just because someone claimed to be his representative and asked for money without his knowledge?"

None of them had any real reply to that.

"We're glad that the NCAA was in agreement with us that Auburn University and Cameron Newton have done nothing wrong. Cameron will be our starting quarterback (against South Carolina) as he has been the previous twelve weeks. I think that's pretty self-explanatory and will answer most of the questions you may have had.

"Cam has been a tremendous leader for our football team, and I think our football team sees that. He's just an unbelievable competitor."

—Gene Chizik, on the Friday before the SEC Championship Game

Steve Spurrier was his usual quotable self during that same Friday press conference. A reporter pointed out that South Carolina had won its last three games. Spurrier replied, "We've played pretty well lately. We're on a three-game winning streak. I thought that was pretty good until I noticed Auburn is on a 12-game winning streak."

When asked about the scandal surrounding Newton, Spurrier said, "We haven't paid any attention to it. He's played all year, and it wouldn't be right for him not to play when the championship is on the line. I remember Joe Paterno saying one time, 'You want to beat the other team when all their best players are playing.' "

He added, "I'm glad he's playing. He deserves to play. We haven't even thought of the other stuff."

He was then asked if Newton should win the Heisman Trophy.

"I think I've already said that Cam Newton will get one of my votes. We get three. I think he deserves the Heisman, no question."

Van Allen Plexico

It's amazing to me how much more I liked Steve Spurrier when he was at South Carolina, than I did when he was at Florida.

Auburn had more success against his Gators teams than most did. Even so, the whole "folksy humor" bit didn't go down quite as well when he was beating everyone else's brains in.

At South Carolina, it seemed like he got humbled a little bit. And that was good for him. It certainly made him more likeable, as far as I was concerned.

Finally Saturday arrived, and it was time for Auburn to state its case for an SEC title and a spot in the BCS National Championship Game.

In even-numbered years, the SEC East team enjoys home field designation in the SEC Championship Game. That meant that, in a reversal of their earlier game that season, Auburn would be wearing all white, while the Gamecocks wore their garnet home jerseys with white helmets.

In the Georgia Dome locker room before kickoff, Chizik exhorted the troops: "Your heart's gonna be pounding, you're gonna be pumping, I want to see a locked-in in your eyes right now. Because I truly believe this today, man. I truly believe this. I truly believe that today's gonna be our finest game." He pointed to one player after another, calling them out by name, saying, "This is ours. This is ours." Then, before leading them out of the locker room and into the tunnel, he added, "No one's taking this from us. We've got sixty minutes... Let's go."

"If we win this next one," said Ted Roof, the defensive coordinator, "we're getting a ring, man. We're champions of the Southeastern Conference."

"Going into the (second) South Carolina game, I felt very confident," added Chizik, "because we'd played them earlier in the year and I felt we'd left a lot on the table."

Zac Etheridge, the safety, agreed. "Going into that game, we were very confident that Round Two (with South Carolina) was going to be nothing like Round 1. When we took the field, from the first snap, from the first series, it was all about dominance."

Auburn came out strong against the Gamecocks, scoring their first touchdown in only four plays, covering a minute and forty seconds. The key play was a 62-yard pass from Newton to Darvin Adams, setting up a short toss to McCalebb for the score.

South Carolina struck back with a touchdown of their own, as quarterback Stephen Garcia hit Patrick DiMarco for a 25-yard touchdown.

Earlier in the season, this would mark the point where Auburn's offense went into a lull, while the defense gave up two or three more scores, resulting in perhaps a 24-7 deficit by the second quarter. That was very much what happened against Clemson, Georgia, Alabama, and even against this South Carolina team, back in September.

But something had changed about this Auburn team, ever since the first half of the Iron Bowl. This time, they did not lie down and allow the Gamecocks to strike for multiple unanswered scores. Instead, the Tigers marched right back down the field and scored again.

It seemed as if the offense suspected or feared the defense might give up a lot of points in the first half, as they'd done all year—so they decided to put the game out of reach first. Newton and Dyer ran the ball on most of the plays of this drive, and Cam carried it into the end zone from 5 yards out. Now Auburn led, 14-7 with 5:31 to go in the first quarter.

After a Gamecocks punt, the Tigers rang up their third TD of the quarter, moving 76 yards in 4 plays and consuming less than a minute of game time. Darvin Adams caught a 54-yard pass from Newton for the score. Now it was 21-7 Auburn.

The game became muddled for a time in the second quarter, with turnovers on both sides. Eventually, South Carolina scored to bring themselves within one touchdown, at 21-14.

The Tigers got the ball back with seconds remaining before halftime and one last chance to score. Operating near midfield as the clock expired, Cam rolled out and flung a Hail Mary into the endzone, where it appeared half the rosters of both teams stood waiting. Somehow the ball deflected off the first one or two defenders to touch it, and into the hands of (who else but) Darvin Adams, who caught it for a touchdown.

"You could feel the air sucked out of the stadium," observed Ryan Pugh, Auburn's center, "and you could feel the air sucked out of their sideline."

> *"I don't think I've ever been around a Hail Mary that worked. The chances of those working are slim-to-none. Be it luck or not, call it what you want, somehow or another, miraculously, we came down with it. And we went into the locker room with incredible momentum."*
> *—Gene Chizik*

> *"No, I didn't draw it up like that, but it worked out the way we wanted it to. In a big game, you have to make plays and that's a big play in a big game and it helped us loosen up a little bit to come out in the third quarter and put the game away. The pressure was off of us a little bit then."*
> *—Gus Malzahn, Auburn offensive coordinator*

"I just knew in my mind, nobody's gonna beat us," said Kodi Burns, looking back later. "Everything's going our way. We beat Alabama from down 24-0. We just got a Hail Mary right before halftime of the SEC Championship Game. I just knew at that point, we were destined. We were going to win the whole thing."

At the half, Auburn led South Carolina, 28-14. The game had felt about as close and contested as their first matchup, back in

ALL THEY DID WAS WIN

September. But the last-second score from Newton to Adams changed the game, more than most observers realized in the moment.

In the third quarter, Auburn removed any semblance of doubt about how the game would play out. The Tigers scored two touchdowns, and the one that put Auburn up, 35-14, came on a 1-yard plunge by Cam. It was his 20th rushing touchdown of the season and would be his final one on the ground as an Auburn Tiger.

The Tigers added another touchdown in the fourth, to extend the lead to 49-14. South Carolina finally ended their scoring drought with a field goal to make it 49-17. But then the Tigers struck again, this time under the direction of reserve quarterback Barrett Trotter, who led the backups down the field for a Mario Fannin score. This would be Auburn's last rushing touchdown of the season.

> *"At no point did I think I'd be standing on the sideline of the SEC Championship game, knowing (we were) going to the national championship game. Just seven days earlier, at the start of the Alabama game, and over the course of eight quarters, you go from, 'Well, boys—we'd better enjoy this one (because we're losing to Alabama and not going to the BCS),' to a week later, standing on the sideline saying, 'We're going to the national championship game.'"*
>
> *—Ryan Pugh, Auburn center*

Moments later, the game was over and Auburn had won a massive, crushing victory over Steve Spurrier's Gamecocks, 56-17.

Rod Bramblett summed it up thusly: "Your Auburn Tigers, for the seventh time in school history, are SEC Champions. And Auburn now has a date in the desert."

Not only were the Auburn Tigers the SEC Champions, they were the number 1 team in the BCS rankings, and they were going to play Oregon in the BCS national championship game in Glendale, Arizona on January 10.

"It wasn't going to be like 2004," said Chizik, "when we went undefeated and didn't get a chance to play for the national championship. I knew if we won this one, we'd get a chance to play for it all."

Van Allen Plexico
I like that Chizik was also part of that 2004 team.

Playing for the national championship would be big for any coach, sure.

But Gene Chizik *knew*—deep in his bones, he *knew*—what it had felt like for Auburn to be left out of the BCS national championship game that year. And he understood just how important, and how huge, it was for Auburn to finally get there in 2010.

This was Auburn's best, most complete game of the season, where everything clicked. Even the luck mostly went the way of the Tigers, with Darvin Adams making that miracle catch in the end zone on the final play of the first half. Cam Newton, meanwhile, impressed even the former Auburn quarterback doing the radio commentary: "What a performance," declared Stan White. "It's one for the ages."

Ryan Pugh, meanwhile, enjoyed the fact that a frantic comeback was not required, for once. "That was the only game that season where we sat back in the fourth quarter, knowing we were going to win the game."

> "I couldn't be more proud of our football team, and our fans deserve this. The Auburn Family deserves it. Our football team has been probably one of the most resilient groups of young men I've seen in 25 years of doing this. Everything they got tonight they deserved.
>
> They worked extremely hard over the last four months to be able to get to this point. It's a team that, as I've said before, they're brothers and they have a lot of love in that locker room between them. I think that's one of the huge reasons we're sitting where we're at.
>
> As I told them before the game, I felt like this was going to be our finest hour tonight. I felt like we were going to play great. They were prepared. They were focused. They were locked in. And I think they played like it."
> —Gene Chizik

Tight end Philip Lutzenkirchen agreed: "We have a lot of heart. It's the first game we have played four full quarters and that's good going into Glendale. Cam Newton was freakish as usual. Him and Darvin are both freaks."

"It was our best-played game of the season," Chizik later said, "and perhaps Cameron's, too. He accounted for six touchdowns, four passing and two rushing, in a performance that once again had me marveling at his ability to block out the distractions that had been swirling around him for a full month now."

Newton was named the game's MVP. He completed 17 of 28 passes for 335 yards and 4 touchdowns. He also ran 14 times for 73 yards and 2 more touchdowns.

South Carolina's coach, Steve Spurrier, was impressed by what he saw, particularly from the Auburn offense. Four years later, the "Old Ball Coach" would look back at this game and say of the Tigers' offensive coordinator, "Gus Malzahn is one of the best coaches in the country, not just the SEC. I think everybody knows that. They don't win that (2010) national championship unless he was there. I think everybody knows that, too."

> "Auburn folks have waited twenty years to really lay the wood to Spurrier in a meaningful game... Old Visor Boy wrecked a lot of Auburn seasons in his Florida heyday, and while the Tigers were able to return the favor a few times, they never did so with an old-fashioned butt-kicking until Saturday. For everybody who lived through 1990 and 1996 and 2000, this one was particularly sweet."
>
> —Will Collier, AuburnSports dot com

Van Allen Plexico

It seems like every other game Auburn ever won over a Steve Spurrier-coached team was super-close and won at the very last second. There are a couple of exceptions, maybe, but the general rule—even noted by Spurrier himself once—was that when his teams won, they crushed us, and when Auburn beat his teams, it was on some miracle play at the end.

So—as much as I like the Old Ball Coach—it was great to finally beat the stuffing out of him!

Auburn finished the season with the top scoring offense in the SEC, at 42.7 points per game, the best rushing offense, at 287.2 yards per game, and the best total offense, at 497.7 yards per game. They led the SEC in pass efficiency (174 of 261 passes with just 6 interceptions, for a 66.7% completion rate, and 29 touchdowns), third-down conversions (77 of 145, 53.1%) and first downs (316 overall, for an average of 24.3 per game).

> *"I think a lot of people thought Auburn should have played for the national championship six years ago. This is just poetic. And to think the state of Alabama could have two national championships, two Heisman trophy winners, and the biggest rivals of any colleges in the country, in back-to-back years? It's just historic. And, like this team at the end of the half, they are just not going to be denied."*
> —Terry Ingram, longtime Auburn fan, quoted in the Montgomery Advertiser

By the end of the season, all but one team from the SEC West would be represented not just in the top 25 rankings, but in the top 15. The tigers had played, and beaten, every one of them.

In the east, only division winner South Carolina was ranked, and Auburn had beaten them twice.

- 26 -

TWO LETTERS

On Saturday, December 11, 2010, at the Best Buy Theater in Times Square, Cam Newton was awarded the Heisman Trophy. He became the third Auburn player to win the award, after Pat Sullivan (1971) and Bo Jackson (1985).

In any other circumstances, his victory would have been more than assured. It would have been a complete blowout. There is no question he was the best player in college football that season. He should have run rampant to victory, the way he'd run over, around and through the LSU defense on that October day when it had first become apparent to anyone watching that he was the clear favorite and the only real choice. Given the rumors and innuendo swirling around him, however, some small doubt remained as to whether the Heisman voters would do the right thing and vote for him, or be influenced by unsubstantiated allegations and conjecture.

In the end, quite a few of the voters did buy into the "where there's smoke there's fire" idea. More than 100 of the 886 voters left him off their ballots entirely.

Fortunately, he was such a dominant player with an incredible body of work that plenty of others voted for him. And nearly all of those who did vote for him ranked him first.

"Obviously, like most people, I have my suspicions," said *Sports Illustrated* writer and Heisman voter Stewart Mandel, "but I don't think it's my position to pretend to know what is happening with the NCAA investigation."

Asked about the controversy before the Heisman ceremony, and about his father's enforced absence, Cam replied, "I'd be sitting up here lying to you if I didn't say it hurt. This is a once-in-a-lifetime experience. I love my father. He gave me words of encouragement before I came up here. I know he's with me in spirit."

Alone on the theater's front row, from left to right, sat Stanford quarterback Andrew Luck, Boise State's quarterback, Kellen Moore, Cam, and Oregon running back LaMichael James. Each had experienced a standout season of college football in 2010; each was a formidable opponent with a strong body of work and a solid argument for being a Heisman winner. In another year, any of them could have been the winner. But this was not any other year. This was the year of Cam Newton.

When the host called out, "The winner is: Cam Newton of Auburn University," Cam turned to his left, clasped hands with James, then stood and shook hands with Moore and Luck. His mother stood as she clapped, followed by Chizik and then the rest of the crowd. Cam went straight to her and wrapped her in a bear hug that seemed as if it might go on all night.

"When I reached my mother, I really didn't want to let go," he later explained. "It's been hard for me, but it's been extremely hard for her just to see how much her son has been through and I just wanted to hug her the whole night to make her feel at ease."

He embraced Chizik and a few members of the Newton family before finally climbing to the stage. There he was met by 1985 winner Bo Jackson, who gave him another big hug. Then he moved to the podium at last, where the host handed him the card that had announced him as the winner. "Keep this card," he told Cam. "You should keep it."

As Cam stood at the podium, Pat Sullivan, Auburn's 1971 winner, smiled from just behind his right shoulder. Three Auburn Heisman winners stood together in one room for the first time ever.

He started out thanking God and his mother and father, but became emotional and took a moment to compose himself. After a second someone in the audience shouted out, "We love you, Cam!" The audience burst into spontaneous applause. Cam laughed at that and the tension was broken.

He thanked his parents again, Coach Chizik, Auburn president Gogue, AD Jay Jacobs—and even the troops fighting overseas. He thanked Chizik again, along with coaches Malzahn, Luper and Taylor, as well as the Auburn Family. He finished up by thanking his teammates, whom he credited with his being there. And he ended his speech with those two magical words: "War Eagle." He was emotional and incredibly open and sincere.

Of course, that didn't stop those that preferred to disparage him from taking shots later.

Even Cam's touching remarks at the podium about his parents were dissected by critics. When he said, "I'd like to thank my beautiful mother and my father. My parents do a lot of things behind the scenes that go unnoticed," some at the ceremony snickered at the possible hidden meaning there—intended or not.

"Thank you for all you did for me," he added. "To my father, I love you so much."

Despite the fact that most in attendance likely would have preferred to pretend his father didn't exist, at least for that one evening, Cam was determined to make him a part of the proceedings. He never seemed to feel his father had done anything wrong. Years later, he would tell an interviewer that his father "fell on the grenade" to make sure Cam's eligibility wasn't taken away. Whether that meant Cam didn't believe his father had asked Mississippi State for money, or he just didn't think doing so was wrong, he did not say.

After the ceremony, Cam was asked if he was concerned that, like Reggie Bush after the 2004 season, he might eventually be forced to return the trophy. He replied, "Two letters for you, my friend. N-O."

He noted that, a year earlier, he'd been on an official visit to the Auburn campus, and now he was in Manhattan. "I went from visiting and seeing the best Auburn has, to a year later, seeing what New York has."

During the weekend in the Big Apple, he carried himself with nothing but class and distinction—something noted by his head coach, who was there as well.

> *"Those of us who were in New York with Cameron for the weekend were proud of how he conducted himself during the different functions. He was truly humbled by the honor and grateful to the people who had helped him along the way. Over the entire weekend of Heisman activities, I think he thanked everyone but himself."*
> —Gene Chizik, All In

Ninety-three percent of those who included him on their ballots at all listed him first. The voting finished with Newton at 2,263 points, more than double the total received by his nearest competitor, Stanford quarterback Andrew Luck (1079).

Writing for the *Athletic* a decade later, Justin Ferguson noted, "What makes Newton's Heisman-winning campaign even more impressive in hindsight is the (lack of pro) talent around him. None of the receivers he threw to or running backs he lined up with were drafted into the NFL. Only two of his linemen, Lee Ziemba and Brandon Mosley, were." (And together they played in only 28 games there.)

Ferguson added that the recent national champion closest to 2010 Auburn in winning despite a lack of top blue-chip players was 2016 Clemson, and even then, Deshaun Watson had no fewer than five NFL-drafted wide receivers catching his passes.

He concludes, "Depending on your perspective, the 2010 Auburn offense was either the greatest one-man show in modern college football history, a collection of top-notch role players surrounding a generational talent or something in-between."

Once the New York trip was over and Newton was back in Auburn, Chizik brought him back down to earth and tried to refocus him on the team's unfinished business. The coach told him, "Okay, you've won the Heisman… Your job now is to win the national championship with your team. So let's make sure we're on the same page with what your goal is." Cam replied, "Coach, I'm all in. We're going to win the national championship."

It would be the perfect, storybook ending to an incredible saga that nobody could have imagined mere months earlier—and that looked like it might yet get derailed mere weeks earlier.

But standing in the way of that last piece of the puzzle was Auburn's opponent in the BCS National Championship Game: the undefeated Oregon Ducks.

The third-place Heisman finisher, seated a couple of seats down from Cam that night in New York, was Oregon running back LaMichael James.

He and Cam would be meeting again, very soon, with another trophy on the line. The biggest trophy of all.

- 27 -

UNPRECEDENTED

Thirty-seven days.

That's how much time passed between the Tigers beating South Carolina in the Georgia Dome and lining up to face Oregon in the University of Phoenix Stadium in Glendale, Arizona.

"That was eleven more days than the time we have to practice in the spring," Chizik observed later. "And six more days than the time from the beginning of our preseason practice to our first game of the season."

The Auburn coaches had to decide what to do with those thirty-seven days. Would they use the time to work with the underclassmen? Or would they devote the entire time to preparing for Oregon? After discussing their choices, they opted for the latter—to go "all in" on the national championship.

But then they had to decide how exactly to do that. They didn't want to over-practice or under-practice.

Chizik decided to lay out a specific plan and stick to it: "We will never practice for more than an hour and a half," he told the team. "We'll meet, do a walk-through, we'll break, and then when we come back, you're going to practice for an hour and a half. That time is going to be focused and locked in. The pace will be fast and furious, and we're gonna be moving. Let's get our work done in an hour and a half, and then you're outta here."

Those thirty-seven days felt like an eternity. All the other bowl games played out across December and early January. All the other good teams, including some Auburn had defeated, played in their bowls.

Then, finally, it was Auburn's turn. And the country was ready for it.

Football fans all over America grew increasingly excited as the BCS National Championship Game drew closer. The matchup of Auburn and Oregon probably seemed odd and unorthodox to many at first. They were not exactly two teams who regularly challenged for the national title. But each team possessed a high-octane offense capable of scoring in the 40s and 50s in any given game. The possibility of a titanic offensive slugfest—a once-in-a-lifetime clash of scoring machines—captured the attention of fans everywhere. As Ryan Pugh put it, the game "was billed as a shootout between the two best offenses in college football history, meeting in one game."

Because of this, ticket prices on the secondary market skyrocketed.

Five days before the game, resale prices on StubHub had escalated from a starting point of $3,899 to $15,995 on the 50-yard line. On the Zigabid ticket site, tickets were going for an average of $5,000 each.

> *"Right now, it's unprecedented. It's absolutely the craziest scene we've ever seen. I mean, this is bigger than any Super Bowl we've seen in 20 years."*
> *—Dan Rubendall, founder of Zigabid ticket brokers*

"Right now this game is tracking as the top-selling event in the history of StubHub," said that company's spokesman, Glenn Lehrman. That price was up 40 percent from the previous year's BCS championship game between Alabama and Texas. "The average ticket price is currently at $1,107 per ticket." He confirmed that orders from the state of Alabama were outpacing orders from Oregon by a 2-1 margin.

Just days before the game, ticket brokers ran out of tickets to resell and actually began contacting their earlier customers, asking to buy back the tickets at a premium in order to sell them to someone else at an even bigger price.

Van Allen Plexico
They called me. The company I'd bought our two tickets from, back after the LSU game, wanted to pay me a bunch of money to buy my tickets back, to resell them. I'd paid right at $1500 for the pair—just over $500 each, plus another $500 in taxes and fees and so forth. They offered me so much more that I was tempted, though I can't remember now how much it was. I do know it was a lot. I told my wife I would feel bad not accepting such a big profit on selling them. Surely we needed the money and I should take the offer, I said. She just looked at me and replied, "If you sell those tickets, you will never forgive yourself." I thought about that for maybe two seconds, and then told the ticket brokers, "No thanks."

And I've never regretted it for a second.

Longtime AU Wishbone Podcast listener Lane Middleton confirmed that he experienced the same thing. "I had two tickets and (StubHub) offered me $5,000 plus my original purchase price to sell them back." He refused the offer.

The *Oregonian* newspaper, reporting on the ticket situation, speculated that demand was being fueled in part by the long wait since Auburn's last national championship and the fact that Oregon had never even played for one before. And in addition to that, "The venue for Monday night's game, 73,000-seat University of Phoenix Stadium in Glendale, Arizona, is much smaller than the host of the 2010 title game, the 92,000-seat Rose Bowl in Pasadena, Calif."

For the Alabama-Texas game the previous season, "ticket prices on Zigabid peaked at about $1,000, then declined to about $350, or just over the $300 and $325 face values."

Van Allen Plexico
Alabama-Texas tickets were just not in demand. And that despite the fact that Alabama fans were acting in 2009 as if this would be their only chance to see their team play for the national

championship. It's funny to think about that now, having just lived through the entirety of the Nick Saban Era in Tuscaloosa. But when Tide fans were talking about going to that Texas BCS game, they were literally calling it "a once-in-a-lifetime opportunity," and doing things like putting a second mortgage on their double-wide trailers.

The only thing better than that is thinking how many of them went ahead and bought tickets early to the 2010 BCS game, only to get Auburn instead of Alabama. At least most of them were able to sell those tickets for a good profit—so, you're welcome for our game being so huge and in demand that it drove up your profits, Alabama fans.

Though some still showed up, to root for Oregon. Because Auburn cannot play a sporting event anywhere, in any sport, without Alabama fans showing up in full regalia. It's the most inevitable thing in the world.

The tricky thing for Auburn fans had been making the early decision to buy BCS tickets in the first place. It required the faith that this team would be allowed to do what the 1983, 1993 and 2004 teams had all been denied the opportunity to do: play for the title on the field. Some Auburn fans, having been burned so many times in the past, were understandably reluctant to spend perhaps thousands of dollars on what could have turned out to be another bitter disappointment.

Others boldly took the leap.

And it was the win over LSU that convinced many that this could be the year.

Van Allen Plexico

As I said before, I wasn't expecting anything like an undefeated season and a run to the BCS title game this year. So we were several games into the season before the thought even crossed my mind. But when it did, I kind of panicked, wondering if I'd already waited too late and there wouldn't be any more available. And of course, if I had waited much longer, there wouldn't have been.

I'd had that epiphany and purchased our game tickets back after the LSU game, but I held off on buying plane tickets until we knew for sure Auburn was in. I figured I could always resell the BCS tickets, but I'd be stuck with airline tickets. And since we would be flying out of St Louis rather than Atlanta or Birmingham, I didn't anticipate difficulties in getting flight tickets at the last minute. There wouldn't be a lot of competition for seats to Phoenix from St Louis in January.

And, in fact, Alabama and Georgia had a winter storm that week and quite a few Auburn fans down there were unable to get a flight out. Meanwhile, up here in the frozen North, we had very little snow on the ground and no problems getting out of town at all. It was plenty cold, though, and I have to say it felt very good to land in Arizona and spend a few days in the desert!

There was one other obstacle for me to overcome before I could go to Glendale: The game would be played on January 10. That was just before my birthday, which was an extra bonus. But it was also the first day of what we at the college where I teach call "opening week," the super-important week of faculty meetings that no one is allowed to miss.

Sometime in between buying the game tickets and the plane tickets, I emailed my boss, the dean of our college, and told him Auburn could possibly be in the BCS national championship game, and I asked if I could miss the first two days of opening week to go, if that happened.

Like just about everyone who knows me for longer than ten minutes figures out, he knew what an Auburn sports fanatic I am. Bless him, he emailed me right back and said:

"Dear Van,

"If Auburn is in the national championship game, you have permission to go."

The Oregon Ducks posed unique challenges for any opponent. Head coach Chip Kelly's offensive style was not just "hurry-up, no-huddle," like Malzahn's Auburn offense. It was a quantum leap beyond even that—and it was helped by the fact that it was the *head coach's* system, meaning nobody was leaning on the Oregon OC to "slow down." Quite the contrary.

The Ducks were averaging 49 points per game while running tons of plays, lining up very quickly after the whistle and then getting the ball snapped almost immediately. By keeping their foot on the metaphorical gas pedal, they also made it very difficult for defenses to substitute fresh players in and tired players out. It was an approach that had exhausted the defenses of many of their opponents throughout the season. Over and over, players on the other team would be seen standing with their hands on their hips, gasping for breath, even as Oregon was snapping the ball for the next play. Stanford had even resorted to having players fake injuries and fall down on the turf, in order to get the referees to step in and stop Oregon from running their next play so quickly.

"They were playing at warp speed (that season)," noted Chizik. "(Their opponents') tongues were dragging. This was as explosive an offense as I'd seen. I felt like we could score points on offense. I didn't know if we were going to be able to stop them."

Countering this revolutionary offensive approach was a major challenge facing the Auburn coaches and players. They all had to be ready for it. They needed to be able to send in defensive substitutes and play signals quickly, and then get the players lined up properly before the snap. And they had to be able to do this at breakneck speed, over and over, when the opportunities arose.

During bowl practice, Auburn employed a variety of approaches that allowed them to prepare for Oregon's speed. Chizik instructed Malzahn to have the offense snap the ball and get a play off every twelve seconds, to accustom the Auburn defense to what the coaches expected to encounter in the game. Meanwhile, on the other side of the ball, DC Ted Roof was urging his players to show no mercy, taking advantage of the size and strength possessed by an SEC defense. "We wanted to make the game into a physical, physical battle," he later stated. "We wanted to make it into a bloodbath."

That size and strength advantage was something Chizik felt was not being talked about enough, headed into the game. He noted how the media were all fascinated with Oregon's offensive style, and in particular their tempo and speed. He told his players, "Here's what they're missing: This will be a physical fight. And that's where we're gonna beat 'em. We're gonna play SEC physical, downhill, 'hit them in the mouth' defense and offense. And that's where we're gonna win it. Once you get into the game, everything you've heard about their tempo and speed is gonna become a myth. We'll take the game over and we'll win it because we're gonna make it more physical."

Days before the BCS clash, the players from the two teams were taken to a game between the NBA's Lakers and Suns. When Oregon was introduced, the fans cheered. When Auburn was introduced, boos rained down. That was when the Tigers remembered they were in a PAC-10 state.

That didn't hold true, however, for the actual fans in the stadium on Monday evening. The game crowd was decisively pro-Auburn.

Van Allen Plexico
I hadn't thought of this before, but I wonder if more Oregon fans sold their tickets back to the brokers than Auburn fans did? And if those formerly Oregon—owned tickets then wound up in Auburn people's hands? It would make sense. As this book has argued, we were desperate for that championship. We'd waited so long. I'm sure Oregon figured this would just be the first of many visits for them over the next few years. I could be wrong, but I somehow doubt the game carried quite the same urgency for them as it did for us.

"When I walked out onto the University of Phoenix Stadium field for pregame warm-ups, I was blown away by all the fans wearing orange and blue. The stadium seated almost eighty thousand, and I'd say there were twice as many Auburn fans as Oregon fans. Each school had received an allotment of 17,000 tickets to sell, and each had sold all its tickets. The demand for tickets was so high that this was called one of the most difficult games to acquire tickets for in sports history."
—Gene Chizik, *All In*

Van Allen Plexico
I saw way more Auburn people than Oregon people the entire trip. There was maybe one Oregon fan on the flight with us out of St Louis. We went all over Phoenix that week and didn't see very many at all. Some Ducks fans were tailgating in the parking lot of

the stadium when we arrived before noon, and there were a few around us in the stands, but mostly it was Auburn people everywhere.

I have to note, when they saw us in Auburn gear, several of the Oregon fans tried to be clever and shout out the battle cry of that other institution over in Tuscaloosa. I've said this many times on our podcast: I just do not understand the mentality there. I wasn't going around yelling, "Beavers! Beavers!" (And honestly, I might have been arrested if I had!) Not to mention, we'd just beaten them. They weren't taunting us with the memory of a game we'd lost. So, what is the point of that? What does Alabama have to do with this? It remains a mystery to me.

Beginning with the Mississippi State game, Auburn players had developed a tradition after the team meal, the evening before a game. They would stand, link arms, and sing "Lean On Me." They did that again on Sunday night, 24 hours before the BCS title game.

> *"When we reflected on all the close games we'd played and all the comebacks we'd made and all the adversity we'd overcome to reach that point, we knew very well that this could be a once-in-a-lifetime opportunity."*
> —Gene Chizik, All In

Thousands of Auburn fans milled around outside the University of Phoenix Stadium all day on January 10. Tostitos was sponsoring the game, and so virtually everything in the area bore a "Tostitos" logo. Various Tostitos products were ubiquitous at the official tailgate party held next to the stadium.

Van Allen Plexico

We got there early and spent much of the day at the "official tailgate party" being put on by Tostitos. There really wasn't anything else to do, since the stadium is out in the middle of a big barren area with nothing around it but parking lots and desert. Tickets to the "party" were included with our game tickets. It turned out to be just a sea of Auburn fans mostly sitting on the grass, eating all these free Tostitos chips.

Later that day, a whole bunch of us—it must have been thousands of Auburn people—attempted to do a Tiger Walk when the team arrived, but it proved impossible. We weren't allowed to get very close to the part of the stadium where players entered, so we lined up on both sides of the road leading towards it. The Auburn team buses finally arrived—and they rolled right past us without even slowing down. Presumably the drivers were under orders to proceed directly into the stadium. You couldn't even see the players or coaches inside, because the windows were tinted jet black. They zoomed down the hill and disappeared into the stadium and that was that. We had waited over an hour for "Tiger Walk," and if you blinked you missed it.

Finally we were able to go inside the stadium, whereupon we discovered the tickets we'd bought way back in October turned out to be really, really good. We were fortunate to have a great view from about the 20 or 30 yard line, far enough up that we could see the whole field very well, but not in the nosebleed area.

Down on the field, the Auburn players were warming up. When that was done, Coach Chizik approached Cam Newton and Nick Fairley and told them he wanted them to be the team captains for the game. They considered this and replied that they thought he should choose senior players instead. "Coach," Cam said, "I don't feel comfortable doing that. I wish you'd find a senior because they deserve it. I don't." Fairley echoed Cam's sentiments. Chizik was impressed with both players and agreed with their request.

Before kickoff, Erin Andrews of ESPN asked Chip Kelly, the Oregon coach, what parts of his game plan he was most confident in. "We're confident in all of it," he stated. "That's why we're here."

Tom Rinaldi asked Gene Chizik, "What's the one thought you want these players to carry onto this field?"

"I want them to do what we do, Tom," he replied. "I want them to come out here and play just like we have the first thirteen games, we're gonna be fine."

Leading into the game, analyst Kirk Herbstreit told play-by-play man Brent Musberger that he suspected Oregon quarterback Darron Thomas would be "the X-factor" in the game. "I think Auburn is determined to take away the running of LaMichael James and those fleet-footed backs," he explained. "Thomas is going to have to run and throw to get this Oregon offense in synch."

Onterrio McCalebb summed up what many of Auburn's players and fans were thinking, pre-game: Oregon was just not ready for what the Tigers planned to hit them with. "They already knew we were coming from the SEC," he said, "and we were coming to hit them in the mouth. Our defense was coming to smash them."

- 28 -

THE BCS NATIONAL CHAMPIONSHIP GAME, PART 1: ANYBODY'S BALLGAME

Auburn's team ran onto the field just as the video screens finished the final showing for the season of the "All They Do is Win" hype video.

As the number 1-ranked team, the Tigers wore their traditional navy blue home jerseys, white pants and white helmets. Oregon, as the visitors, were expected to wear white jerseys. Known for rolling out a different uniform look for every game, however, it was a point of interest to see what the Nike-outfitted team would match with those tops, for their first-ever appearance in a national championship game. As it happened, the Ducks played it a bit more conservative than usual and toned things down. They omitted their more common (and more flashy) green and yellow elements entirely, and instead went with metallic gray helmets and pants. Their white jerseys featured gray feather patterns on the shoulders, along with optic yellow highlights around the numbers. They completed the ensemble with socks and wristbands of that same tennis-ball-color, along with a matching yellow "O" logo on the helmet.

Both teams wore a yellow and red "Tostitos BCS National Championship Game" patch on their jerseys.

One interesting note: While (as discussed earlier) Gus Malzahn signaled in plays to the Auburn offense using a clock-radio-like board with flip numbers and color codes, Oregon had created a system that used poster-board-sized signs that players would hold up on the sidelines. Each board was divided into four squares, with each square containing some kind of pop culture image, like a cartoon character, athlete, musician or movie star. They were effective in that offense because the players couldn't be affected by a loud stadium crowd while seeing the play call, and all it took was a glance at them for the key players to understand what to run.

Of course, to this day there is no agreement as to what any of the signs or images on the boards actually meant.

Van Allen Plexico

Beginning the next season, Gus Malzahn would move to the Oregon boards system of play-signaling. Clearly he, at least, understood the concept and saw the value in them.

I've always wondered whatever became of his old flip-card board thing. It ought to be in the Auburn museum, or at least the archives!

Oregon won the coin toss and opted to receive the ball to start the game.

Taking the opening kickoff, Oregon's returner slipped twice and barely recovered his balance before finally being brought down. On the same play, a freshman defensive back playing for Auburn's coverage team also slipped on the grass and was injured, stopping play for some time. You may have heard of him—he went on to figure into another very big Auburn win, three seasons later. His name was Chris Davis, of Kick Six fame.

Davis was barely touched by any Oregon players. He was injured when his legs went out from under him as he tried to change direction on the kickoff, and bent his knee the wrong way.

ESPN commentator Brent Musberger noted that the grass in the University of Phoenix Stadium seemed inordinately slick.

ALL THEY DID WAS WIN

Van Allen Plexico

I have to note that everyone seemed to think the grass surface of this field was extremely slippery. Players slipped down multiple times during the game, particularly when trying to change directions, as on kickoffs. That may have also contributed to the injury to Chris Davis.

The field at that stadium is unique: It's on a movable bed that is kept outside to be exposed to sunshine and the rare raindrop (there in the desert). But when game time arrives, they slide the entire field into the stadium, aboard that rolling bed. That way they can have a natural grass field inside an enclosed dome. For whatever reason that day, however, the grass was extremely slick.

Oregon and Auburn exchanged punts on their first drives. In this and succeeding Ducks possessions, the Auburn defense swarmed all over quarterback Darron Thomas and college football's leading rusher, LaMichael James, tackling them in the backfield as often as not. Meanwhile, on Auburn's first possession, Newton was sacked while dropping back to pass on third down, fumbling the ball. Fortunately for the Tigers, an offensive lineman was able to recover it.

On Oregon's second possession, Demond Washington intercepted a pass from Thomas at the Oregon 47 yard line.

Chizik later observed that his team's preparation for Oregon's speed had paid off. He noted that his defensive players "came off the field after that series saying the pace of the game seemed much slower than what they had been accustomed to in practice."

But then Newton threw a rare interception of his own, giving the ball right back to Oregon.

Just as he had in the first quarter of the Iron Bowl, Cam Newton appeared to be struggling a bit. He wasn't finding much running room on the ground, had thrown an interception on this drive, and had fumbled on the previous one.

The Ducks moved the ball down to Auburn's 20 before the turnover bug struck again. Nick Fairley came almost untouched up the middle and utterly destroyed Darron Thomas, but not before the quarterback could sling the ball downfield—right into the waiting arms of Zac Etheridge. It was Thomas's second interception of the first quarter, and marked three consecutive drives overall that were ended by interceptions.

Again Auburn failed to move the ball and punted. And just like that, the first quarter was over. In what everyone had predicted would be a high-scoring pinball machine of a game—an epic shootout for the ages—the score was 0-0.

Oregon's new option run game wasn't working at all, but little dink-and-dunk screen passes to their backs, Clemson-style, were finding more success. As the second quarter got underway, they were driving deep into Auburn territory and threatening to score.

Nick Fairley had something to say about that, however. He blew up a Ducks play at the Auburn 3 yard line, stopping what looked to be a sure touchdown. Oregon settled for a short field goal, and someone was on the scoreboard at last. Unfortunately, it was Oregon, who now led, 3-0.

Finally Auburn's offense came to life. The Tigers covered 82 yards in 8 plays, starting with some great runs by Michael Dyer and culminating with a 35-yard, over the middle, catch-and-run score by Kodi Burns. Now it was 7-3, Auburn.

Van Allen Plexico

How fitting was it that Kodi Burns should catch the first touchdown pass for Auburn in the national championship game? He also scored the first touchdown in the first game of the Chizik Era, at the start of the previous season. So he bookended the two-year run to the title.

After everything he'd gone through in his four seasons on the Plains, I love that he got to go out in style and in glory. And the *Sports Illustrated* cover photo from the game shows Kodi in the foreground, being lifted up in the end zone after this play.

Oregon came right back, and in dramatic fashion. Starting their next drive from their own 7, Thomas connected with receiver Jeff Maehl for 81 yards, down to the Tigers' 12 yard line. Three plays later, James caught a short pass and took it in for the score.

ALL THEY DID WAS WIN

Van Allen Plexico
Somehow it wouldn't have been a 2010 Auburn game without the defense giving up at least one long pass completion in the first half that led to a touchdown.

Oregon under Chip Kelly liked to go for 2 after scoring their first touchdown of a game. They did it here, successfully, with Rob Beard running it in for 2 points. The Ducks were back ahead, 11-7.

Van Allen Plexico
I liked Oregon's unorthodox approach to football, which included their idiosyncratic habit of going for 2 after their first touchdown. I suspect Chip Kelly believed it would be easier to score a 2-point conversion early in a game than later, perhaps with the win on the line. And there was a psychological component to it: "Our TD counted for more points than yours." This was another thing Gus Malzahn borrowed from Oregon going forward, and he attempted it several times after becoming the Auburn head coach in 2013.

It's also funny to note that, while Oregon had several good backs, we all enjoyed the fact that one of them was named Kenjon Barner. That's a nickname some use for Auburn fans, as in "AuBarn," and thus, "Barner." We were joking at the time that we must have a spy on their roster, and that it was probably very confusing to any Alabama fans who were watching and wanting Oregon to win. "I can't root for somebody called 'Barner'!"

Ultimately, Barner wasn't much of a factor in the game, for either team.

The Auburn offense didn't miss a beat. Newton completed a string of passes to Adams and Zachery, down to the Oregon 25. From there, the Tigers went to the run game, eventually ending up at the Ducks' 1 yard line and facing fourth and goal. Chizik and Malzahn decided to go for the touchdown. "We called a pass play that we hadn't run all season," Chizik explained later, "but that had been successful every time we ran it the year before." But that had been with Chris Todd at quarterback, not Cameron Newton. Cam attempted a short pass in the flat to H-back Eric Smith, but he shorted the throw and the ball fell incomplete. Oregon took over at their own 1.

Van Allen Plexico

The national championship is on the line, points are at a premium, we get to the opponent's 1 yard line, we have Cam Newton at quarterback—and we throw a pass?

I was in agony at that moment.

Clearly Cam wasn't feeling too great, either. He couldn't have been 100 percent healthy in this game. If he had been, deciding what play to call there would have been as obvious as sending Bo over the top against Alabama.

The offense had faltered, but it had left the ball right up against Oregon's goal line. It was time for the Auburn defensive front to make its presence known again.

Mike Blanc charged in and took down LaMichael James in the end zone for a safety and 2 points. Auburn still trailed, but now it was 11 - 9. And Auburn would receive the ball following the safety.

This time, the offense didn't self-destruct when it mattered. Emory Blake and Michael Dyer dominated the ensuing series, moving the ball rapidly down the field. Dyer ran the ball with authority and Blake caught a 30-yard pass from Newton for a touchdown. Wes Byrum's extra point made it 16-11.

It would turn out to be Auburn's final touchdown of the season.

And with that, the first half ended.

Van Allen Plexico

I was feeling pretty good at halftime.

There had been plenty of things to be concerned about. Cam had started the game by throwing an interception, and later he'd thrown an incomplete pass on fourth down on the Oregon 1 yard line. So it wasn't his greatest game ever. And we only had 16 points to show for it.

But the defense was playing well. We'd held a team that usually rang opponents up for like 50 points to just 11. And we always played better in the second half.

There was one minor disappointment for the fans: We were surprised that no halftime entertainment was provided. Instead, the Auburn University Marching Band did their usual performance. I wasn't necessarily expecting a Super Bowl-type halftime show with major celebrities or anything, but I did think we'd get something. Of course, we love the AU Marching Band, but still—it was the BCS National Championship Game. I figured they'd bring somebody of note in to sing or something. Usually they do, right? Maybe just some dogs catching frisbees. But—nope. It might as well have been a home game against Louisiana-Monroe.

That really didn't matter, though. As the players like to say, it was a business trip. And we were there for one reason only: to win the national championship.

In the locker room, Chizik told the team, "The second half is going to be old-fashioned football—tough, physical SEC football." That, he felt, was to Auburn's advantage. "I told them eventually we would wear Oregon down." Nothing about the game plan was changed before the third quarter began.

Only 5 points separated the two teams at the half. With thirty minutes left to play, it was anybody's ballgame.

> *"I remember going into the second half thinking, 'This is precarious ground for Auburn. If Oregon can hang around, and they hit a big play on offense, Auburn could be in big trouble."*
> *—Chris Low, ESPN*

Van Allen Plexico

As good as our defense tended to play in the second half, if you had told me at halftime that Auburn had scored all the touchdowns it would score...? That we would only score two more field goals—6 points!—the rest of the way, and against that Oregon offense?

If I'd known that at halftime, I would have bet you nearly anything that we would lose the game.

- 29 -

THE BCS NATIONAL CHAMPIONSHIP GAME, PART 2:
HERE IN THE DESERT

Auburn received the kickoff to begin the third quarter.

Cam ran the ball for a few short gains, then hit a 39-yard pass to Philip Lutzenkirchen down the left sideline. The drive stalled out, and Wes Byrum kicked a 28-yard field goal, increasing Auburn's lead to 19 - 11.

> *"We put up a lot of yardage, but we never finished those drives."*
> —Ryan Pugh, Auburn center

Van Allen Plexico
Again—if you'd told me that field goal would be our last scoring play until the final seconds of the game, I probably would've hidden under the seat. Surely Oregon was going to find a way to score more points than that before it was over.

After an exchange of punts, Oregon drove the ball to Auburn's one yard line, setting up their own fourth-and-goal.

The most overwhelming offense in college football that season, set up on the 1 yard line? Surely the Ducks were about to score, right?

Not so fast, my friend. Just as Oregon had stopped Auburn at their goal line earlier, Auburn's defensive front now stopped Kenjon Barner in the backfield, giving the Tigers the ball on their own 1.

Unlike the Ducks, Auburn did not give up a safety on the ensuing drive. Instead, the Tigers moved the ball 46 yards in 10 plays, getting safely away from the Auburn end zone before punting it away.

Neither team could get anything going. Oregon punted, Auburn punted, and Oregon punted again, as the clock ticked and the third quarter melted away and became the fourth. Finally Auburn found a different way to give the ball back to the Ducks: they fumbled.

> *"All we had to do, as we had done so many times in the season, was crank out one of those game-ending drives where we eat up the clock, and the championship would be ours. But on our second play, Cameron fumbled on a run and Oregon recovered. Cameron never fumbles, but one of Oregon's defenders made a nice play, coming from behind and punching the ball out of his arm."*
> —Gene Chizik, All In

With less than 5 minutes to go in the game, Auburn had given their opponents new life. Oregon wasted no time as Darron Thomas passed the Ducks down into the red zone. LaMichael James took it in from 2 yards out with 2:33 remaining to bring the score to 19 - 17 Auburn. Thomas hit Jeff Maehl for the 2-point conversion and the game was suddenly tied at 19.

> *"It doesn't matter how you win. A win is hard to get. I don't care who you play. I don't care if it's a high school team. A win is hard to get."*
> —Kodi Burns, Auburn receiver

Van Allen Plexico

Cam fumbled. Again, not enjoying his best game as an Auburn Tiger, and at a really bad time for it to happen.

And then Oregon's offense suddenly looks like the one we'd been expecting all along. They zip right down the field and tie the game.

With any other team, in any other year, I might have been in a panic. But with this team, I felt a strange degree of calmness and confidence. We'd seen them deal with adversity like this over and over. We knew what they could do, when they absolutely had to do it.

If they were ever going to do it, this would be the time. It would be their last chance ever—and with everything on the line.

After the kickoff, Auburn started the final drive of the game at their 25.

"When our offense jogged onto the field, I thought, 'Been there, done that—here comes more of the same.' I knew, in a season filled with comebacks, we'd find a way to win this one too."
—Gene Chizik, All In

After a 15-yard pass from Newton to Blake on first down, Michael Dyer took the ball and was involved in what would become the most-talked-about play of the game.

He was tackled after a 5-yard gain—or so it appeared. But the referees didn't blow the whistle. Realizing this, the Auburn sideline erupted in frantic motions and signals for Dyer to GO! Keep running! Somehow, he wasn't down!

In fact, he'd rolled over the would-be tackler and never actually touched the ground with any part of his body that would cause the play to end.

As he took off down the field again, the Oregon defenders chased after him, finally bringing him down—for real this time—at the Ducks' 23 yard line. The play, which at first appeared to have been stopped after 5 yards, went for 37.

Ducks fans howled their outrage, then and forever after. The referees took a look at it on instant replay.

"Following the review, the ruling on the field stands."
—Head referee Bill LeMonnier

"I can tell you, in Oregon they think he was down."
—Chris Low, ESPN

"The man was not down."
—Gene Chizik

The officials ruled the play stood as called on the field. First down Auburn, at the Oregon 23.

After short runs by Dyer and Newton, Dyer again got loose down the middle of the field and was tackled as he tried to cross the goal line with 10 seconds to go. At first, the referees signaled a touchdown, but this time the review went in Oregon's favor and the ball was placed at the 1.

Van Allen Plexico
There's an argument to be made that Oregon should have let Dyer score. It's like the famous ending of the 2005 Auburn-Georgia game: we were about to score a touchdown to go ahead of Georgia, but our receiver fumbled the ball into the end zone, where we recovered. By rule, the ball was placed on the UGA 1. It meant we still had to kick a short field goal to take the lead, but it also meant we were able to run the clock down before we did so, denying them any opportunity to respond. The same thing held true here: If Dyer had scored on the run, Oregon would've at least gotten the ball back, and could have thrown a couple of Hail Marys. Instead, Cam took a knee and we ran the clock down to 2 seconds remaining.

ESPN's graphic pointed out that Byrum had made five game-winning field goals in his career, including two that season.

Van Allen Plexico
Of course this is the one he'll always be remembered for—winning us the national championship, on the final play of his college career. But we also should remember back when he was a freshman, in 2007, and Auburn went down to Gainesville and beat Urban Meyer's Gators on a Byrum last-second kick—one he had to execute twice, because Meyer called a timeout just as he

was kicking it the first time. His running around in front of the Florida bench, doing the Gator chomp at them, will live forever.

"Once (the Dyer not-down play) happened, I think we kind of knew that Wes had it in the bag because of just who Wes is. The guy is cool, calm and collected no matter what situation he's ever in. So we knew he had it in the bag then. It was just up to us to block for it."
—Lee Ziemba, Auburn offensive lineman

"I remember going back to 2004—it flashed in my mind—2004 we were undefeated and never got a chance to have this moment. And I thought it was really cool. I remember looking up in the stands right before the field goal and seeing the whole side in this sea of orange. And I remember thinking, 'Man, all of these people behind me, all these people outside, that traveled here through bad weather, never knowing if they're ever going to get an opportunity to even witness this again, to ever see this again in their lifetimes.' I remember thinking, 'How awesome is that?'"
—Gene Chizik

Van Allen Plexico
Wes Byrum goes out there, a senior, with his final kick as an Auburn Tiger, to try to win the national championship.

John Ringer
No pressure there!

"Wes Byrum was one of these guys that just didn't get rattled," noted Chizik later. "You always want a quarterback who wants the ball in his hands at the end of the game. Well, he was kind of like that as a kicker. He wanted to be able to kick that last field goal, and he'd done it before, several times. This was nothing new. A chip shot, a 19-yarder. And he just smiled—not a lot to say. There was no question in my mind he was going to make it. He was money."

Ryan Pugh agreed. "I just remember being the left tackle on the field goal team, and thinking to myself, 'We've got the most clutch kicker in college football behind us. Dude's kicked more game-winners than anyone I know. He's not even nervous, so why would I be nervous?'"

"There was no doubt about the outcome," said Will Collier on AuburnSports dot com. "After four years of nailing clutch kicks, Oregon would have needed machine guns to prevent Wes Byrum from knocking through his career capper."

"Everything on the final play was perfect," said Chizik later. "Josh Harris's snap from center, Neil Caudle's hold, and Wes's kick."

Byrum's 19-yard field goal was good. The clock expired as the ball passed between the uprights. Auburn had won the game, 22-19. In doing so, and at long last, Auburn had won the national championship.

That bears repeating:

AUBURN HAD WON THE NATIONAL CHAMPIONSHIP.

> *"The 1983 team. Thank you for the memories.*
> *"The 1993 team, my fellowship friends and seniors. Thank you for the memories.*
> *"2004—Jason Campbell and Cadillac—thank you for the memories.*
> *"The 2010 BCS national champions: Thank you for our memories."*
> *—Stan White, Auburn Network broadcast*

Cam Newton finished with 265 yards passing on 20 of 34 attempts, with 2 touchdowns and 1 interception.

Van Allen Plexico

It wasn't just in our imagination that Cam struggled a bit against Oregon.

Mark Inabinett, writing for AL dot com, noted that Cam entered the national championship game with a passing rating of 188.2, which had him on pace to set the all-time NCAA FBS single-season record. But then, against Oregon, he completed 20 of 34 passes for 265 yards, 2 touchdowns and 1 interception. As solid as those number sound, they dropped his overall rating down to 182.05. Not only did that prevent him from surpassing

Hawaii's Colt Brennan (in 2006) for the *all-time* single-season record, it also dropped him below one of his Heisman rivals, Boise State's Kellen Moore, who topped the 2010 season with a 182.64 passer rating.

That said, I think Cam would have preferred winning the game and the championship over setting a random individual record.

Michael Dyer won the offensive MVP award after rushing for 143 yards on 22 carries. Cam rushed for 64 yards, also on 22 carries (and with two fumbles; one lost), while Onterrio McCalebb added 47 yards on 6 attempts.

Cam spread the ball around. Emory Blake and Darvin Adams each had 4 catches for 54 yards. Terrell Zachery had 6 for 48. Philip Lutzenkirchen added 2 for 48, while Kodi Burns and Mario Fannin caught one each, and McCalebb had 2 for 10 yards.

Oregon's Darron Thomas threw for 363 yards but was intercepted twice. No Ducks back rushed for as much as 50 yards, including much-hyped Heisman finalist LaMichael James, who finished with just 49 yards and no touchdowns. The Auburn defense came into the game intending to stop the run, and they accomplished that. Nick Fairley won Defensive MVP after disrupting the Ducks offense all night long.

Oregon had averaged over 300 rushing yards per game and 6.1 yards per carry. The Auburn defense held them to 75 yards on the ground and 2.3 yards per carry. More importantly, they held Oregon to a staggering 30 points below their scoring average.

Auburn had scored only 6 points after halftime, and only that last field goal after the first drive of the second half. Yet the defense had limited Oregon to just one score during all that time. Oregon won the second half, 8-6, but lost the first half 16-11, and that was the difference.

Van Allen Plexico

I fully expected the Oregon game to be a lot like the Arkansas game: two powerful, ultra-fast offenses just putting the pedal to the metal and rolling up and down the field. In hindsight, I suppose we should have expected more of a defensive struggle. When teams have that much time off to prepare, defenses usually move ahead of offenses. But I went into the game expecting fireworks—not that I'm complaining in the slightest that our defense decided to show up from the very beginning for once, and not put Cam and company in a 21-0 hole in the first quarter again!

> *"The reality is this wasn't a game like Arkansas where we'd be able to go up and down the field offensively. We couldn't do it. So we had to win that game with defense that night, and the defense came through."*
> —Gene Chizik

> *"Everybody thought it was going to be this high-scoring game, and I remember our seniors saying, 'Nah, they're not going to do that on us.' They had some ballers—LaMichael James and all those guys. But we knew we had a better team, better players, and we could dominate them on the defensive line."*
> —Nosa Eguae, Auburn defensive lineman

Just as they had against Alabama, the Auburn defense had bailed the Tigers out in the second half, when they needed to keep their opponent off the scoreboard.

In fact, Auburn's defense had been stellar in the second half all season.

In the first half of games, not so much. They remained in the lower half of the defensive stat charts for the SEC all year. Over the course of entire games, they'd performed only slightly better in 2010 than they had in 2009, when they'd been downright porous. But that was because they tended to give up yardage and scores early.

Late in games, however, it was an entirely different story. The 2010 Auburn defense allowed an average of just 3.7 points in the fourth quarter, and completely shut out five of their opponents in that period—including Georgia and Alabama. They'd held Oregon's mighty offense to zero points in the third quarter and just 8 points in the entire second half. And that was enough for two field goals to win it.

This game would be the only time an SEC and PAC-10 team played one another in any bowl game during the 16-year history of the BCS system. Because the two conferences lacked any common bowl tie-in, the only way teams from the two conferences could meet would be for both to secure spots in the BCS National Championship Game. This year was the only time that happened.

Seven BCS National Championship Game records were broken or tied in this game, including the most plays run (85, by Auburn, surely warming Gus Malzahn's heart) and 639 yards of combined passing by the two teams.

Van Allen Plexico

Man, this was a fun Oregon team to watch. They had been building towards this for a couple of years. Just an unbelievable offense. They didn't have great, 5-star playmakers and athletes, but they'd been running Chip Kelly's system for several years, and they knew it inside and out.

We thought our offense under Gus Malzahn was fast, but theirs was insanely fast.

John Ringer

They were a really good team. They were well-coached. This was the peak of the Chip Kelly era. They had a lot of explosive players and they had a really fun offense, too, in the same way that we did.

But the biggest thing in this game was Nick Fairley. They hadn't seen anyone like him. His ability to disrupt the middle of their offensive line and mess up the timing of their offense—I thought it was going to be the biggest thing in the game, and for a lot of the game, it was.

They were a very good team. They were good on both sides of the ball. They were well-prepared. We knew it would be a close game—we weren't going to just show up and blow them out of the stadium. And we didn't play our best game.

Van Allen Plexico

They'd never seen a defensive line like ours. In fact, Chip Kelly put in a bunch of option run plays they didn't normally use, specifically because of our defensive front. They were desperate to find some way to nullify our defensive line.

It didn't work.

Our defense wasn't just big, it was also fast. They couldn't fool it. Nick Fairley was getting penetration up front every play. Their quarterback, Darron Thomas, as good as he was, was getting killed. Their All-American running back, LaMichael James, got almost nothing. We shut him down. He didn't do anything in this game.

If this game had been played the weekend after the SEC Championship Game, it might have been 60-59. But it was played more than a month later, and the two defensive coordinators had a lot of time to think about the other team's offense and prepare. Those defenses were ready. Both teams were having to scratch and claw to score points.

The game was popular with viewers and fans all across the country. It earned ESPN the largest overnight TV rating in cable television history. Not the largest rating in *ESPN* history; not the largest *sports program* rating. No, it earned *the largest TV rating in cable TV history, period*.

It turned out Cam and company could even work miracles with the Neilsen ratings.

Before we turn the page on this game, however, there's one more thing worth noting.

One of the reasons this season and this game meant so very much to Auburn fans was not just that the Tigers had won all their games and earned the BCS trophy at the end. Many Auburn people also felt that the season and the subsequent number 1 ranking in the polls provided—at long last—a sort of validation for Auburn Football. A demonstration that Auburn could conduct a national-championship-caliber season—go out and win every game—and actually be *acknowledged* as champions by the rest of the country. Unlike after the 1983, 1993 and 2004 seasons—seasons where something always happened—this time everyone had to admit that the Tigers were the best. And that felt different, to Tigers fans. Different, and long overdue.

Will Collier, however, made a very compelling argument for a different perspective on the season; an argument that all that really mattered was winning the games. What the rest of the country thought about it wasn't worth our time or concern. It's a point of view worth considering, at the very least. Will states that for him, the emotions after beating Oregon and being ranked number 1 in the country were no different than those he felt at the end of the 1983, 1993 and 2004 seasons.

"Whether you or I or anybody else calls the outcome a 'national championship' is immaterial in my mind. The achievement of winning all your games against a ferocious slate of competition is the most important achievement.

"When I saw the final A.P. poll the next day, my reaction was basically, 'That's nice,' quickly followed by a check on the current weather in ice-encrusted Atlanta.

"The results on the field matter. The opinions of a bunch of sportswriters and/or coaches, not so much. That's as true today as it was in any other year."

—*Will Collier, AuburnSports dot com*

- 30 -

CELEBRATION DAY

Twelve days after winning the BCS National Championship Game in Arizona, the champs reconvened on the Plains for a celebratory ceremony to mark the occasion.

> *"When we got back home and had the celebration, I started seeing how many of my friends and people in Auburn who had actually made it out to that game and spent the money to go out there and get a ticket. That's when you kind of realized how special it was for everybody and for the Auburn Family. What a blessing to be a part of something like that. Unbelievable."*
> —Lee Ziemba, Auburn offensive lineman

The crowd was bundled up in jackets and hoodies and scarves and hats. It was cold—it was, after all, January.

It was also huge.

Van Allen Plexico

I watched the celebration on streaming video. I wanted to be there so bad, but I just couldn't afford to go. The trip to Arizona had cleaned me out financially for like a year afterwards! I was so broke, I didn't even make it to DragonCon that fall—the only one I've missed since 1997!

But it was great to see so many folks in attendance. It almost looked like a regular game crowd, on video.

It nearly was. Just under 80,000 fans showed up for the national championship celebration event on January 22.

University officials had not planned to open the upper decks but had to, due to the size of the crowd—roughly the same size as the one that had watched the Tigers win in Glendale, Arizona.

"It's so fitting. I'm not surprised we had so many people there because that's who our fans are. It's awesome to see them all show up and celebrate with us."
—Gene Chizik

Before the Celebration event had even started, a massive crowd of fans gathered for Tiger Walk, greeting the coaches and players as they entered the stadium at the southwest corner. The Auburn University Marching Band played as Aubie and the team filed through the crowd.

A new blue banner had been strung across the back of the big scoreboard at the south end of the stadium. It read:

NATIONAL
CHAMPIONS
1957   2010

Van Allen Plexico
I wish they'd included at least a couple of others on there. It gives the sense that we don't acknowledge them at all, when in fact several other years that official selectors named Auburn national champions are listed on the Auburn Football website.

But that's an argument for another day, and another book.

Inside, the same "national champions" message was repeated along the space above the press box. On the big scoreboard, the game clock displayed 20:10 and the score display read 22-19.

> "This is vindication for 2004. It has been a long time coming. I feel like they've been a good team for years, but it's always been cut short. They never really had an opportunity to show who they really were, but they did this year. For them to win a national title means a lot to me."
> —Adrienne Crane Stewart, 2005 Auburn grad, at the Celebration

A huge stage had been erected at the south end of the field, extending from the end zone out to about the 30 yard line. A podium stood at the center of it, emblazoned with a large "AU" logo. Cam Newton's Heisman Trophy sat on a round table to the left of the podium. The BCS crystal ball trophy and other trophies and awards secured by this team sat on a table on the right. They included the SEC Championship trophy, the AP national championship trophy, Nick Fairley's Lombardi Award, Gus Malzahn's Frank Broyles trophy (for the nation's top assistant coach), and the Grantland Rice trophy (Football Writers Association national champion).

And that wasn't all: Later that day, Auburn would be entertaining the University of Alabama's basketball team in the recently-opened Auburn Arena (later renamed Neville Arena). At halftime of that game, Auburn was slated to pick up another piece of hardware: the ODK Sportsmanship Trophy, presented to the winners of the Iron Bowl.

In addition to the packed lower ring of stands and much of the upper decks, thousands of fans—in this case, students—filled the center of the football field itself, their ranks extending almost to the north end zone.

The fans in attendance were as excited and emotional as if the team had just won the championship game that day.

> "I remember thinking, 'This is my Auburn family.' I felt so connected to them, even though I didn't know a lot of them. I was overwhelmed. I even cried.
>
> "They had a really good presentation. David Housel, when he spoke, I was bawling. Everything he was saying was true. He talked about how it changed people to come to Auburn, and he talked about the Auburn spirit. It was special."

—Adrienne Crane Stewart, 2005 Auburn grad, at the Celebration

"The excitement of the day and the electricity in the stadium was hard to describe. It was absolutely out of this world. It was one of the best experiences of my life."
—Meighan Julbert, Auburn student, at the Celebration

Former players and other university and state dignitaries spoke, including the Alabama governor and the university president, as well as the quarterback of the other national championship team recognized by Auburn:

"Our team had some of the same qualities (as this year's team). You are dedicated, you work hard, you are determined, you believe in the coaches and you believe in each other. And with a crowd like this, you have to believe in Auburn fans.

"Remember you represent more than a football team. When you put that championship ring on, just remember what it means. Wear it with pride, wear it with class, and believe in Auburn."
—Lloyd Nix, Quarterback of the 1957 National Championship team

"At every one of this season's games, there were two great teams on the field: the Auburn offense and the Auburn defense."
—Dr Jay Gogue, Auburn President

The fans were emotional. The players felt that same emotion, and some reflected upon it, when they spoke:

"The Auburn fans are the best in the country. It just makes you feel honored and special to be a part of the family... and then to have this last reception like this, words can't describe it. It's something I'm going to remember for the rest of my life because it's people that became a part of me."
—Kodi Burns, Auburn receiver

> *"I have been here through bad seasons and good seasons alike, and the Auburn Family just doesn't change through any of it. All these trophies and rings will fade away. But when I have gray hair and I have one foot in the grave, I'm not going to remember this championship. What I am going to remember is the warmness and the kindness of the Auburn people and what 'this Family' means to me."*
> —Lee Ziemba, Auburn offensive lineman

The loudest cheers were for Newton, Nick Fairley and Kodi Burns, who continued to have the love and appreciation of the Auburn family for his selfless behavior back in 2009, as well as for his on-field performance since then.

When Cam Newton came to the podium, he struck the classic Heisman pose and delivered a unique, singsong version of "War Eagle!" The Heisman was ceremonially handed to him by former Auburn quarterbacks Stan White and Randy Campbell. Then he thanked the Auburn fans for their support through a trying time.

> *"You never stopped believing in me. People have asked me over and over: How did I handle the distractions? The simple answer is, God, family and you, my Auburn family. You never lost faith in me and that means more to me than words can ever say. You will be in my heart forever.*
>
> *"This is my last time on this field as a part of the Auburn football team. I want to go out saying this: I believe in Auburn and love it. War Eagle."*
> —Cam Newton, at the Celebration

Then Nick Fairley hugged him. It was a rare moment; usually a quarterback would be terrified of having Fairley's arms wrapped around him.

> *"I felt proud that I could say that I was someone who stood behind him. I heard all the negative comments, but I didn't believe it. His personality and the way he's carried himself, it's hard not to believe him. When he acknowledged the fans, it*

made me really feel like we were part of their success. It was amazing."
—Adrienne Crane Stewart, 2005 Auburn grad

Gene Chizik lifted the crystal football aloft, as he had after the game. "You are the best fans in the United States of America," he told the crowd. "And you have helped us and been a huge part of being the best football team in the United States of America."

"It's kind of a bittersweet situation that we're in right now, because what other way can you picture us going out than the way we went out this year?"
—Cam Newton, when asked about his decision to turn pro after the season

Asked about the size of the crowd, Newton replied, "I was speechless for the most part. I really didn't expect it to be like that."

"There was no doubt in my mind we had the blueprint to get this done."
—Gene Chizik, at the Celebration

"Forever, this team will be known as champions."
—Jay Jacobs, Auburn athletic director, at the Celebration

Months later, Auburn's players and coaches visited the White House and met President Barack Obama. Kodi Burns presented him with a blue Auburn jersey with "OBAMA" and the number 1 on the back.

The president praised the team and called out one player in particular.

"There's a guy named Cam Newton who had a pretty good season and went on to win the Heisman Trophy. So obviously that's really extraordinary."
—President Barack Obama, at the White House ceremony for Auburn

Obama and Chizik also briefly discussed the tornadoes that had recently hit Tuscaloosa and other areas of the state.

"You don't understand the devastation until you see it firsthand," Obama said. "But what was also inspiring was the amount of strength and generosity that was shown by so many people in the midst of so much tragedy. And that includes the members of this program. Two days after the tornado, almost 70 Auburn coaches, players, and athletic department staff—led by Coach—traveled to Pleasant Grove and Cullman to help out with relief efforts.

And even though one of the toughest-hit areas by the storm was the home of the Crimson Tide, this team knew what we all know in situations like this, which is we're all on the same team."

- 31 -

ONE MORE BRICK

Pat Dye had once said that getting Auburn's home games in the Alabama series moved out of Legion Field in Birmingham and to Jordan-Hare Stadium in Auburn in 1989 represented "the last brick in our house." It was the last obstacle that had to be overcome to prove that Auburn's football program was on the same level as the other top teams.

But it turned out there was one more brick we were missing: the national championship.

Auburn had earned a national title in 1983, finishing 11-1 against by far the toughest schedule in the country, only to have it stolen by Miami.

Auburn had earned a national title in 1993, as the only undefeated team in major college football still standing at the end of the season—only to have it denied because of probation.

Auburn had earned a national title in 2004, going undefeated and winning the SEC, only to be stuck in third place and left out of the BCS game.

That one last brick was still missing from our house.

As stated earlier in this book, a few college football teams win national championships with some regularity. They approach every season with hope—and beyond hope, the confidence of potential success at the highest level.

Auburn has never been that kind of program.

Other teams never win national championships at all, and know they probably never will. They have no hope of doing so, and they understand that.

Auburn has never been that kind of program, either.

The fans of both of those types of teams have no need of hope. They don't need hope because they'll win without it, or they don't need hope because they simply won't win, regardless of it.

What they both do know is a kind of peace, whether it be the peace of constant success or the peace of not having to give it any thought at all.

Auburn fans have never known either of these kinds of peace.

There is the constant striving to win, knowing it is possible. There is hope. But, all too often, it is a faint hope, at best.

And there is also the constant frustration of coming up just short, or of being somehow denied a championship even when the team did everything it had to do to win, as in 1983, 1993, 2004, and other years.

One reason—one of so many reasons—why 2010 was so important was that Auburn, in that year, finally broke the curse, ended the drought, and proved they could win a consensus national championship.

There had been one championship that was generally recognized by all: 1957.

But it had been 53 years since that one. There was a growing danger that, at some point, Auburn winning in 1957 was going to start seeming like Army winning in 1945: ancient history, and very unlikely to happen again.

Auburn University desperately needed to disrupt that narrative before it could take root. The Tigers needed to demonstrate that they were among the legitimate contenders, and that national championships were possible there.

Winning the national championship in 2010 truly was the "last brick in our house."

It proved that, at Auburn, anything was possible. And that there was always hope—a realistic hope. And that the biggest dreams could become reality.

"It showed Auburn could win a national championship in the modern era. There was the woulda coulda shoulda of 2004. The fact that they were able to win a national championship—an official national championship—it made it as special an Auburn season as there's ever been.

"You can't talk about Auburn in this state without talking about Alabama, and vice versa. And Alabama's coming off a national championship (the previous year). Auburn could win some Iron Bowls and some state championships and some SEC championships, but Alabama owned the national championship trophies. Until 2010. And that's one reason why, I think, that season bothered, hurt, angered, disturbed Alabama fans maybe more than any other Auburn season."

—Kevin Scarbinsky, columnist, AL dot com

Van Allen Plexico

I was determined to hold onto that incredible feeling—the feeling I'd longed for my entire life, up to that point—for as long as possible. I didn't want to let the fact of what Auburn had accomplished slip far from my thoughts for a moment; not for as long as we were the reigning champs. My fear was of going days at a time not thinking about it, and then waking up one day and realizing our time was over and some other team was now champion. I wanted to feel that championship, to think about it, to embrace it, for at least part of every single day, until our year was done.

So, on Twitter, I created a new hashtag: #BCS365

Whenever I tweeted about Auburn that year—and if you know me, you know it was a lot!—I would include that hashtag. Other AU people there started doing it, and for a little while it was a neat little thing—a thing that helped remind us all to be grateful, to remember it, and to celebrate and enjoy it every single day.

John Ringer

I have a framed image in my office at work of the final score of that game in Arizona. I put it specifically in a place where I would be looking every day, to remind myself of what happened. And I do remember. I remember how good that day and that game made me feel and how this championship title will live in history. And that we got to experience it together.

> *"You see (teams) winning national championships and they've got seven, eight, nine, ten draft choices on one team. We didn't have that in 2010. We had really good college football players, and the best offensive player in America, and the best defensive player in America, in Cam Newton and Nick Fairley."*
> —Gene Chizik

During and after this season, some said this Auburn team was "a one-man team," as if Cam Newton did it all by himself. As if Nick Fairley didn't exist, let alone the rest of the players on the team—the offensive line that protected Cam and created all those running lanes for him and the great and varied stable of backs; the touchdown catches of Philip Lutzenkirchen and those talented wide receivers; the incredibly gritty and tough play of the defensive line; the secondary that always, always woke up in the second half and shut down their opponents; Josh Bynes and the other linebackers; and the kicking of Wes Byrum and Ryan Shoemaker. And all the rest.

"It takes a team, a player-led team, really to win a national championship," noted Kodi Burns. "And that's what we had. Leaders. Guys that, when things got rough, they found a way to get it done."

Added Zac Etheridge, "The difference from the year before was all of us coming together and playing for one another."

Not to mention the coaches.

"That team was special," said Gus Malzahn. "That coaching staff was special. Gene Chizik did a great job of keeping everything together. All that we went through—not just our players but our staff and everything that goes with it."

Justin Ferguson, writing for the *Athletic* in 2020, argued that the 2010 Auburn Tigers were the first team of their kind to win the BCS national championship, and could well be the last of their kind as well.

How were they different? Ferguson pointed out that 2010 Auburn was the only BCS national champion to allow more than 22 points per game. It was the only BCS champion not built on a foundation of elite recruiting classes. It had the lowest-rated overall talent in the recruiting ratings of any BCS champion—and is arguably the only one ever to not meet the "Blue Chip Ratio" standard for having more 4- and 5-star recruits than lower-rated players. (Auburn's 2010 roster met that standard at the time, but changes to the formula and to historical recruiting rankings since then have brought it into question.)

"Before Auburn's run to the national title in 2010," he said, "there hadn't been another team quite like it in the BCS era. The ever-accelerating CFP (College Football Playoffs) era has made it increasingly unlikely that a repeat performance (by any team similar to them) will happen."

Even if the defense did tend to give up an inordinate amount of points earlier in games, though, they always managed to lock things down by the final frame. As Ferguson noted, "The two national champions before (2010 Auburn) allowed 12.9 and 11.7 points per game. The two after it allowed 8.2 and 10.9 points per game. Auburn's 24.1 points per game made for quite the change of pace for what was expected from a title-winning team."

But that doesn't tell the whole story. Ferguson argues that Newton and company's repeated late-game heroics wouldn't have been possible without the Tigers' defense shutting their opponents down in the fourth quarter, over and over.

"In 14 games during the 2010 season," he concludes, "Auburn allowed just 49 fourth-quarter points — an average of 3.5 per game. No team scored more than eight points on the Tigers in the final frame. In the seven wins decided by a single possession, Auburn allowed a combined 32 fourth-quarter points."

So it wasn't a one-man team. Not at all. Cam may not have had blue-chip, NFL Draft-bound receivers to throw to or hand the ball to, but he had tough, solid college players at those positions—and lots of them. And the defense could adjust when it had to, if only to keep things interesting.

That said, at the end of the day, it is true and fair that the one person above all others who will be remembered from this team is the quarterback. For a few months in 2010 and early 2011, he truly was Superman, Camzilla, and the Blessed Individual.

Of course, he was not the first transcendent, demigod-like figure to carry the ball for the Tigers on the way to a Heisman Trophy. Just 25 years earlier, Vincent "Bo" Jackson had lit up the SportsCenter highlights with his seemingly impossible feats of athleticism, on the way to becoming a nationally-beloved, two-sport star and media figure.

After the 2010 season, Van and John asked Reynolds Wolf, noted Auburn fan and famed meteorologist for the Weather Channel, if he would rather have Bo Jackson or Cam Newton on his Auburn team, if he could only have one of them.

Reynolds replied, "That is so difficult. It breaks my heart (to have to choose between them).

"I think I would take Cam Newton.

"And the reason is that Cam Newton, as the head of the offense, made every single person around him better. Whereas Bo Jackson, although he was incredible—in my opinion, the greatest athlete who has ever lived—he could not make Pat Washington a 3,000-yard passer. He's not gonna make the defense better. He's not gonna make the offensive line better.

"But Cam Newton had the ability to lift up everyone. I think even the defense could watch him and be inspired by him. He lifted up the entire team. He lifted up the university."

– EPILOGUE –

Cam Newton and Nick Fairley turned pro after the 2010 season. Newton was the first player taken in the NFL Draft, by the Carolina Panthers. In 2015, he was the league MVP and led his team to the Super Bowl, but came up just short of a win there. Fairley was the 13th player selected overall, and played for the Lions, Rams and Saints over the course of a seven-year pro career. He was plagued by injuries and never made the huge impact he had in college. By 2018, he was out of the league.

Without those two generational players, Auburn's fortunes in 2011 predictively declined. Early in the season, sophomore running back Michael Dyer looked capable of carrying the offense. Eventually, however, off-field issues caused him in 2012 to transfer to Arkansas State, to play for his former offensive coordinator, Gus Malzahn. He was dismissed from the Red Wolves team by Malzahn that same year after a police stop involving drugs and guns. After a brief stay at Arkansas Bible College, his playing career finally ended at Louisville, where he was ruled academically ineligible for the Cardinals' bowl game in 2014. He never came close to reaching the vast potential hinted at during his first year at Auburn, when he'd broken Bo Jackson's freshman rushing record.

Onterio McCalebb, Emory Blake and Philip Lutzenkirchen enjoyed good but not stellar seasons for Auburn in 2011, as the Tigers finished 8-5. The defense continued to struggle in the first half of games, and now it struggled in the second half as well. At the end of the year, Chizik dismissed defensive coordinator Ted Roof.

The Tigers lost their offensive coordinator at that time, as well. Nearly everyone had predicted, back during 2010, that Gus Malzahn soon would be offered at least one head coaching job. He departed the Plains to take over at Arkansas State, where his good friend Hugh Freeze had just spent one year in that same position. He too, would spend one year in Jonesboro with the Red Wolves before returning to Auburn in 2013, this time as the new head coach.

Auburn radio play-by-play announcer Rod Bramblett won the 2010 Alabama Sportscaster of the Year Award, given by the National Sportscasters and Sportswriters Association, for his work calling the Auburn Tigers in their championship season. He won again after the 2013 season, which included his immortal calls on "the Prayer in Jordan-Hare" against Georgia and "the Kick Six" against Alabama. On May 25, 2019, he and his wife, Paula, were killed when their vehicle was struck from behind by a driver under the influence of marijuana.

Philip Lutzenkirchen finished his Auburn career as the school's all-time leader in touchdown receptions by a tight end. He went undrafted but signed as a free agent with the St Louis Rams.

On June 29, 2014, he was involved in a late-night, single-vehicle accident. He and the driver were killed, while two others riding in the vehicle were injured. He was not wearing a seatbelt and was thrown from the back seat. The driver was legally intoxicated and Lutzenkirchen himself registered a high blood alcohol level of 0.377 at the time of the accident.

Following Auburn's win in the 2010 Iron Bowl, Alabama fan Harvey Updyke poisoned the oak trees at Toomer's Corner in Auburn with a powerful herbicide. He then called in to Paul Finebaum's radio show to brag about what he'd done.

"The weekend after the Iron Bowl," he told Finebaum and his listeners, "I went to Auburn, Alabama, because I lived thirty miles away, and I poisoned the two Toomer's trees. I put Spike 80DF in 'em."

When Finebaum asked him if the trees had died, he replied, "They're not dead yet, but they definitely will die."

"Is it against the law to poison a tree?" asked Finebaum.

"Do you think I care?"

"No."

"I really don't! Roll Damn Tide!"

The call was traced and Updyke was arrested. He argued that his killing the ancient and beloved trees was justified because an Auburn fan in Tuscaloosa after the Iron Bowl had put a "Scam Newton" Auburn football jersey on the statue of Bear Bryant. He later attempted to excuse his actions by stating he "had too much Bama in him."

Updyke first pleaded "not guilty by reason of mental disease or defect." He later agreed to a deal whereby he pleaded guilty to "criminal damage to an agricultural facility." He received a sentence of three years in prison and a monetary fine, with probation after six months in jail. He died of natural causes in 2020.

The trees Updyke poisoned were not able to be saved, and had to be replaced twice, along with all of the soil around them. Even when new trees at last took root there, they could not be rolled until they reached a proper maturity. At last, in August of 2023—twelve years after the initial poisoning—Auburn University announced fans could once again roll the trees at Toomer's Corner in celebration of Auburn victories.

Prior to the championship season, Auburn had approved plans to erect statues of its previous two Heisman Trophy winners, Pat Sullivan and Bo Jackson, outside Jordan-Hare Stadium. With Cam winning the third of Auburn's Heismans, the university simply added a third statue to the order.

Van Allen Plexico

Cam's statue being added so quickly gave rise to my all-time favorite meme: A genuine photo of Cam walking to class, book bag over his shoulder, passing by a certain statue in the background. The meme text reads, "WALKS TO CLASS IN FRONT OF HIS OWN STATUE."

In May of 2011, with the final ruling from the NCAA on the Newton case still pending, Auburn AD Jay Jacobs was asked by John Zenor of the AP if he had any reservations about adding a statue of Newton alongside the other two, when they were installed later that year. Jacobs replied that he had no issues with doing so, because he was confident that both Auburn and Newton ultimately would be cleared of all charges.

"Out of respect for the NCAA process, technically it's still an open issue," Jacobs noted. "But when Dr. Emmert, the president of the NCAA, comes out in February (and says) that he's found no wrongdoing on Auburn's part, I'm not sure how you can be any more confident than that. And no circumstances have changed since then."

In response to Jacobs's statements, NCAA spokeswoman Stacey Osburn issued a cautionary note. She pointed out to the AP that Emmert's comments regarding Newton and Auburn had related only to the reinstatement decision (prior to the SEC Championship Game). She went on to say that a school is notified when an investigation is closed. Auburn had not yet been sent such a notification.

At the SEC meetings in July of 2011, NCAA representative Julie Roe Lach met with all twelve SEC coaches as a group. A report leaked out that, during the session, Gene Chizik had "confronted" Roe Lach about the continuing investigation of Auburn's recruitment of Newton. The initial report hinted that Chizik had essentially cornered the NCAA representative and demanded to know when the investigation would be over. "We will let you know," she reportedly snapped back at him.

ALL THEY DID WAS WIN

Chizik refuted the report. He stated that, during the session with all of the conference coaches, he had merely inquired about the investigation's progress, and asked her to clarify a couple of points about it, and that she had been "happy" to oblige.

On October 12, the NCAA released a statement that it had closed its 13-month investigation into Auburn and Cam Newton. Auburn was completely cleared of all charges and allegations. Auburn was notified in a letter sent to the university by associate director of enforcement Jackie A. Thurnes.

In the letter, Thurnes stated that the NCAA enforcement staff, along with Auburn University, conducted "more than fifty interviews into whether Newton was paid to sign with Auburn, and examined documents including bank records, tax filings and phone and email records." They concluded that "any allegations of major rules violations must meet a burden of proof, which is a higher standard than rampant public speculation online and in the media." There had certainly been plenty of "rampant speculation," but absolutely no proof whatsoever.

Just like that, Cam Newton and Auburn were both cleared of any wrongdoing.

All that smoke, but not a single fire to be found.

And all that smoke was part of the problem. The NCAA was bombarded by every would-be "insider" and his brother trying to get in on the feeding frenzy—clogging up the actual investigation with an overflow of garbage.

Will Collier, who covered the Newton story for AuburnSports dot com, points out "how crazy those two or three weeks were (after the initial reports appeared). Not just every day, but every few hours some outlandish new rumor or story would pop up and send people into a frenzy. Not only were ESPN and the rest of the sports media running 24/7 with 'Camgate,' every variety of insanity was popping up on the then-dominant blogs and message boards, all credited by posters to 'my sources on the inside,' of course.

"NCAA investigators said later that it had taken them much longer than it should have to resolve the real issues, simply due to all the red herrings that had been dropped in their laps by what turned out to be baseless media stories and 'tips' from all over the place."

Eventually, of course, the "real issues" were resolved.

Those who had predicted the Tigers would be stripped of their BCS trophy and Newton would lose his Heisman were left with egg on their faces. As of this writing, fifteen years later, both trophies are still securely in the hands of those who won them.

Van Allen Plexico

This is the hill I will die on until someone someday proves me wrong:

Auburn did *not* pay Cam, Auburn never offered Cam any money, and Cam did *not* ask Auburn for money.

For more than a decade, I would make that argument against anyone who wanted to challenge me. I would then back it up with, "The NCAA did a thorough investigation and found nothing!"

But, in the last few years, with the advent of NIL and players being paid, and for my own amusement, I've taken to changing it a little:

"Auburn did not pay Cam, and Cam did not ask Auburn for money," I still start with, nowadays—and then I add, "but if we *did* pay him, we got a bargain—and you should have outbid us."

Even on the way out of the stadium in Arizona, and while I was eating a late supper at In-and-Out Burger, I was getting texts and tweets from people I knew—some of them even friends!—telling me that I was wasting my time being there, wasting my time celebrating, because Auburn would have to forfeit this trophy and Cam would certainly have to give up his Heisman, possibly within days.

I couldn't believe people I knew and thought of as friends could be so casually cold and callous. Frankly it came close to ruining one of the most joyous days of my life, and I still haven't forgotten it.

To this very day, I enjoy occasionally pointing out to them and everyone else that we still have the crystal football, and Cam still has his Heisman.

Will either ever have to be given back?

To quote a certain Blessed Individual: "Two letters, my friend. NO."

In response to the NCAA's final report on the matter, Gene Chizik stated, "As I've said many times, I feel very confident about the way we run this program. I've said many times that we haven't done anything wrong, so quite frankly I moved on a long time ago."

Years later, Cam Newton in an interview publicly scoffed at the idea that he or his family had been paid for his services. He found the idea absurd, noting that any sudden infusion of cash into his family's coffers would've been easily noticed by their friends and neighbors back home.

Gene Chizik made out very well financially from the 2010 season. On top of his base salary of $2.1 million, the 2010 season provided Chizik with $1.3 million in incentive-based bonus payments. He later sat down with Jay Jacobs to renegotiate his contract to bring it closer in line with what Nick Saban and Les Miles were making at Alabama and LSU, respectively. The following season looked to be a rebuilding year, for sure. But clearly Chizik had earned a raise.

Few could have imagined what lay just ahead.

The following season, 2012, with Malzahn and his unique offense gone to Arkansas State, Gene Chizik decided to embark on what looked to be a long-term rebuilding project. He chose to move toward a more NFL-style offensive scheme, similar to what Alabama was running. He felt that, once this transition was made—and it could take some time—Auburn would be in a better position to recruit top players and to compete with its big rivals.

However, given that the players on Auburn's current offense had been mostly recruited by Malzahn to run a very different offense, there were always going to be challenges in 2012. New offensive coordinator Scot Loeffler was going to have to rebuild the offense from the ground up, using players not suited to that style of play. Chizik assumed his staff would be given the time to do this, especially considering the good will he felt he had bought for himself in 2010.

He was wrong.

It seemed few fans wanted to give Chizik the credit for 2010. Instead, many credited Cam Newton, Gus Malzahn and Nick Fairley for the championship. When Chizik's book, *All In*, was published in 2011, he revealed that he hadn't even wanted to recruit Cam Newton as a quarterback—it had been Malzahn and the offensive staff that had pushed him to even consider it. Now fans wondered even more openly about Chizik. By the end of what became a 3-9 season, in which Loeffler's offense finished last in the SEC in total yards and passing yards, much of the Auburn family was no longer "all in." Some concluded Chizik was indeed a 5-19 coach who had gotten extremely lucky with a particular coaching staff and a couple of spectacular players.

Astonishingly, just two years after going undefeated and winning the national championship, Gene Chizik was fired by Auburn. True to his nature and his style, Chizik appeared to take it all in stride.

Van Allen Plexico

There's no question that, by the end of the 2012 season, we all felt something had to change. The team was just playing terribly, especially on offense. It was making us long for the offense of 2008—and that's a horrifying thought. Every week on our podcast, we referred to the previous Saturday as "another trip to the dentist," meaning you kept doing it regularly, but it was no longer a pleasant experience you looked forward to.

ALL THEY DID WAS WIN

I don't think Gene Chizik did himself any favors with his *All In* book. I have to admit I enjoyed reading it while we were researching this book, and obviously we used several important quotes from it here. And he comes across as a very likeable person. But in the book, I think Chizik is in some ways too honest. He talks over and over in it about how shocking it was for Auburn to want to hire him, especially after he went 5-19 in two years at Iowa State. He explains—very convincingly, I think—why he believes his Cyclones teams only won 5 games. But he dwells more on what he believes the perceptions of others will be to his record, rather than on why it was so poor. He all-but-says, *Can you believe Auburn hired me?*

And it's particularly frustrating for him to do that, knowing he won the national championship just two years later. Other coaches would've spent a lot more time talking about winning the things they won in 2010, and a lot less time dwelling on perceived shortcomings. But that, apparently, is just how Chizik is.

He also hurt himself in that book and its accompanying speaking engagements when he openly admitted that he hadn't wanted to bring Cam Newton in for an official visit to Auburn, or even look at game film of him. Gus Malzahn and Curtis Luper really had to twist his arm to persuade him to even give Cam a chance. And it wasn't because of anything wrong with Cam—his situation at Florida or whatever. It was because he just stubbornly didn't want to consider signing a junior college transfer at quarterback. We Auburn folks are very lucky Luper and Malzahn were convincing in their arguments. Unfortunately for Chizik, I think this only made the fans wonder why we needed Chizik at all, if it was the offensive coordinator and the running back coach who'd brought in the star player—and over the head coach's objections, no less.

All that said, however, one thing I've learned from researching and working on this book is that Chizik was probably treated too harshly. Yes, bringing in Malzahn as the head coach worked out pretty well—in the short term, at least. But Chizik was thinking long-term all along. He

353

brought in Scot Loeffler—an NFL offensive coordinator/quarterback coach—for a reason. He felt that Auburn needed to move away from the unique, gadget-oriented offense of Malzahn and toward a more standard, NFL-friendly offense that he believed would assist him in recruiting and in competing against rivals like LSU and Georgia and Alabama. Making such a huge change in the offense would have taken multiple years to fully enact, requiring the recruitment of different types of players at both the skill positions and on the line.

Chizik assumed, especially after winning the national championship, that he'd be given the time to make such a massive change to the structure of the team. I would argue that he was *not* given that time, and the reason in part was because he didn't receive much of the credit for that championship. In his book he states that, had he known he wouldn't be allowed the time to make that transition, he probably wouldn't have attempted it. I think perhaps he should have asked up front.

Am I saying Auburn should have kept Chizik after 2012? No.

Should Chizik have been a bit more guarded about the behind-the-scenes events leading up to Cam Newton's signing? Yes.

Should Chizik have tried a more gradual change to the offense he wanted? Without question.

And finally, was Chizik the right guy at the right time, during the national championship season? Absolutely.

In addition to his various duties as head coach, I can pinpoint two other things he did spectacularly well; two things that possibly meant the difference between 14-0 national champions and coming up short and disappointment.

One, he perfectly managed Cam Newton, as a player and as a human being. With rock-steady resolve, he kept Cam focused and on task while all the controversies swirled around him and around the program. At the same time, he managed those controversies with the media and the public and the fans as well as anyone ever could have.

And two, his steady, Zen-like resolve kept the entire team on an even keel throughout the season. He always, always demonstrated a level-headed and even-tempered demeanor and served as a terrific example for his players to never get too high or too low.

In my view, without Gene Chizik leading the way, Auburn would not have been able to come from behind in more than one or two of the several close escapes this team pulled off in 2010. Say what you will about 5-19 and about 3-9 in his final year at Auburn. The Tigers could not have asked for a better head coach in 2010. He was every bit the X-factor that Gus Malzahn and Nick Fairley and even Cam Newton were for that team. I honestly don't think Auburn wins its first recognized national championship since 1957 without him.

John Ringer

Was Chizik treated unfairly? Possibly.

But the 2012 season was so bad, with the team clearly quitting at times and off-the-field issues increasing in frequency and severity, that changes needed to be made.

Gene Chizik was an excellent defensive coordinator in the early- to mid-2000s. As a head coach he was the right man at the right time to assemble and lead this Auburn team to heights no one imagined possible. But, as Van mentions, his honesty and directness in his book and speaking engagements served to undermine him.

I think Gene Chizik deserves credit for being the coach that led Auburn to a national title, but I also think he deserved to be dismissed for the way the team fell apart in the post-title years. In any successful endeavor, people always end up believing that they themselves are the secret ingredient to success. In this case, Chizik joins Ed Orgeron of LSU as someone who won a national title but did not last through the years afterward.

Following Chizik's dismissal, AD Jay Jacobs hired Gus Malzahn to return to the Plains, this time as head coach. Many of the players he had recruited previously were still on the roster. To this mix he added an unorthodox transfer: Nick Marshall, a speedy former defensive back from the University of Georgia who wanted to play quarterback. In his first season as head coach, Malzahn took this Auburn team to within one play of winning a second national championship in four years. Malzahn would continue at Auburn through 2020, though he never quite matched the success of that first season.

For the rest of the decade, Auburn would remain the last SEC team to go undefeated and win the national championship. The feat would not be matched until the 2019 LSU Tigers, another team with a generational quarterback and a spectacular offense.

In 2020, on the tenth anniversary of the championship season, defensive lineman Nosa Eguae reflected:

> *"It was one of those surreal moments where I think if you're in it, you just can't fully appreciate it. But now, ten years later, you look back on it and you just know it was a complete blessing. More than that, I think we were all destined for it. Everything just happened to work out in our favor that year because we were meant to win the championship, we were meant to have the season that we did, and we were meant to do it for the Auburn Family."*
> *—Nosa Eguae, Auburn defensive lineman*

Destiny or not, the 2010 Auburn Tigers set records and worked miracles. As the Football Study Hall website put it in 2019, "Auburn pulled off a series of magic acts that only Auburn could pull off. S&P+ (team measurement) sees this Auburn team as basically an 11-win team and ranked them sixth in the updated rankings, only the Tigers won *seven* games by a touchdown or less and won the national title."

They described the Iron Bowl as "an extremely statistically unlikely Auburn win" with a "post-game win expectancy of 16%," and the likelihood of the Tigers beating Alabama,

Kentucky, Georgia and South Carolina (the first time) at a combined 4%.

They sum 2010 up with, "If we play this season out again, Auburn goes about 9-3, and we maybe get a matchup of 12-1 Bama vs. 11-1 Ohio State for the title. I'll take this version, thanks. The best team on paper didn't win the national title, but the most dramatic did. Worth it."

Worth it indeed.
We'd certainly waited long enough for it.
Fifty-three years!
Rod Bramblett expressed it in four perfect sentences, uttered at the end of the BCS National Championship Game:

"And now, here in the desert, Auburn's journey is complete.

"Fifty-three years of waiting, of hoping, of dreaming, of coming so close. It's all over. The Auburn Tigers are on top of the college football world, and the view from here is sheer perfection."

One sign being waved in the stands after the game summed it up more succinctly—summed up all those years of frustration, and this year of redemption and joy, in one simple word:

—*Van Allen Plexico and John Ringer*
Summer 2025

– NOTES –

Much of this book was assembled from firsthand recollections by the authors and their friends and associates, as well as from carefully rewatching video footage of games from the 2009 and 2010 seasons (in some cases, over and over!).

Most game and player statistics come from ESPN's online box scores and from the Sports-Reference website.

Gene Chizik's autobiographical book, *All In*, was a source for a number of the coach's quotes. It was published by Tyndale House in 2011.

Former Auburn AD Jay Jacobs appeared with host Ronnie Sanders on the Auburn Undercover podcast in May 2025, just before this book went to press, in which he discussed the hiring process for Gene Chizik. He is quoted in Chapter 2.

The chapters on the games prior to Alabama in 2010 benefitted from the "Perfection on the Plains" series by Jeff Shearer, a series that ran in 2020 at AuburnTigers dot com.

Longtime friend of the authors, Will Collier, contributed his original AuburnSports dot com reporting from during the 2010 season, and also wrote new material especially for this book.

The Jeffrey Whittaker and Greg McElroy quotes in the chapters on the Iron Bowl are from an article by Evan McCullers, *Plainsman* Assistant Sports Editor, printed in Alabama's student paper, the *Crimson White*, in 2015.

Andy Staples wrote an article in 2020 about the 2010 Iron Bowl for the *New York Times*, as part of its look at the 40 greatest comebacks in sports history: "The Comeback, No. 31: The play that preserved Auburn's chance at a championship."

A number of quotes throughout the book come from interviews featured in "Undefeated Auburn: Revisiting Auburn's Historic, Championship-Winning 2010 Season," a video retrospective feature published by AL dot com.

Some of the information on ticket prices for the Oregon game came from "BCS National Championship: Ticket prices make Oregon-Auburn 'bigger than any Super Bowl," by Rachel Bachman, published by *The Oregonian* on January 5, 2011.

Some of the information about the Auburn BCS celebration event came from "Auburn faithful Celebrate as Champions," by Lindsay Slater, published by the *Times-Journal* (Ft Payne) on January 24, 2011.

Justin Ferguson revisited the 2010 season in 2020 in an article for the *Athletic*, and we have quoted him and some of his stats in multiple chapters.

Some of the 2010 Kentucky game retrospective material was written by Dick Gabriel, published on the WKYT Website in 2020.

The "Finally" photo on the last page of the Epilogue is a screenshot from the ESPN game broadcast.

ALL THEY DID WAS WIN

Additional information was gathered from:

Matt Hinton, Yahoo Sports
Philip Marshall, *Auburn Undercover*
ESPN website
The Bleacher Report
Chris Brown, *Smart Football* website
Reporting by Charles Goldberg
Reporting by Mark Inabinett
Reporting by Jon Solomon
Reporting by Jay Tate
Reporting by John Zenor

– BONUS –
2004 AUBURN vs 2010 AUBURN

John Ringer

In the pandemic summer of 2020, we did an actual simulated play-by-play of a theoretical game between the 2004 and 2010 Auburn teams.

The 2004 team got out to an early lead (as nearly everybody did against the 2010 first-half defense), and then Cam brought the 2010 team back late (as happened quite a few times that season) to tie the game and force overtime.

Van Allen Plexico

Yes! And if folks want to find out how that simulated game ended—you can find "The 2004 vs 2010 Auburn Tigers Showdown" episode of our podcast at www dot AUWishbone dot com, under "Our Greatest Hits!"

– APPENDIX 1 –
2009 AUBURN TEAM ROSTER

Player	Class	Pos	Summary
Chris Todd	SR	QB	
			198 Cmp, 328 Att, 2612 Yds, 22 TD
Neil Caudle	JR	QB	
			15 Cmp, 20 Att, 170 Yds, 1 TD
Ben Tate	SR	RB	
			263 Att, 1362 Yds, 5.2 Avg, 10 TD
			20 Rec, 105 Yds, 5.3 Avg
Mario Fannin	JR	RB	
			34 Att, 285 Yds, 8.4 Avg, 0 TD
			42 Rec, 413 Yds, 9.8 Avg, 3 TD
Jason King	JR	RB	
Onterio McCalebb	FR	RB	
			105 Att, 565 Yds, 5.4 Avg, 4 TD
			6 Rec, 58 Yds, 9.7 Avg, 0 TD
Eric Smith	SO	RB	
			20 Att, 99 Yds, 5.0 Avg

Davis Hooper	SO	RB
3 Att, 1 Yds, 0.3 Avg		
Darvin Adams	SO	WR
60 Rec, 997 Yds, 16.6 Avg		
Kodi Burns	JR	WR
5 Rec, 46 Yds, 9.2 Avg		
Terrell Zachery	JR	WR
26 Rec, 477 Yds, 18.3 Avg		
Anthony Gulley	FR	WR
Travante Stallworth	FR	WR
2 Rec, 21 Yds, 10.5 Avg		
Emory Blake	FR	WR
9 Rec, 66 Yds, 7.3 Avg		
Deangelo Benton	FR	WR
6 Rec, 88 Yds, 14.7 Avg		
Jay Wisner	JR	WR
3 Rec, 56 Yds, 18.7 Avg		
Quindarius Carr	SO	WR
2 Rec, 78 Yds, 39.0 Avg		
Tim Hawthorne	JR	WR
1 Rec, 3 Yds, 3.0 Avg		
Derek Winter	SO	WR
1 Rec, 16 Yds, 16.0 Avg		
Philip Pierre-Louis	FR	WR
Tommy Trott	SR	TE
11 Rec, 144 Yds, 13.1 Avg		
Gabe McKenzie	SR	TE
Philip Lutzenkirchen	FR	TE
5 Rec, 66 Yds, 13.2 Avg		
Mike Berry	JR	OL
Lee Ziemba	JR	OL
Byron Isom	JR	OL
Ryan Pugh	JR	OL
Josh Harris	SO	OL
Andrew McCain	SR	OL
Bart Eddins	JR	OL
John Sullen	FR	OL
Morgan Hull	JR	K
Wes Byrum	JR	K

Mike Blanc	JR	DL
Michael Goggans	JR	DL
Antonio Coleman	SR	DL
Jake Ricks	SR	DL
Antoine Carter	JR	DL
Zach Clayton	JR	DL
Nick Fairley	SO	DL
Robert Hill	SO	DL
Chris Humphries	FR	DL
Derrick Lykes	FR	DL
Dee Ford	FR	DL
Eltoro Freeman	SO	LB
Josh Bynes	JR	LB
Craig Stevens	JR	LB
Wade Christopher	SO	LB
Watson Downs	FR	LB
Jonathan Evans	FR	LB
Harris Gaston	FR	LB
Adam Herring	SO	LB
Ashton Richardson	SO	LB
Zac Etheridge	JR	DB
Daren Bates	FR	DB
Walter McFadden	SR	DB
Neiko Thorpe	SO	DB
Gabe Barrett	JR	DB
Drew Cole	SO	DB
D'Antoine Hood	SO	DB
Ikeem Means	FR	DB
Woody Parramore	JR	DB
Mike Slade	SO	DB
Harry Adams	SO	DB
T'Sharvan Bell	FR	DB
Demond Washington	JR	DB
Clinton Durst	SR	P

– APPENDIX 2 –
2010 AUBURN TEAM ROSTER

Player	Class	Pos	Summary
Cam Newton	JR	QB	
Passing			185 Cmp, 280 Att, 2854 Yds, 30 TD
Rushing			264 Att, 1,473 Yds, 5.6 Avg, 20 TD
Barrett Trotter	SO	QB	
			6 Cmp, 9 Att, 64 Yds, 0 TD
Neil Caudle	SR	QB	
			1 Cmp, 1 Att, 42 Yds, 0 TD
Clint Moseley	FR	QB	
Michael Dyer	FR	RB	
			182 Att, 1093 Yds, 6.0 Avg, 5 TD
			1 Rec, 9 Yds, 9.0 Avg, 0 TD
Eric Smith	JR	RB	
			5 Rec, 49 Yds, 9.8 Avg
Onterio McCalebb	SO	RB	
			95 Att, 810 Yds, 8.5 Avg, 9 TD
			7 Rec, 86 Yds, 12.3 Avg, 1 TD

ALL THEY DID WAS WIN

Mario Fannin	SR	RB
61 Att, 395 Yds, 6.5 Avg		
17 Rec, 173 Yds, 10.2 Avg, 2 TD		
Davis Hooper	JR	RB
12 Att, 37 Yds, 3.1 Avg		
Kodi Burns	SR	WR
11 Rec, 177 Yds, 16.1 Avg		
Terrell Zachery	SR	WR
44 Rec, 633 Yds, 14.4 Avg		
Darvin Adams	JR	WR
52 Rec, 963 Yds, 18.5 Avg		
Emory Blake	SO	WR
32 Rec, 526 Yds, 16.4 Avg		
Shaun Kitchens	FR	WR
1 Rec, -3 Yds, -3.0 Avg		
Ralph Spry	JR	WR
Trovon Reed	FR	WR
Quindarius Carr	JR	WR
3 Rec, 103 Yds, 34.3 Avg		
Derek Winter	JR	WR
3 Rec, 44 Yds, 14.7 Avg		
Deangelo Benton	SO	WR
1 Rec, 15 Yds, 15.0 Avg		
Antonio Goodwin	FR	WR
Philip Lutzenkirchen	SO	TE
15 Rec, 185 Yds, 12.3 Avg		
Brandon Mosley	JR	OL
Mike Berry	SR	OL
Byron Isom	SR	OL
Ryan Pugh	SR	OL
Lee Ziemba	SR	OL
A.J. Green	JR	OL
Wes Byrum	SR	K
Cody Parkey	FR	K
Antoine Carter	SR	DL
Zach Clayton	SR	DL
Nosa Eguae	FR	DL
Nick Fairley	JR	DL
Mike Blanc	SR	DL

Kenneth Carter	FR	DL
Dee Ford	SO	DL
Michael Goggans	SR	DL
Corey Lemonier	FR	DL
Derrick Lykes	SO	DL
Jamar Travis	SO	DL
Jeffrey Whitaker	FR	DL
Craig Sanders	FR	DL
Craig Stevens	SR	LB
Josh Bynes	SR	LB
Wade Christopher	JR	LB
Jessel Curry	FR	LB
Watson Downs	SO	LB
Jonathan Evans	SO	LB
Eltoro Freeman	JR	LB
Harris Gaston	FR	LB
Jake Holland	FR	LB
Chris Humphries	JR	LB
Mike McNeil	SR	DB
Neiko Thorpe	JR	DB
Daren Bates	SO	DB
Zac Etheridge	SR	DB
Demond Washington	SR	DB
Drew Cole	JR	DB
Chris Davis	FR	DB
Demetruce McNeal	FR	DB
Ikeem Means	SO	DB
Woody Parramore	SR	DB
Aairon Savage	SR	DB
Ryan Smith	FR	DB
Ryan White	FR	DB
T'Sharvan Bell	SO	DB
Demetruce McNeil	FR	DB
Anthony Morgan	SO	DB
Steven Clark	FR	P
Ryan Shoemaker	SR	P

– APPENDIX 3 –
1,000-Yard Rushing Streak

Beginning with Ben Tate in 2009 and then Cam Newton and Michael Dyer in 2010, the Tigers had at least one 1,000-yard rusher in 9 straight seasons, from 2009-2017, and 11 overall during that span of time.

This is, by far, the SEC record for most consecutive seasons with a 1,000-yard rusher.

YEAR	PLAYER	RUSHING YARDS
2009	Ben Tate	1,362
2010	Cam Newton	1,473
2010	Michael Dyer	1,093
2011	Michael Dyer	1,242
2012	Tre Mason	1,002
2013	Nick Marshall	1,068
2013	Tre Mason	1,816
2014	Cameron Artis-Payne	1,608
2015	Peyton Barber	1,017
2016	Kamryn Pettway	1,224
2017	Kerryon Johnson	1,391

– APPENDIX 4 –
MEMORIES

We asked the patrons of the AU Wishbone Podcast for their thoughts and memories about the 2010 season.

Winston Boddie

My favorite memory from the 2010 season is one that I will carry with me forever. My dad was a 1951 graduate of API and a lifelong Auburn football fan. Growing up every Saturday my dad and I either watched or listened to the games. When I became an adult, no matter where I was in the world, I would call my dad after the game to talk about it.

My dad passed away on Father's Day in 2010 so that happened to be my first season without getting to talk to him after the games. As the season unfolded, and the team continued to win I thought about him often and dearly missed talking to him every Saturday. I have special memories of almost every game, but none are more special than the championship game. I watched the game in the middle of the night from my apartment in Algiers, Algeria, and it just so happened to be on my birthday.

As the clock hit zero and Auburn had won my thoughts immediately went to my dad. How ecstatic he would have been to see them win the championship. I'm not gonna lie—I may have shed a tear or two that morning, not only because they won, but because I did not get to call my dad and talk about the game.

Chris Thrash

I was in my second year of residency at UCLA working in the cardiac ICU during the Iron Bowl. After that first quarter, I got disgusted and went back to work. Shortly after the T-Zach TD to open the 3rd quarter, my intern said, "Hey Dr. Thrash, you better get back in here." I watched the remainder of the game in an abandoned patient room. My work colleagues gave me an Auburn SEC championship T shirt for Christmas that year.

Anne Pridgen

I lived in Rome (Italy, not Georgia) during the 2010 season, so unfortunately I missed some of the games. I did the best I could, but the time difference and challenges of streaming worked against me. But there was no way I was going to miss the National Championship game! I went to bed that night but set my alarm to get up in the middle of the night. The game was on Armed Forces Network, and miraculously we were able to tune in. (If you're not familiar with AFN, it's known for its riveting commercials that air instead of your typical ads. You can learn about school zone safety on Misawa Air Force Base, for example.)

I'd bought canned boiled peanuts at the American Embassy in order to have some semblance of familiar football food. So there I was in Rome, Italy, in the middle of the night, eating boiled peanuts, watching my Tigers play for it all. And of course, after we won, I was not able to get back to sleep, so that was one long—and happy—day!

Bill Minor

I was in my last year of graduate school in 2010 and I remember several of the earlier games being a little tough with the team getting their sea legs before they hit it in stride. My favorite memories of that year were watching the LSU game, arguably the most exciting game that year, at a bar on College Street with one of my friends from graduate school and being around the rest of the fans who didn't go. It had a surreal atmosphere, dare I say a family one, even though not in the stadium, was hard to match.

Fast forward to January 10th. We picked the same bar to watch the national championship game. The best part about it was once Wes Byrum kicked it through, we ran out the door and were at Toomer's Corner to celebrate! Although an Auburn fan my whole life, it was a surreal time to be there. Oh and classes were cancelled the day of and day after the game due to ice, so that was fun too.

Wade Ward

After we graduated from Auburn in 1989, my wife and I lived in Madison, Alabama for 18 years and then moved to Texas. I had grown up in Mobile and a year before I moved to Texas, my parents retired in Florida. We'd had season tickets since I was in seventh grade until my son started playing soccer in first grade. Even though we no longer had season tickets, my parents and I still met at as many Auburn games as our schedule allowed and went to almost all of Auburn's bowl games. When we found out Auburn was going to the National Championship game, we had to go.

My parents purchased us a package. They drove to Alabama and flew with a charter. My wife and I drove my new Mustang. When I purchased the car, I asked the salesman if there was anything I needed to do to break the car in. He said something along the lines of "unless you are driving the car 2000 miles on a trip, you don't have to do anything... Who would purchase a new car and do something like that?" I smiled and explained my plans. To my surprise, he said he was a big Cam Newton fan, said "War Eagle," wished us the best and said to not use the cruise control.

For my previous job in Huntsville, I had traveled to the Phoenix area frequently and had told my parents I knew where to eat. To everyone's surprise, we ate dinner where an

Auburn and Oregon pep rally was scheduled. The Oregon "O" cheer was nothing compared to the Auburn fight song!!!

The game was AUsome. I remember Cam not having his best game, but the Dyer run followed by Wes Byrum's field goal was super-exciting.

We celebrated back at the hotel with a bottle of Dom Perignon we had won at my wife's Christmas party. A trip I will remember for the rest of my life.

A footnote: I drove the same car to Pasadena (after the 2013 season), met my parents and brought a bottle of Dom hoping for the same results, but that story will be for another book :).

My parents are still in Florida and we are in Texas. I hope I can pay for the next one.

Kathy Bright

The day after watching our Tigers win the SEC Championship I jokingly suggested to a friend that if they decided to take the family jet to the BCS Championship Game then me and my mom wanted to hitch a ride. The same day we all bought tickets! We got a good deal compared to what I heard prices went for up until gametime, but we could pay a little more because we didn't have to pay for a hotel or a flight!

The weather in Birmingham tried to keep us away but we met the plane in Mississippi and flew out the morning of the game. I have never felt more like the MVP. We got off the plane on the tarmac and into a car that took us straight to the game. We had incredible seats in the lower corner of the Auburn side of the field at the winning endzone!

We had some very nice Oregon fans in front of us that were shocked that we also cheered for our band. The game was stressful but to this day was one of the best days of my life. Being in that stadium with my mom, my friends, my Auburn family, the toilet paper flying, and War Eagle playing over and over will forever be etched into my memory. I am forever grateful I made the decision to take the chance and buy the ticket!

Jarrod Alberich

So there I was in the stadium in Arizona, very very nervous, as the Auburn Tigers lined up for the final kick at the end, to win the game. It's germane to the story that I was there with my very good friends Ezra and Delvin, and it's also germane that none of us are under six-foot-two and 250 pounds. We are big, burly, manly men. Delvin and I have both served in combat zones. We are military guys. Self-defense guys. We are the manliest of men.

So now I will tell you the story of how I made our whole section cry.

Back to the field goal: Snap, kick, good. The whole place just erupts.

I, on the other hand, just drop to my seat, almost as if every bit of life is out of my body, extremely overwhelmed. I sit there for what felt like thirty minutes but was probably thirty seconds, dumbfounded. I just never thought I would see this day. I never thought I'd see it.

So I get my faculties back and I stand up and I look over to my good friend Delvin, and I have tears welling up in my eyes. I'm so emotional. I honestly never thought I'd see this day. And I just give him a hug. And Delvin, he tears up a little bit too. We're good friends; we've been through a lot, and we're both sort of tearing up. And then I turn to my other side, and there's my very good friend, Ezra, and I've got tears rolling at this point, and I hug him. And he's a manly man, too, but starts to have a little bit of tear action and emotion too. And these two middle-aged women turn around to give us high-fives and they see these three big, burly men with the tears welling up in their eyes and they say, "Oh my gosh," and they're very touched, and then they start crying. And then the people next to them start crying. And well, the whole section ended up crying. And it was all on me. I led the Great Cry at the National Championship Game.

I don't regret it. I'm proud of it. And War Eagle.

(Jarrod Alberich is "the Yard Sale Artist" and AU Wishbone "Guess-the-Game" segment host)

ALL THEY DID WAS WIN

Walt Austin

I spent all of 2010 deployed to Kosovo, so my memories were of trying to find ways to plan waking up in the middle of the night to watch games and following along with whatever game thread might be going on *The War Eagle Reader*. I had to celebrate as I could from afar with all of the victories, and struggle through the wondering what would happen with Cam Newton all by myself, with no other Auburn fans around. It ultimately culminated in this piece I wrote and Jeremy (Henderson) published at *The War Eagle Reader*:

https://www.thewareaglereader.com/2011/01/celebrating-a-championship-alone-in-kosovo-with-an-expensive-cigar/

I was home in time for A-Day and the unveiling of the statues of the Heisman winners. That A-Day game was one of the first dates I had with my now-wife.

Auburn Elvis

So much of the 2010 season seems like a blur, but I recall going to the spring A-Day game and hearing the people around me excited about a new quarterback we'd gotten. And I vividly remember seeing the three main quarterbacks standing together on the sidelines, and remarking at how much taller one of them was. I guessed that one must be the new kid everyone was so excited about. I mean, he was no Barrett Trotter on the field that day, but he sure was large.

Tony Perry

I have been a lifelong Auburn fan. 2010 was my freshman year at Auburn! I was one of the lucky few freshmen to get a full home slate of student tickets, and I attended every one. Then, as if I wasn't lucky enough, I won a discounted $200 student ticket to the National Championship Game in the lottery.

I sat in the opposite endzone of the game winning kick. My favorite memory was hearing the crowd *erupt* after Michael Dyer wasn't down and began running again after getting up. I will never forget that special end to a special season. War Cam Eagle!

Chad McDowell

We had great "old money" seats a few rows up around the 50 for the "Camback." Though there was a little tension in the air due to the playing of "Take the Money and Run" pregame, people were friendly enough—until the first-half onslaught started.

Since we had a nine-year-old girl with us, and with the game seemingly out of hand, we contemplated leaving at halftime as the level of vitriol and profanity towards us had increased to an almost intolerable level. Fortunately, the Newton-to-Blake connection with a few minutes left in the half was enough to give us hope.

Needless to say, we couldn't have been in a more perfect place during that second half. Carried that momentum and excitement to Atlanta and then to Glendale—same nine-year-old in tow—who in fact just graduated on the Plains! WDE!

George Gaston

I remember attending the Georgia game that season with my childhood best friend and fellow Auburn graduate who had since moved to Atlanta. Walking back to the car after the game, I called my wife in Mobile. She had bought two tickets for us to the SEC Championship Game without discussing it with me, and she had been terrified the Tigers wouldn't make it that far (in part because we might get stuck with the tickets, but mostly because she'd have felt like she jinxed it!). Sometimes we talk about whether we should have tried to plan to travel to Glendale instead, but we loved our experience in Atlanta. I remember being blown away when Cam Newton completed that Hail Mary pass to Darvin Adams at the end of the first half. I was coming from the concession stand when it happened and hadn't quite made it back to my seat! Little did I know they were serving "Cam Cam Juice" on the sidelines.

Patrick Williams

I have been an Auburn fan all my life. My dad, a pharmacist, was a 1969 graduate of Auburn University, and my parents had season tickets while I was growing up. So I have been in the Auburn Family literally since birth. I had never experienced the Auburn Family as much as I did following the events of October 2, 2010.

My mom had taken my son Peyton and my nephew Wesley to the Auburn—Louisiana-Monroe game that day to celebrate the boys' birthdays, which were about a month apart. Peyton's was October 3, so he was to turn 14 the next day. During the day, he had texted me some things about his experience including just after Tiger Walk, when he sent me a text that read, "Just touched Gene Chizik and Cam Newton — will never wash!" Little did I know that that would be the last communication I ever received from him.

On the way home just after merging onto Highway 280 to head back to Boaz, Alabama, our hometown, my mom hit a patch of gravel, lost control of the car, and Peyton was ejected through the back window. He did not survive the wreck, and our lives that day changed forever.

The days after the accident are a bit of a blur, but word about the accident began to reach many members of the Auburn Family, including people within the athletic department. We began to receive messages from people. Athletic Director Jay Jacobs sent us a care package. Flowers were sent to the funeral from the athletic department. Head Swim Coach Brett Hawke came to Peyton's viewing with quite a few pieces of memorabilia for our family. (Peyton was a swimmer.).

A few days after the funeral and burial, we received a phone call from Laura Meadors, Coach Chizik's administrative assistant. She was calling to let us know that Coach and Mrs. Chizik wanted us to be their special guests at the homecoming game that year vs. Chattanooga. My wife LaShea, our daughter McKenna, and I traveled back down to Auburn for the first time since October 2. It was an extremely emotional trip passing right by the very site on Highway 280 where our son and brother had taken his last breaths on earth.

When we got to the stadium, Laura escorted us in and we were allowed to be on the field pregame. We interacted with numerous people on the field including Coach Trooper Taylor and Travis Williams. Mrs. Jonna Chizik hosted us during the day, and we made our way up to her suite. During halftime, Tim and Kim Hudson came in, and we chatted with them for the entire second half.

After the game, we were scheduled to meet and spend some time with Coach Chizik. Unfortunately, that was the week where all the allegations about Cam had come out, and there was a lot of media to do. While we waited, we got to interact with a number of players and coaches as they were exiting. At one point, Cam came out, and he was told who we were. He stopped and said, "Oh, your story has touched my heart!" You could see him get choked up. We posed for pictures with him and thanked him for his time.

After Coach Chizik finished his media obligations, Laura and Mrs. Chizik took us into a room in the stadium called the Heisman Room. Coach Chizik came in and we spoke for a few minutes about Peyton, his love for Auburn, and our sadness at our loss. Laura handed him a wrapped box. He told us that in the box was something very special just for us. He told us to wait and open it when we got home, but he wanted to tell us about its contents. He said, "Our team knows Peyton's story. We've talked about him and his love for Auburn. In this box is the Auburn flag that flew over the stadium the day Peyton died. All of our players and coaches have signed it. We know it won't bring Peyton back or keep you from being sad, but we just wanted to help you get through one more day." Obviously, the tears flowed with everyone in the room.

My wife LaShea grew up an Alabama fan in an Alabama family. She and Peyton used to spar over the rivalry. That day, however, she became a member of the Auburn Family, and she has never looked back. The kindness that Auburn people have shown us over the past fifteen years has been amazing and unforgettable.

We were able to go to the SEC Championship that year to watch Auburn beat South Carolina, and some family members and friends made a way for us to go to the BCS National Championship game in Glendale, Arizona. Watching Auburn win the National Championship was a sweet salve for our souls. When Wes Byrum made the championship-winning kick, I just sunk down into my seat and cried, thinking about Peyton up in heaven watching his beloved Auburn Tigers win it all. Little did we know that the autographed flag that was presented to us would become a National Championship signed flag just a few weeks later.

A couple of years later, a group of teachers from Boaz went to a conference at the Auburn Hotel and Conference Center. They saw Trooper Taylor in the lobby, and they went over to talk to him, several of them being Auburn fans. They chatted for a few minutes, and he told them he was entertaining a recruit who was staying at the hotel. He asked them where they were from and they told him Boaz. He said, "Oh! That's where Peyton Williams was from!" He talked about the impact that Peyton's death had had on the team that year and how it served as an inspiration to them.

Through our loss, we saw the love and care of the Auburn Family in many real and tangible ways. It gave us great comfort that we remember to this day. God truly blessed us through the entire experience, and He still does to this day. War Eagle!

ABOUT THE AUTHORS

Van and **John** have been recording episodes of the **AU Wishbone Podcast** almost every Monday since fall 2012.

Van Allen Plexico is an award-winning author who managed to attend Auburn (and score student football tickets) for some portion of every year between 1986 and 1996. He teaches college near St Louis, and also hosts a number of different podcasts, appears at pop culture conventions, and writes and edits novels, stories, nonfiction works and articles for a variety of publishers. Find links to his various projects at *www.plexico.net*.

John Ringer graduated from Auburn in 1991 (which may be the greatest time ever to be an Auburn student — SEC titles in 1987, 88 and 89 and the 1989 Iron Bowl). His family has had season tickets every year since well before he was born and he grew up wandering around Jordan-Hare on game days. He currently lives in Richmond, Virginia where he spends way too much time reading about college football and basketball on the internet.

You can hear Van and John discuss the latest in Auburn Football—with lots of humor and fun thrown in—every single week:
Just search "AU Wishbone" on your favorite podcast app, or go to
www.AUWishbone.com

ALSO FROM THE AU WISHBONE CREW:

FIRST TIME EVER:
The Untold Story of How Auburn First Brought Undefeated Alabama to Jordan-Hare Stadium—
AND BEAT THEM

The complete story of the 1989 Iron Bowl.
How and why did Alabama try every trick in the book to avoid coming to Auburn, and how did Pat Dye and company finally win that fight—and the game itself? It's all here!
Includes a play-by-play breakdown & analysis of the game!
At over 300 pages, it's available in paperback and hardcover wherever books are sold!
ISBN: 978-1962993012
www.whiterocketbooks.com

WE BELIEVED
A LIFETIME OF AUBURN FOOTBALL
Vol 1: 1975-1998

Meticulously researched and created using the same style as AUBURN BASKETBALL: FROM BARKLEY TO BRUCE, WE BELIEVED Vol 1 dives deep into the Pat Dye era of Auburn Football. Filled with memories, full game descriptions, player stats and much more, it's the indispensable work on Auburn in the 1980s & 1990s. At nearly 500 pages, it's $19.95 wherever books are sold!
ISBN: 979-8536996751
www.whiterocketbooks.com

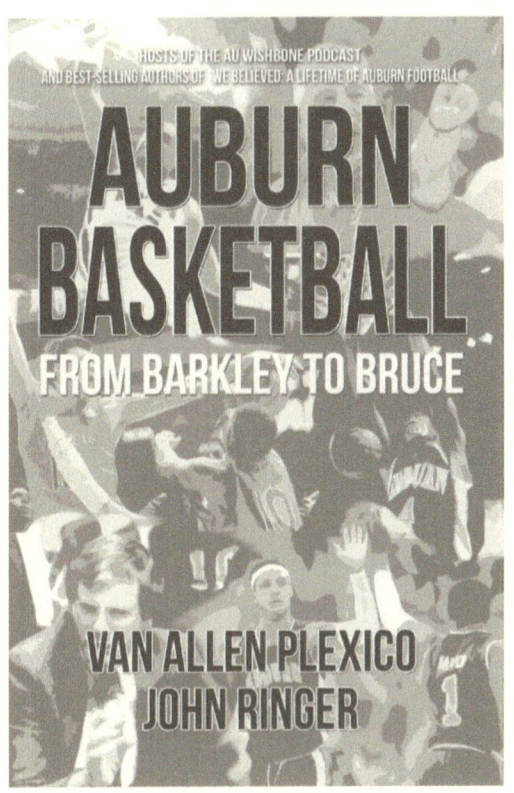

AUBURN BASKETBALL:
From Barkley to Bruce

"The best and most comprehensive book ever written on Auburn Basketball." —David Housel, Auburn Athletic Director Emeritus
Covering every basketball season from 1978 — 2022 and featuring a new interview with Auburn's legendary Coach Sonny Smith, this book takes you from Charles Barkley in the Olympics and NBA (and Waffle House!) to the hiring of Bruce Pearl and his magical Final Four run, and everything in between.
It's $16.95 wherever books are sold!
ISBN-13: 9798353194996
www.whiterocketbooks.com

www.ingramcontent.com/pod-product-compliance
Lightning Source LLC
Chambersburg PA
CBHW030243010526
44107CB00030B/1323/J